The Free and Open Press

The Free and Open Press

The Founding of American Democratic Press Liberty, 1640–1800

Robert W. T. Martin

NEW YORK UNIVERSITY PRESS

New York and London

NEW YORK UNIVERSITY PRESS
New York and London

Library of Congress Cataloging-in-Publication Data
Martin, Robert W. T., 1967–
The free and open press : the founding of American democratic
press liberty, 1640–1800 / Robert W. T. Martin.
p.   cm.
Includes bibliographical references and index.
ISBN 0-8147-5655-7 (cloth : alk. paper)
1. Freedom of the press—United States—History.   I. Title.
PN4738 .M37 2001
323.44'5'0973—dc21   2001002577

Manufactured in the United States of America

10 9 8 7 6 5 4 3 2 1

For Gretchen

Contents

Acknowledgments		*ix*
Note on the Text		*xi*
Introduction		1
1	The English Inheritance: From Milton to Cato	16
2	The Coming of the Crisis	35
3	The Pre-Revolutionary Crisis	68
4	The Making of the First Amendment	93
5	The Emergence of Modern Democratic Press Liberty	125
	Conclusion: The Foundation of American Press Liberty	155
	Notes	*169*
	Bibliography	*215*
	Index	*233*
	About the Author	*239*

Acknowledgments

As a student reading scholarly works for the first time, I would occasionally glance upon various authors' acknowledgments, and I was struck by two things: the number of people and institutions they felt they had to thank and the conventional expressions of absolution they would make for colleagues who had commented on the work "but were in no way responsible for its remaining shortcomings." I now understand better both of these matters, and so, if I have learned nothing else while writing this book, I have learned a good deal about authorial debts and duties.

A number of institutions have played a critical role in supporting and encouraging this project, and I am grateful to them—or rather, to the people who directly or indirectly make them flourish. At the University of Minnesota, both the Department of Political Science and the Graduate School provided me with extra financial assistance, which allowed me to focus on my research and enabled me to pursue my work at the American Antiquarian Society in Worcester, Massachusetts. The Society's staff is legendarily helpful, and they proved their reputation is well earned: They helped me maximize my use of their vast and valuable resources, pointed out important materials I did not know existed, and jump-started my car when the need arose. The staff of the Wilson Library at the University of Minnesota has been similarly helpful, especially the patient and quiet folk at the Rare Book Room. And the staff of the Acquisition and the Cataloging departments kindly trusted me to use materials long before they had a chance to record and process them. I would also like to thank the staffs of the Beinecke Rare Book and Manuscript Library (Yale University), the Watkinson Library (Trinity College), the Connecticut State Archives, and the New-York Historical Society. Finally, the editors of *History of Political Thought* have kindly granted permission to use in chapter 3 material first published in *History of Political Thought*, vol. No. 15 (1994), pp. 505–534. Copyright © Imprint Academic, Exeter, U.K.

If the number of institutions I have to thank is limited, the number of individuals is not. As it would be impossible to list them all, I would like to express my deep gratitude to a few people who most richly deserve it. Intellectually, my greatest debt is to James Farr, who has been my trusted adviser, friendly mentor, and keenest critic. By treating me like a colleague, he has made me one. My debt to Terence Ball is also great, for he has been a source of insight, encouragement, and inspiration. The other members of my dissertation committee, John Howe, the late Paul Murphy, and, especially, Mary Dietz, generously provided perceptive criticism and solid advice at an early stage. More recently, Jim Read was munificently helpful as I revised the work for publication. All of these scholars read and commented on the book at various stages—in Jim Farr's case, repeatedly. Yet they really are not responsible for its weaknesses, for, as I now understand, even the best advice can be poorly heeded.

I am also indebted to the past teachers and advisers who helped me along my academic journey, most notably, Jeffrey Isaac, Russell Hanson, and Howard Reiter. My colleagues at Hamilton College have made the last few years of this project enjoyable and productive. I thank them, and especially Philip Klinkner, for their support and encouragement. I have also been assisted by the gifted staff at New York University Press, and I am very grateful for their assistance. Stephen Magro, in particular, has helped keep my mind on the big picture even as he introduced me to the fine points of book publishing.

It is a delight to acknowledge the immeasurable contribution of my parents, for it is their faith in education that has made me the student and teacher I am. I would also like to thank my family and friends, whose encouragement and support has made this whole business possible and who have made the time away from the project both enjoyable and invigorating. Two friends in particular deserve special mention here: Paul Soper, for always making time for wide-ranging discussions of early American political thought, and Stacey Hunter Hecht, for our continuing conversations about everything else.

And, finally, I would like to thank Gretchen Herringer, who often had to put aside her own professional duties to read my work, charitably. Indeed, the reader, too, should thank her for making the text both more direct and less inelegant, not to mention a good deal shorter. She has taught me much else over the years, and for that I owe her everything. Happily, that is a debt that will take a lifetime to repay.

Note on the Text

In general, I have chosen to leave the text of quotations, as well as titles, with their original spelling, italicization, capitalization, and punctuation. I have done this in part to retain the flavor of these early tracts and in part to avoid unduly biasing the reader's interpretation of ambiguous passages. More important, many printers actively used italicization, capitalization, and punctuation to augment the message conveyed by the text. However, it has proven necessary on occasion to quote from modern, edited collections in which the text has been modernized.

For the dates before England and her colonies switched to the New Style (Gregorian) calendar in 1752, I have followed the standard convention of stating the year as if 1 January—not the Old Style (Julian) calendar's 25 March—were New Year's Day.

And though all the windes of doctrin were let loose to play upon the earth, so Truth be in the field, we do injuriously by licencing and prohibiting to misdoubt her strength. Let her and Falshood grapple; who ever knew Truth put to the wors, in a free and open encounter[?]
—John Milton, *Areopagitica,* 1644

It has ever been . . . our fixed resolution to keep *our Journal* free and open . . . yet we do not mean that it should be a vehicle of . . . inflammatory declaration.—In the present unhappy controversy between G.B. and these colonies . . . we defy any one . . . to say they were denied a place for their pieces in our paper; yet, at the same time, we look on it as a right to judge [what to omit] and have always followed our own judgement.
—William Bradford, *Pennsylvania Journal,* 17 August 1774

Introduction

Writing in the wake of the McCarthy era, James Morton Smith concluded his monumental study of the Sedition Act controversy (1798–1800) and its struggles over press liberty with these words by the novelist John Dos Passos:

> In times of change and danger when there is a quicksand of fear under men's reasoning, a sense of continuity with generations gone before can stretch like a lifeline across the scary present.[1]

Happily, the specter of McCarthyism has long since been dispelled. Yet, for many advocates of free expression, the present era *has* been scary. Certainly, the last two decades were a time of great challenges to settled ways of thinking, causing "much agony and soul-searching."[2] From pornography and "hate speech" to the right to privacy and the public's "right to know," a series of controversies have flared up, and Americans have responded by renewing their free speech dialogue in public fora as diverse as local newspapers and law reviews, lunch counters and the Supreme Court bar.

This dialogue has not been idle chatter. Free speech is crucial to American democracy, most notably in its manifestation as the foundation of the "fourth branch" of government. More important still, it is fundamental to our very way of thinking about politics; increasingly, significant matters of public (and even private) affairs become disputes over freedom of expression.

These important debates over free speech are critical episodes in America's continuing discussion about the competing priorities of individual rights and community concerns. Broadly, such issues animate much of current democratic theory. More specifically, however, the tensions they reveal are central and longstanding features of the American free speech tradition. In contemporary jurisprudence, this debate over competing priorities is seen in the differences between those who regard individual liberty as the central value of the First Amendment and those who contend that democratic self-government is paramount. In fact, as the constitutional scholar Robert C. Post explains, "this tension is internal to the domain of democracy." The laws and norms that are intended to make democratic discourse possible are "intrinsically contestable," always open to the criticism that they overly stress either social cohesion or individual autonomy, both of which are "necessary for democratic legitimacy."[3]

These and related tensions, I contend, have been with us from the first major episode of Anglophone conflict over press liberty. More important, in our very efforts to address these controversies—in the repeated calls for a "free and open debate"—we employ the distinctive language of the "free and open press" that reflects the persistence of these tensions.[4] It was the early American concept of the "free and open press" that would at first unite, and later bifurcate, the potentially contradictory demands of community and individual. Instead of tackling recent press issues, then, I trace this contradictory discourse from its emergence through the very founding of our current concept of democratic press liberty.

The Founding of Modern, Democratic Press Liberty

"I thank God, *there are no free schools* nor *printing,* and I hope we shall not have these hundred years," Sir William Berkeley, Governor of Virginia, wrote of his colony to the House of Lords in 1671. "For *learning* has brought disobedience, and heresy, and sects into the world, and *printing* has divulged them, and libels against the best government. God keep us from both!"[5] A century and a quarter later, a fellow Virginian, James Madison, would write his national legislature in a remarkably different spirit, declaring that "to the press alone, chequered as it is with abuses, the world is indebted for all the triumphs which have been gained by reason and humanity, over error and oppression."[6]

The considerable rhetorical chasm between Berkeley and Madison is reflective of a theoretical divide that is deeper still. Berkeley, for example, would certainly have agreed with the position taken formally by his successor, Lord Culpeper, prohibiting any printing without prior royal approval and proper license.[7] Madison, to the contrary, maintained that freedom of the press was necessary, and he further required "that it should be exempt, not only from previous restraint by the executive . . . but from legislative restraint also; and this exemption, to be effectual, must be an exemption not only from the previous inspection of licensers, but from the subsequent penalty of laws."[8]

The extreme divergence of these statements reflects the reformation in political discourse that culminated in the founding of the American tradition of press liberty. The striking conceptual shift that took place involved not simply matters of definition but also competing understandings and justifications of free expression. The transformation cut to the very core of Americans' evolving theories concerning government, the public sphere, and, ultimately, democracy. The primary aim of this book is to explain these evolutions through a conceptual history of press liberty. This conceptual history begins by examining the legacy of some of the earliest debates over freedom of the press in England and concludes by analyzing the pivotal political and theoretical struggle over the Sedition Act of 1798.

As I explain shortly, the extensive secondary literature on this important topic has been polarized by a contentious debate that has raged for almost half a century. One side tends to overemphasize eighteenth-century efforts to suppress the expanding public sphere of early America, while the other has overreacted by focusing almost exclusively on "libertarian" rhetoric and practices. Predictably, the results of this exchange have been mixed. One outcome is a scattered but rich body of research that has been a crucial resource for this study. Another outcome, however, is a pair of competing interpretations, neither of which helps us understand the sound evidence uncovered by the other side. The burden of this book, then, is to furnish a new conceptual framework that explains both bodies of evidence.

That conceptual framework is the ambivalent tradition of the "free and open press." Praising the freedom of political expression, the colonists of North America frequently lauded the "free and open press," by which they referred generally to the public sphere of unhampered political discourse. Until the 1760s, press liberty was seen as a unified concept, even though it comprised a number of separate claims. Increasingly during the first half of the eighteenth century, these various claims coalesced into two strains of argument that I call "free press" doctrine and "open press" doctrine (drawing the terms from midcentury colonial discourse). Free press doctrine lionized the press as the prime defender of public liberty in its role as a bulwark against governmental tyranny. Open press doctrine, on the other hand, stressed the individual right of every man to air his sentiments for all to consider, regardless of his political perspective or the consequences for the people's liberty.

The distinction between these doctrines was brought to the surface only during the pre-Revolutionary crisis of the 1760s and 1770s and was probably clear even then to only a few colonists. Nevertheless, I seize on it and expand on it, employing it in a more systematic way than the colonists ever did. (For example, I use the terms "free press" and "open press" exclusively to refer to these doctrines.)[9] I take the liberty of employing these terms retrospectively precisely because my doing so enables us to understand a legacy of both suppression and liberation. For, as we shall see, the free press and the open press could be complementary (and relatively libertarian), as when a printer who favored the nascent patriot movement published a critique of a Tory administration (thus defending public liberty by airing his sentiments). But the same printer just as easily suppressed a Tory response by contradicting open press values and trumping them with the free press claim that the danger to public liberty would be too great if he were to open his paper to tyrannical efforts "calculated to inflame and divide."[10]

This framework, then, can explain both bodies of evidence uncovered by the secondary literature. But our press liberty tradition continues to exhibit contradictory impulses toward liberation *and* suppression. In important ways, these impulses are the legacy of the free and open press of the eighteenth century. Thus, in providing this historical analysis, I further hope to inform current debates over free speech by revealing the essential ambivalence that continues to plague the very foundation of modern American democratic press liberty.

Though the main substantive focus of this book is press liberty, analysis of the founding stages of this fundamental debate reveals a great deal about the character of American political thought more generally. The recurring rhetorical controversy over press liberty acts as a particularly illuminating window into early American political discourse precisely because it allows the analyst to view, often all at once, a great many crucial elements of that developing body of thought. The philosophical yet practical debates over press liberty involved questions of individual rights, the public good, liberty, commerce, sovereignty, and the nature of the public sphere; ultimately, the issue of press freedom forced early Americans to reexamine and reconceive the very nature of democracy. Capitalizing on this revealing perspective, this book also seeks to inform and advance current scholarship on the character of early American political discourse.

Contested Academic Terrain

Given contemporary battles over press liberty such as those concerning pornography and racist "hate speech," it is perhaps not surprising that the historiography of eighteenth-century American free press discourse is rife with debate. One press liberty historian observes that those new to the topic "may feel as if they wandered into the middle of an argument. They have."[11] Actually, it is worse than that. Investigating the conceptual history of American press liberty in its founding stages, one immediately and unavoidably finds oneself in the middle of not one but two enduring scholarly debates. The first controversy involves the history of press freedom, and the second regards early American political thought and culture more generally. In both cases, the way I examine and relate this history serves to undermine and recast these debates.

Press Liberty or Suppression?

One of the heated arguments into which we have wandered began in ear-nest about forty years ago, though its roots go back to much earlier in the century. By 1950 or so, the weight of informed opinion—shared by most legal scholars and Supreme Court Justices—held that the American Revolutionaries and Framers intentionally established a full freedom of expression by wiping out the crime of seditious libel. Seditious libel, though a "damnably difficult concept to define," refers generally to the crime of publishing criticism of the government, its men or measures.[12] Thus, Zechariah Chafee, a preeminent free speech scholar, wrote in 1941 that the First Amendment was intended to make "prosecutions for criticism of the government, without any incitement to law-breaking, forever impossible in the United States of America."[13]

Enter the legal historian Leonard W. Levy. His highly influential 1960 book, *Legacy of Suppression: Freedom of Speech and Press in Early American History,* provided "a useful antidote to saccharine, knee-jerking patriotic versions" of the Framers and free speech that were espoused—without much evidence or investigation—by Chafee and virtually all legal scholars.[14] Against that orthodox belief in the liberating intentions of the Framers, Levy's history presented a radical revisionism.[15] Throughout *Legacy,* Levy offered rich details in support of his claim that eighteenth-century "American experience with freedom of political expression was as slight as the theoretical inheritance was narrow."[16] Early Americans simply accepted and lived by the traditional view, codified most influentially by the English jurist Sir William Blackstone, that freedom of expression meant freedom from prior restraint, not subsequent punishment. Levy's view that the Framers left us with a Blackstonian "legacy of suppression" went on to become the new orthodoxy, even appearing in the landmark free speech ruling, *New York Times Co. v. Sullivan* (1964).[17]

Nevertheless, *Legacy* elicited a storm of criticism.[18] Perhaps most damning was the observation, made first by the historian Merrill Jensen and subsequently documented by many others, that the public discourse of early America was rife with seditious libel.[19] Then, in the early 1980s, major law review essays challenged Levy on the theoretical as well as the practical evidence and presented detailed documentation that undermined his Blackstonian interpretation of the First Amendment.[20] Levy defended *Legacy,* but even then a revision was in the works.[21]

"I am revising myself," Levy announced in the preface to *Emergence of a Free Press* (1985), the "revised and enlarged edition" of *Legacy.*[22] After admitting that he had written *Legacy* in anger and in order to spite liberals who did not want him to publish his revisionist history, Levy made a number of more substantive confessions.[23] He admitted that in *Legacy* he "ignored" evidence of "nearly epidemic" seditious libel and was thus "wrong" in claiming that American experience with press liberty was "slight."[24] He went on to concede that it was misleading to suggest that the Framers intended the First Amendment to provide only freedom from prior restraint. Perhaps most important for our purposes, Levy recognized that many in the Framing generation saw the press as a fourth branch of government and realized that a robust freedom of political expression was necessary for genuine popular sovereignty.[25]

"In the end," however, "Levy is unable to decide how much of *Legacy* to repudiate."[26] Indeed, Levy stuck to his guns on a number of important claims. First, his "principal thesis remain[ed] unchanged:" "The revolutionary generation did not seek to wipe out the core idea of seditious libel, that the government may be criminally assaulted by mere words." Second, and significantly for our conceptual history,

Levy still held that "the theory of freedom of political expression remained quite narrow until 1798, except for a few aberrant statements."[27] And though he conceded that early Americans in fact had plenty of *practical* experience with free political criticism, Levy insisted that such practice is irrelevant to his theoretical inquiry.[28]

To those who found stout roots of American free speech libertarianism in the eighteenth century, Levy's dismissal of the practice and belittling of the theory of press liberty left *Emergence* woefully one-sided. And, indeed, it is.[29] As these "libertarian" interpreters have recently shown, Levy's revision—despite its own solid evidence—still leaves a great deal of data unexplained. David Rabban, for example, in his lengthy and detailed critique of *Emergence,* has pointed to a number of fundamental weaknesses in Levy's approach. First, as we have seen, Levy simply refuses to explain the reality of a "savage," unfettered press. This evidence "amazes" him and leaves him "puzzled," yet he maintains that neither the lack of libel trials nor the reality of an unbounded press illuminates the meaning of freedom of the press.[30] "Levy's refusal to reflect on the paradoxes between practice and theory constitutes a basic weakness of his analysis."[31]

Though it may be true that the practice of press freedom does not directly or simply explain the concept of press liberty, it does help us understand exactly what manner of press freedom historical agents took their repeated justifications to be legitimating. Accordingly, I attempt in this book to attend more carefully to the peculiar context of legal change and the critical interdependence between theory and practice; thus, we may hope to achieve a better grasp of subtle but significant theoretical developments prior to 1798.

A second and central point for Rabban is that Levy's grasp of theoretical developments before the Sedition Act controversy is also impaired by the standard he applies to theories of press freedom.[32] Committed to demonstrating that no trace of our contemporary understanding of press liberty emerged before 1798, Levy concentrated exclusively on our current definition of freedom of the press, which rejects the notion of seditious libel. This standard, however, is a singularly anachronistic yardstick with which to measure a considerably removed historical period. As a result, he missed significant shifts in argument that fall short of the mark. Furthermore, Levy largely interpreted the history as progressing toward a repudiation of seditious libel. But as we see later, to the historical agents themselves, seditious libel per se ceased to be the sole pivotal issue after the trial of the New York printer John Peter Zenger in 1735.

Finally, Rabban's excellent essay also draws our attention to a crucial body of historical scholarship that Levy ignored.[33] Since the 1960s, a mountain of historical research has documented the increasingly dominant "republican" character of American political thought during the eighteenth century. This literature, discussed more fully later, finds in early American political discourse a stress on civic virtue and public, rather than private, good. Neglecting this research, Levy found no broad theoretical change that would have undermined traditional views of press liberty. To the contrary, I maintain that republican ideology played a crucial role in the development of press freedom. As we shall see, republicanism's emphasis on the contest between public liberty and governmental power helps explain early Americans' increasingly rich appreciation of the relationship between press liberty and popular sovereignty.

But the libertarian interpreters' assault on *Emergence* did not end with Rabban's essay. Drawing in part on republican historiography, Jeffery A. Smith has recently investigated the ideology and practice of early American printers, revealing and ably documenting the evidence of what he calls "libertarianism."[34] By focusing on printers such as Benjamin Franklin, Smith was able to correct some of Levy's oversights and misinterpretations while generally demonstrating that "libertarian" practices and principles were more widespread and more important than Levy recognized.[35]

Recent work, then, has provided a powerful counterpoint to Levy's account. But radical revisionism like Levy's invites radical responses. Thus, if only to set the record straight, Rabban's essay and Smith's book heavily stress the most libertarian moments and arguments. To be sure, Smith has noted that the meaning of press liberty "consisted of many strands and many colors."[36] Yet, as one reviewer has observed, Smith still "seeks a core 'libertarian' position." As a result of this sharp focus, much of Levy's solid evidence "emerges largely untouched."[37] Moreover, the thinking of conservatives is left unexplained.[38]

This, then, is the crux of our problem. Having wandered into this academic argument, how are we to explain an ambivalent legacy that presents indisputable evidence of efforts at suppression that exist alongside attempts at liberation? How, for example, are we to understand Patriot defenses of their publicly condemning and even hanging in effigy a Tory printer simply for making his newspaper open to contributors of every political stripe, precisely when monumental public issues were being discussed? We might, with Smith, simply label such instances "inconsistencies," or failures of "libertarian" self-control.[39] But that will not do, because, as we shall see, many moves to suppress the press were defended—with sincerity and acumen—as efforts to *protect* press liberty.

Happily, we are not alone in our effort to make sense of this ambivalent legacy. An excellent essay by the historian Richard Buel directly confronts some of Levy's evidence and explains it by noting that republicanism would permit some suppression of press freedom if it was necessary to defend the people's liberty more generally.[40] This certainly accords with my analysis, since I document a longstanding emphasis on the press as a bulwark against governmental encroachment and thus the prime defender of public liberty (the free press). However, Buel's essay fails to appreciate the interdependent, if potentially contradictory, role of open press doctrine: the strain of argument that posits the right of every man to air his sentiments for all to consider, regardless of the political viewpoint advanced and its impact on public liberty.

One scholar who suggests a distinct open press approach is the late Stephen Botein. For Botein, however, developments in press discourse are best explained as part of reactive "business strategies," such as maintaining an impartial newspaper open to all sides so as to serve all possible customers.[41] The printers examined here certainly were businessmen, and, as we shall see, economics played an important role in the conceptual history of press liberty. Yet, whereas Botein saw economics as the main determinant of press theory and practice, I demonstrate that these forces were subordinate. The main forces of change were ideological and political. Indeed, it is only by examining these contexts that we can begin to explain the pivotal conceptual evolutions of the eighteenth century.

Previous studies, then, for different reasons and from different perspectives, fail to explain fully our ambivalent legacy of suppression and liberation. To be sure, the heated exchanges and extremist positions of the current debate suggest the high stakes—in terms of cultural clout and legal authority—of this historiographical dispute. But the polarized academic landscape also provides fertile ground for this book's effort to synthesize this disjointed literature by employing some new analysis and certain new material. Ultimately, I hope to reveal the central dynamic of the founding of American press liberty. That dynamic involved two interconnected yet potentially contradictory doctrines (free press and open press) that developed within an evolving tradition (the free and open press). By taking account of this central dynamic, the present study explains a great deal more of the evidence, both practical and theoretical, than either strand of the existing scholarship. This analysis thus allows us to better understand the foundation of modern American democratic press liberty.

This clearer understanding is, of course, valuable to scholars. For example, the historian John Nerone can see only irony in the Patriots' antipress violence against Tories in the early 1770s, given the Patriots' repeated praise for press liberty.[42] My analysis, however, offers a richer understanding of this critical moment when Patriots and Tories forced each other to rethink the unitary free and open press discourse, ultimately causing its bifurcation into two clearly distinguished and potentially contradictory doctrines. But appreciating the conceptual evolution of press liberty and accounting for more of the evidence is not only a matter of getting the history right. The current standoff between Levy and the libertarian interpreters is deeply troubling for contemporary free speech thinking because both stories imply that defending press liberty is a simple and easy business. Levy used an anachronistic standard and ignored actual press practice to demonstrate that the Framers fell short of "true" press liberty, only to claim that it appeared abruptly around 1800; this leaves the reader satisfied that we have since largely succeeded where eighteenth-century statesmen failed. Smith, Rabban, and others rescue old myths by stressing the grand struggle for republican liberty while largely ignoring Levy's solid evidence of recurrent suppression. According to either interpretation, liberty of expression is something we need not spend a lot of time or effort on: We can be ensured success simply by continuing to surpass—or by merely following—early heroes. But, as this study demonstrates, explaining both bodies of evidence reveals a much more demanding, ambivalent legacy, one we need to appreciate fully if we are to address our contemporary free speech struggles in any depth and with any success.

A "Notorious Debate"

As I suggested earlier, revisiting and reinterpreting early controversies over free expression teaches us a great deal about early American political thought. Thus, in this book I hope to recast the second argument into which we have wandered: the longstanding and remarkably persistent debate over the general character of eighteenth-century American political thought. This debate between "liberal" and "republican" interpreters is well known and well documented, so I will not tax the reader with yet another lengthy summary.[43] Suffice it to say that "liberal" students of early American political thought, such as Joyce Appleby and John Patrick Diggins, see a stress on individual rights and responsibilities in commercially expanding eighteenth-century America. They emphasize the role of John Locke and other early theorists interpreted as liberals and stress the emergence of motivating norms focused on individual rights and liberties in the maintenance of contract and commerce.[44] The "republican" school, alluded to earlier, is frequently associated with Bernard Bailyn, Gordon Wood, and J. G. A. Pocock, among others, and sees as central to early American political thought a concern with the people's common good as threatened by either a power-hungry administration or the inevitable decay of republican forms of government. This interpretation stresses the place of civic virtue in the thought of the colonists and considers Locke but one influence among many.[45] Finally, much of this debate centers on differences over when republicanism "ended" and liberalism "began."

In the past decade or so, there has been a welcome recognition that the relationship between liberalism and republicanism in early American political thought is more complex.[46] The present study contributes to some recent attempts to reconsider this academic debate by elucidating a certain degree of historical and theoretical consonance between republican and liberal thought.[47] Fitting neatly within neither side of the debate, my analysis demonstrates the need to recast this scholarly discourse. As we shall see, a predominantly "republican" stress on public liberty and the public good (free press doctrine) and a more nearly "liberal" notion of individual rights (open press doctrine) coexisted in a single, ambivalent tradition throughout much of the eighteenth century. The way these two doctrines of press liberty played out during the second half of that century suggests the inadequacies of any approach that assumes an adversarial relationship between liberal and republican political "languages."

But what, then, are we to make of this ambivalent tradition? Acknowledging the plethora of solid, textual evidence that supports each of the competing interpretations, one recent approach, advanced by

Michael Zuckert, seeks to explain both bodies of evidence. Early Americans' appeal to both liberal and republican themes makes sense, according to this view, because the themes existed on different "levels" of political thought. Republicanism is really political thinking on the level of political science, while what is often called "liberalism" exists on the plane of political philosophy.[48] Elsewhere, the distinction is characterized as that between "fundamental ends and necessary means," or simply as that between "theory" and "practice."[49] However described, this distinction saves early Americans from their contradictions by harmonizing republican and liberal themes on parallel levels, thus returning the liberal Locke to his central role of theorizing about the fundamental ends of government for which the republican politics of America would be fashioned.

This ends/means distinction is clearly a very promising approach, furnishing as it does a rather tidy resolution to a longstanding and influential scholarly muddle. On the other hand, in this book I investigate a pivotal political concept from its seventeenth-century roots through its puzzling eighteenth-century mixture of liberal and republican themes. And, contrary to this recent interpretation, I demonstrate that, as the concept of press liberty evolved, liberal and republican themes exhibited discord, as well as harmony. Specifically, we shall see the open press priority on individual rights and the free press emphasis on defending the public good coexist in one vague but unified tradition until the unprecedented contexts of the Revolutionary and Founding eras revealed previously unseen contradictions, which in turn forced that tradition to bifurcate and subsequently evolve.

None of the ideological twists and turns I analyze in this book would be problematic for Zuckert's approach if they involved discursive moves between distinct levels of thought, between philosophical fundamentals and the practical means of governing men. However, for the issue of press liberty at least, no such distinction is tenable. Press freedom was and is a topic given to clashes that involve both practical politics and abstract philosophy. For early Americans, press liberty was an end as well as a means, a matter of both the philosophy and the science of politics. As a practical "means," free speech was taken to be the primary "bulwark" of all other liberties, private as well as public. But, as we shall soon see, free speech was also a matter of "the general principles of liberty, and rights of man, in nature and in society" for Thomas Jefferson and his contemporaries.[50] Thus, the penetrating issue of press liberty suggests the untenable nature of any attempt to resolve the "notorious" liberal/republican debate through a distinction between ends and means.

The Conceptual History of Press Liberty

How, then, are we to resolve the dilemma presented by illustrious ancestors who undeniably spoke and wrote in two distinctive and often irreconcilable idioms? Unfortunately, the resolution I advocate is not nearly as orderly as that explored by Zuckert; indeed, it is not really a resolution at all. Rather, I begin by conceding—with Michael Lienesch and others—that the thinking of eighteenth-century Americans was "ambivalent, contradictory, and sometimes flatly paradoxical."[51] That is, I pay the "terrible price" that scholars following Zuckert seek strenuously to avoid: "the resolute concession to human self-contradiction."[52] In fact, I have argued elsewhere that the existence of some contradictions in any individual's thinking is an unavoidable part of human life.[53] Given the breadth and depth of human thought, the almost infinite implications that those thoughts carry, and the ceaseless transformation of the world around us, it is not at all surprising that some of our views, beliefs, and practices are in conflict with others. Rather, it would be a miracle if we could keep them all in perfect harmony.

Given all these contradictions, how can we—or our historical subjects—remain functional? Actually, most of these contradictions exist on the margins of our consciousness or buried beneath the innumerable assumptions we use to make sense of the world. Thus, many of these contradictions remain *potential* contradictions until new circumstances or new criticisms highlight tensions in our (until now) seemingly coherent worldview. When we respond by attempting to justify our beliefs and actions, we occasionally (and often unintentionally) contribute to conceptual evolution[54] in the process of verbal justification.[55] My approach to studying conceptual history, then, does not mean that we must believe that eighteenth-century Americans "lived easily" with confusion.[56] Rather, it simply means that they, like us, could not always see all the distant implications and unintended consequences of their beliefs, actions, and practices.

Allowing for contradictions in the discourse of those we study, however, is not without its risks. We might easily and anachronistically see contradictions where they did not exist for the historical agents or depict the agents as oblivious to the tensions in their views when, in fact, they were quite mindful of them. But, as the "notorious" liberal/republican debate has made abundantly clear, ignoring the ambivalence of early American discourse is no guarantee of avoiding anachronism. We must, I argue, listen carefully to the historical agents themselves and do so in a way that avoids too much abstract discussion without recourse to real issues, events, and arguments. By narrowing our focus to a single issue, albeit a pivotal one, we should be able to analyze accurately the emerging tensions in an ambivalent tradition just as the early Americans themselves began to perceive and address them, often with conceptual change.

Listening carefully and closely to the historical agents requires defining the scope of one's study in a deliberate way. Certainly the conceptual history of press liberty is only a small part of the history of the book in America. This much broader narrative explores elite domination of information, printer self-regulation, and the role of print in everyday lives; I am indebted to this scholarship for informing my analysis, as I am to the emerging literature on the early American public sphere.[57] Yet, seeking to explain the conceptual evolution of the "freedom of the press" that established modern, democratic press liberty, I focus tightly on the discursive use—and, indeed, *innovative* discursive use—of this concept.

In what follows, I concentrate my attention on the explicitly political press. The content of children's literature has a political dimension, and it might well reveal new evidence of interest to historical political philosophy,[58] but it rarely provides thoughtful discourse on the concept of press liberty. Discussions of personal libel, on the other hand, are much more likely to bear on questions of democratic press liberty, especially when either of the parties is a public figure. Such cases are discussed in due course. Furthermore, though I explore the discourse of relatively modest figures such as printers, my focus on the discursive formation of the concept of press liberty tends to exclude those—such as women and slaves—most often excluded from the early debates. Finally, the issues of religious toleration, religious liberty, and free speech often prove to be of great interest. As we shall see momentarily, religious toleration and religious liberty played a critical role in the development of press liberty during the seventeenth century. And the theory and practice of "free speech" is often addressed interchangeably with press liberty in the following pages precisely because that is how the historical figures frequently employed the terms.

To be sure, analyzing the conceptual history of a single momentous issue requires that one look to the many relevant contexts (and changes in those contexts) that might have influenced the concept's evolution. These contexts often range from the material, such as demographics and economic circumstances, to those more obviously discursive, such as religious, linguistic, cultural, and ideological backgrounds. The vast secondary literatures mentioned earlier, and especially those on press liberty and early American political thought, have made a broad study of these various contexts possible. Previous research has also provided an invaluable introduction to an otherwise insurmountable mountain of primary sources. Without this solid scholarship as a guide, an extensive analysis of the thousands of pertinent newspapers, broadsides, pamphlets, sermons, and books—not to mention legal records, legislative journals, private diaries, and personal correspondence—would have been well-nigh impossible.

The academic historian and the informed lay reader will find in these pages some familiar figures and well-worn passages. But they will also find less familiar names and often-ignored texts. More important, my thesis of a conceptual tradition that bifurcated and was later transformed presents a new reading that illustrates the central dynamic in the evolution of early American press liberty. It demonstrates how arguments and elements we might readily label "liberal" and "republican" coexisted in a unified yet ambivalent tradition, at times exhibiting coherence and at others displaying contradiction and tension. Ultimately, I have endeavored to provide a more accurate, if more complex, assessment than is currently available of the founding of modern American democratic press liberty, and of the figures and texts that contributed to it. Such an analysis is necessary if we are to understand fully the ambivalent nature of the political tradition to which we are heir.

1

The English Inheritance
From Milton to Cato

The eighteenth-century Americans who concern us here were not really American at all; they were, for the most part, English. Accordingly, the purpose of this chapter is to analyze the theoretical background from which the colonists of British America could draw. This will provide a benchmark against which later developments can be compared. More specifically, I survey the vast array of arguments that emerged during the seventeenth century, the first era of significant press liberty discourse in Anglo-American political thought. Many of those arguments later fell away because of the end of licensing, increased secularization, and broad philosophical shifts. The remaining arguments coalesced into two strains of argument that I have been calling free press doctrine and open press doctrine, borrowing the terms from the historical agents themselves. Throughout the course of this study we will follow eighteenth-century Americans as they isolate, re-examine, and recast these concepts, ultimately arriving at a recognizably modern, if still ambivalent, understanding of press liberty.

My goal is to examine the English inheritance concerning press liberty and to define and analyze the distinguishable, but as yet indistinct, doctrines of the free press and the open press. In order to do this as succinctly as possible, we stress influential theorists from the three major periods of debate: the radical 1640s, the licensing disputes of the turn of the century, and the response of "Cato" to the unscrupulous politics of the 1720s.

First Flush of Freedom

The three years leading up to the Printing Ordinance of 1643 witnessed the first great explosion of press freedom in the history of the Anglo-

Saxon world. The Ordinance, and succeeding acts, presented real threats to this new-found liberty. Reacting to the dire need to protect press liberty, several religious and political radicals went into print, providing the first concerted defense of the liberty of the press in the Anglo-American tradition.

The press was not new to England in 1640, having been introduced at least by 1476, possibly by 1468. The crown immediately assumed the prerogative over the press, with Henry VIII instituting the first comprehensive royal licensing system in 1538. By 1640, control was considerable, if imperfect, and was founded upon the old Tudor alliance of the crown and the Stationers' Company, whereby the crown let the Stationers monopolize the press in exchange for a commitment to help combat seditious and blasphemous printing.[1]

But if the printing press and its regulation were not new to the 1640s, neither were claims for some measure of press liberty. To be sure, for most sixteenth-century Englishmen, the idea that subjects should have the privilege of publishing their sentiments was seen as dangerous.[2] Nevertheless, by 1600, Members in Parliament, at least, had freedom of speech, though debates would sometimes erupt over whether this allowed Members to discuss certain topics, such as the royal succession. Amid these debates, Peter Wentworth defended freedom of speech in 1570, asking, "how can Truth appear and conquer until falsehood and all subtleties that should shadow and darken it be found out?"[3] Thanks to Wentworth and others, the revolutionaries of the 1640s had several established radical Protestant traditions on which to draw.[4]

In addition to some philosophical precedents, the 1640s were also heir to a history not altogether devoid of practical experience with press liberty or, rather, licentiousness. Black-market printing was by no means unheard of (a third of sixteenth-century books went unregistered),[5] and importation for politics and profit was also a problem the Stationers' Company had to monitor. The Martin Marprelate tracts (1588–89) are perhaps the most famous example of illicit printing, though these Puritan authors bristled at the application, not the principle, of press regulation.[6]

These experiences notwithstanding, the practical freedom of the early 1640s was unique and unrivaled. With the weakening of the crown in the late 1630s, the Stationers moved to ally with Parliament. But the Company was in limbo for three years, from 1640 to 1643, during which time previously suppressed printers openly published attacks on both Parliament and the king. Suddenly, every political or religious extremist found the press available to him.[7]

This new burst of freedom was genuine. It was not, however, intentional. Political pressures and confusion led to a failure of control. Both Houses of Parliament turned to press regulation as soon as it was deemed possible. Nevertheless, during the early 1640s, "the English press operated virtually free of restriction." This liberty is dramatically demonstrated by the almost one hundredfold increase in the number of pamphlets printed during this period, from twenty-two, in 1640, to a peak of 1,966, in 1642.[8] This practical freedom continued throughout the decade, despite repeated attempts by Parliament and the Stationers to reestablish control. Significantly, these conditions provided the occasion for the first explosion of press liberty discourse.

Gifted rhetoricians that they were, the radical defenders of the free press used many different arguments in their tracts, often presenting two or three separate arguments in the same paragraph. Fortunately, these myriad defenses can be aggregated into a handful of general types of claims without too much violence to the texts or their spirit. In what follows, then, I briefly survey and analyze these different types of arguments. I begin with the more practical and rhetorical arguments. While these may be of less interest to us today, they are quite common in the tracts and were central to the propaganda war being fought. As such, examining these gives us a more accurate picture of the pamphlets, as well as a feeling for the debate.[9] From there, we move to examine the arguments that proved most influential to the conceptual history examined in this study.

The Practical and Rhetorical Arguments

Arguments, by their very nature, tend to be rhetorical and aim at some practical end. But the contentions I refer to here are rhetorical in the worst sense: bombastic and hyperbolic, yet lacking in substance. Typically, these barbs involved a sort of guilt by association, usually labeling press regulation as "Papist." There was simply no more efficient way to stigmatize one's adversaries than to associate their principles with those of the "Roman Antichrist." John Milton, the master wordsmith, was quite adept at this tactic, but it is perhaps the Leveller leader John Lilburne who epitomized the strategy, writing, in his open letter to the more moderate John Prynne, "truly, had I not seen your name to your Bookes, I should rather have judged them a Papists or a Jesuites."[10]

If these rhetorical arrows should miss their mark, one could simply claim that regulation could not possibly work or was bound to be counterproductive. Indeed, as the 1640s wore on, press regulation did seem more and more ineffective. Further, Milton and others argued that attempts at legal suppression would be counterproductive by making heterodox views more famous and thus would "prove a nursing mother to sects."[11]

A more reflective, if still practical, tack was to argue that, since licensers (like all people) are fallible, to license the press is to risk suppressing truth. This argument was a favorite of John Goodwin, whose *Theomachia*—"one of the most important publications of the entire period"—bore the subtitle *The Grand Imprudence of men, running the hazard of <u>Fighting against God</u>, in suppressing any Way, Doctrine, or Practice, concerning which they know not certainly whether it be from God, or no.* The centrality of religion, and the ubiquitous scriptural references used by Goodwin and others to make this argument, suggests the fundamental role religious issues played throughout the revolutionary era.[12] Of course, religion and politics were profoundly interdependent at this time; nevertheless, it is significant that, though the Levellers' petitions to Parliament in 1647 and 1648 make this argument without scriptural support, the censorship and subsequent punishment of religious publications are their most pressing concerns.[13]

The One Truth Shall Prevail

Pragmatism and hyperbolic rhetoric can be efficient argumentative tools, and there is no reason to believe they were not effective in the raging debate of the 1640s. Nevertheless, the prevailing assumption, reinforced by recent experience, that free debate would lead to division and disorder had to be seriously addressed if the radical case was to be persuasive. The radicals generally argued in response that the Presbyterian Divines and, before them, the Episcopalian bishops had obscured religious and political issues for their own interests. These obscuring tactics, licensing included, made it all but impossible for the truth to emerge and thereby unite the nation.[14]

In a fair fight, however, the truth—God's Truth—would most certainly prevail. This claim was perhaps the most prevalent argument for press liberty in the middle of the seventeenth century. The argument was biblical in its origins, and chapter and verse would sometimes be cited for anyone who might miss the allusions.[15] The "bible" for the latter-day Revolutionaries of America, however, would be Milton's prose works.[16] And, while *Areopagitica* seems to have gone almost entirely unnoticed by its contemporary audience, this fact may be explained by its decorous presentation and its classical language.[17] This language, of course, is what makes Milton so quotable today. "We do injuriously by licencing and prohibiting to misdoubt [Truth's] strength," he argued. "Let her and Falshood grapple; who ever knew Truth put to the wors, in a free and open encounter[?]." William Walwyn is almost as eloquent: "All mens mouthes should be open, that so errour may discover its foulnes and trueth become more glorious by a victorious conquest after a fight in open field; they shunne the battell that doubt their strength."[18]

The Leveller party, in its Petition of 18 January 1649, provides perhaps the most innovative rendering of this critical argument. Reacting to parliamentary moves to enforce strictly the comparatively draconian Printing Ordinance of 1647, it took this argument onto secular, political ground and explained its logic.

> [I]f Government be just in its Constitution, and equal in its distributions, it will be good, if not absolutely necessary for them, to hear all voices and judgements, which they can never do, but by giving freedom to the Press; and in case any abuse their authority by scandalous Pamphlets, they will never want Advocates to vindicate their innocency.

The "good of the Commonwealth," like religious truth, would also prevail in open debate. And why would it prevail? Because falsity is easily combatted in a fair encounter. Indeed, the Levellers insisted, "scandalous Pamphlets" do "greater mischief" when licensing restricts "proper and effectual answers."[19]

The Necessity of Conscience

The radicals wanted to persuade their readers that press freedom, and free expression generally, was the best and quickest way to end division and bring out the one unifying Truth. Failing that, if the readers were not persuaded or just did not want to let radicals have their opinions, many theorists argued, as Thomas Hobbes soon would, that they simply had no choice but to believe what they believed.[20] Walwyn maintained that "man is by his own reason necessitated to be of that mind he is, now where there is a necessity there ought to be no punishment." Lilburne echoed Walwyn's sentiment, insisting that "it is the incommunicable Prerogative of Jesus Christ alone . . . to raigne in the soules and consciences of his chosen ones."[21]

In *A Helpe to the Right Understanding of a Discourse concerning Episcopacy* (1645), Walwyn truly broke new ground. After extending the argument to "the free and undisturbed exercise" of one's conscience, Walwyn suggested that Parliament is subordinate (at least theoretically) to the very people it is attempting to control. An established Royalist argument had been that Parliament had only those powers the people could grant it, and Royalists knew that most moderate Parliamentarians would concede the people's powers were few indeed.[22] Walwyn, seeking to limit Parliament for differing reasons, simply turned this argument to his own purposes. He abruptly shifted from his religious exegesis to assert baldly that Parliament cannot have any power the people did not grant it; since the people cannot possibly have the right to force others against their consciences, Parliament cannot properly do so, either.

> [T]he people of a Nation in chusing of a Parliament cannot confer more then that power which was justly in themselves; the plain rule being this: That which a man may not voluntarily binde himself to doe, or to forbear to doe, without sinne: That he cannot entrust or refer unto the ordering of any other: Whatsoever (be it Parliament, Generall Councels, or Nationall Assemblies:)

Or, more simply, "what the people cannot entrust . . . [Parliament] cannot have."[23]

This argument is potentially very radical. The Levellers would repeat it, maintaining that Parliament is inferior to those "who chuse them," and Williams would argue that if the people do not have a "*power originally* and *fundamentally*," it is impossible to "derive it *Ministerially*."[24] Nevertheless, to the best of my knowledge, neither Walwyn nor any of his contemporaries drew out the implication of reversing this logic—that, since Parliament has a right to free speech, the people must have it as well. The arguments from the necessity of conscience had begun to chip away at some of the foundation of the arguments against press liberty.

Exploring this innovative logic would have provided the radicals with a convincing thrust to their arguments for the right of press freedom. An easier tactic, however, was just to claim it.

Claiming the Commoners' Right

Walwyn's "grant-of-power" argument, even if someone had traced the logic backward, would have struck many as extremely radical and would have lacked any accepted precedent. It seemed simpler and less novel merely to expand the established Member's right to free expression during Parliament to include subjects who were not in Parliament. Though the First Amendment scholar Leonard Levy stated that no one would employ this extended claim until the turn of the century, in fact Walwyn, Milton, and Lilburne all were willing to borrow from (and perhaps bend) recent history in support of this claim.[25] Earlier, when the bishops had complained that the Divines were attacking them in the press, Walwyn argued, "*some of You* [in Parliament] *made answer, that there was no remedy, forasmuch as* the Presse was to be open and free for all in time of Parliament: *I shall make bold as a* Common *of* England *to lay claim to that* privilege." But, later in the same paragraph Walwyn dropped the historical logic and simply wrote in defense of "just Liberty *in time of* Parliament."[26]

Lilburne was the most straightforward, using a largely unintentional failure of control in the recent past to establish a moral right to press liberty. He appealed to the Presbyterian Divines, "that the Presse might be as open for us as for you, and as it was at the beginning of this *Parliament*, which I conceive the *Parliament* did of purpose, thatso the freeborne *English* Subjects might enjoy their Liberty and Priviledge, which the Bishops had learned . . . to rob them of."[27]

Lilburne's position was the most extreme. He claimed freedom of the press on the grounds of a subject's liberty, even asserting that this liberty had existed at some time before the bishops "robbed" the people of it. Lilburne further suggested that the established reasoning for a free press, the need to debate during Parliament, applies to subjects, as well as to Members. He went on to note, however, that the sitting Parliament provides a punishing body should someone "abuse his penne." This argument is a little disingenuous, since Lilburne well knew that the Long Parliament and its regulations were proving less than effective.[28] Nevertheless, Lilburne made the strongest case for the subject's liberty of the press, while at the same time raising the pivotal issue of just how far this freedom goes.

The Extent and Purpose of the Commoners' Right

Even if the right that Lilburne was claiming for English subjects was meant only to allow debate, the moderate majority might well have insisted that certain ideas were simply beyond the pale, even dangerous. Our radicals surely knew that most people feared the dissolution of society. But even though the masses of people tended (at least in the early 1640s) to be fearful of societal breakdown, we might well expect our radicals to be more revolutionary. We are thus surprised to find them excluding seditious printing from the right of press freedom. Walwyn, for one, concluded his *Compassionate Samaritane* by calling on Parliament to agree "that the Presse may be free for any man, that writes nothing scandalous or dangerous to the State."[29]

These would not be considered libertarian sentiments today. Yet the issue of the extent and purpose of this right claimed on behalf of the common people of England is crucial to an accurate interpretation of these early arguments concerning press liberty. If we read our own current First Amendment freedoms into the radicals' claims, we are sure to overestimate them. Conversely, however, if we are not sensitive to the context, we are likely to overemphasize the limits and misread their positions.

In part, the deference to the idea of *some* limits was most likely tactical moderation in support of strategic radicalism.[30] But part of the reason these revolutionary theorists sometimes bowed to restrictions on seditious printing was that they took the restrictions to be efforts to stop the Royalist press. Lilburne, for one, made it clear that it was the Royalist writings that the radicals took to be dangerous. The licensers abused their powers, he complained, yet they allowed (or rather did not adequately discourage) the printing of Royalist "Malignant Books and Pamphlets, tending to the ruine both of the *Kingdome* and *Parliaments Priviledges*, by likewise [allowing] the sending of Printing matterials to the King, whereby to Print down both Power of Parliament, and freedome of the People."[31] The Levellers knew that the only hope of achieving any long-lasting freedom (including press freedom) lay in pressuring Parliament, not in allowing the king to propagandize freely his way back to power.

When the context shifted, and Royalist success seemed unlikely, the

Levellers began to think more creatively about press liberty. While the notion of the press as a check on tyranny had been hinted at before,[32] it was only when the king was at bay and Parliament had threatened strict regulation that the Levellers were led to apply these notions to a parliamentary despotism. As with the "truth-shall-prevail" argument, it was in the Petition of 18 January 1649 that the Levellers were at their most innovative and explicit.

> [A]ll things being duly weighed, to refer all Books and Pamphlets to the judgement, discretion, or affection of Licensers, or to put the least restraint upon the Press, seems altogether inconsistent with the good of the Commonwealth, and expressly opposite and dangerous to the liberties of the people, and to be carefully avoided, as any other exorbitancy or prejudice in Government.[33]

The notion of the press as a barrier to parliamentary as well as royal tyranny and a defender—indeed, the most essential defender—of the people's liberties would appear again and again.[34] Significantly, however, the Levellers never explained whether, in arguing against "the least restraint" on the press, they intended to put an end to subsequent punishment as well as prior censorship. The issue of subsequent punishment would have to wait for the next century.

The Overt Acts Argument

The grant-of-power claim, commoners' increasingly unrestricted rights, and the press-as-check-on-government argument were all innovative and revolutionary. The claim that only "overt acts" can harm government was at least as radical, for two reasons. First, the notion that words can endanger government was widespread. The "bad tendency" of words to breach the peace and to bring government into disrepute had been a central precept of the Star Chamber until its abolition in 1641. Second, overt acts theory strikes at the heart of the definition of seditious libel, which maintains that government can be harmed by mere words.

Perhaps the earliest hint of this argument is to be found in Roger Williams's *The Bloudy Tenent* (1644). Williams suggests the overt acts argument in several places but is most direct when he posits "a false Religion and *Worship* will not hurt the *Civill State*, in case the *worshipers* breake no *civill Law*: . . . the *Civill Lawes* not being broken, *civill Peace* is not broken: and this only is the Point in Question."[35] Williams is here concerned chiefly with religious toleration, and at no place does he specifically extend this overt acts argument to free expression regarding civil authority.

Walwyn, however, did take this argument explicitly into the civil realm. In *A Helpe*, after defending freedom of the press against claims that it would increase divisions, he countered, "and as for disturbance to the State: admit any mans judgement be so misinformed, as to beleeve there is no sinne; if this man now upon this government should take away another mans goods, or commit murder or adultery; the Law is open, and he is punished a malefactor, and so for all crimes that any mans judgement may mislead him unto."[36]

Walwyn did not develop this line of thinking any further. And his Leveller party, in its Petition of 18 January 1649, suggested only that an "abused" government can readily "vindicate their innocency." Indeed, this argument, and these early arguments more generally, are perhaps not inspiring as developed theory. Nevertheless, this first concerted attempt at press liberty discourse provided the varied and multifaceted grounding on which later defenses would be built.

The Licensing Controversy

January 1649 was at once the high point and the beginning of the end for the Levellers, both as a political movement and as innovating theorists of press liberty. The arrival of the Commonwealth and the Council of State brought with it some of the most repressive press regulations of the Interregnum. When power was centralized in Cromwell's Protectorate in 1653, press control became even more efficient. The Restoration, in turn, brought a new, exhaustive licensing act, which lasted in place, with one six-year hiatus, until 1694.

The longevity of these regulations suggests how the restored monarchy and a conservative balance of power served to remove press liberty as a topic of public debate. This is not to say that control was complete. During Sir Roger L'Estrange's long tenure as licenser (1662–79) it seems that only about half of the published pamphlet literature carried his imprimatur.[37] It is possible that some recycled Miltonian arguments played a role in the Printing Act's expiration in 1679. Still, the major reason was a political calculation in favor of postponing renewal.[38]

Then, once the Exclusion Crisis, the battle to exclude the future James II from the throne, eclipsed all other issues in the press and threatened to become violent, Charles II prorogued Parliament before the Act had been renewed.

This lapse in the licensing provisions was of no help to Algernon Sidney, both because the manuscript found in his study was unpublished and because he was tried and executed for treason, not for unlicensed printing. And while this martyrdom would make him a cherished source for the American Revolutionaries, neither he nor his confederate John Locke did much to develop the philosophy of press liberty. To be sure, both provided occasional interpretations of the truth-shall-prevail argument, and, in keeping with their broader concerns, they stressed the people's right to debate, as well as the people's revocable grant of power to their rulers.[39] Still, when Locke took up the specific issue of the licensing act in 1694, he provided many (ultimately convincing) practical arguments against renewing the Act, pausing only twice to make "sarcastic reference" to the broader principles of licensing.[40]

With Locke's memo circulating, the Printing Act of 1662 expired, never to return. And while Locke did little directly to develop press liberty philosophy, the end of licensing brought recurring exchanges during the next two decades over the merits of licensing and press regulation more generally. An examination of this discourse demonstrates the refining of the vast array of arguments that emerged in the 1640s. This can best be seen in the writings of the radical Deist Matthew Tindal. Before analyzing Tindal, however, we would do well to pause briefly to assess the philosophical context to which he was responding.

In the interests of brevity, focusing chiefly on one frequent contributor to these debates seems prudent, and Daniel Defoe provides an excellent subject. Defoe's essays can be seen as representing "the best work on both sides."[41] His general moderation and his mercenary attitude can make him difficult to characterize. Happily, this is not a biography but a conceptual history, and Defoe is a perfect source for the most articulate expression of the moderate middle ground concerning early eighteenth-century press liberty discourse.

"THAT there should be a Restraint upon the Press, seems a Matter of Necessity: But the Manner of it, a Matter of Debate," John Asgill declared as late as 1712, and many, Defoe included, would certainly have agreed.[42] The reason licensing was needed, Defoe wrote in support of the Whig government in 1699, was that truth does *not* prevail. The mere printing of an assertion makes it seem orthodox; this is especially problematic, he argued, since the "generality of mankind" are unable to detect falsity. The more corrupt among them will use the unclarity of truth as an excuse for evil, while even the indifferent will think there is no difference between truth and falsity. Ultimately, it is the Magistrate's duty to stop people who are in error.[43]

Some would go so far as to argue that the unrestrained press brings a "Tyranny" over men's reputation, since insulting attacks are "irremediable." This is true, Defoe explained, because, with the "poison" already out, the proper response arrives too late to change men's minds.[44] Writing for the Tories in 1705, Defoe concluded that debate is dangerous, since some authors are "like *Guy Faux* with his . . . Candle, walking among the Barrels of Gun-Powder."[45]

Press liberty has a direct tendency to disorder. Indeed, for many, printing *was* an overt act. Seditious authors "are [the] very Assassins of all Government," one anonymous author explained; defending libeling was tantamount to "not only the wearing of private Daggers, but the using them too, even against the Person of the Magistrate himself."[46] A regulated press was plainly necessary to check a licentious world. As for the people's rights and privileges, press liberty was not among them. Press freedom was not one of the ancient or essential liberties, nor was it necessary: "the Lords and Commons," not the people, were "a sufficient Bulwark against any Designs of Arbitrary Power."[47]

Matthew Tindal's works would be "much in Vogue" in mid-eighteenth-century America, but it was against these turn-of-the-century mainstream currents that he was fighting.[48] And it is in response to these moderate views that he fashioned a radical approach to press liberty. Tindal's highly original texts are pivotal because they demonstrate a narrowing of the range of arguments. Furthermore, Tindal's division of his arguments into civil and religious reasons against press regulation paved the way for the "free and open" press tradition that later emerged in the works of John Trenchard and Thomas Gordon.

The argument that the truth shall prevail is perhaps the most central claim that Tindal makes, and it is the essence of his "religious" reasons for press liberty. With the Glorious Revolution of 1688, the issues of religious toleration and freedom of conscience had, in large part, been resolved, leaving the argument from the necessity of conscience to fall away. Conversely, with the need to defend against the return of licensing provisions, arguments that defended the right of everyone to publish his sentiments would prove right on target.

Religious concerns remained a crucial shared basis of agreement, even in this less devout era, and Tindal, a leading Deist of the day, tied many of his arguments for opening the press to the goal of advancing Protestantism, though he was much less likely to cite Scripture than the Puritan revolutionaries of the 1640s. The rhetoric of "popery" was still effective, and Tindal used it, but he did so sparingly, tending to be more positive.[49] Thus, the main point of his advocacy of Protestantism was the promotion of the search for truth.

Press licensing, Tindal complained, hinders our examining all sides of any debate, which is "the only way to discover truth."[50] Indeed, rather than being lost in comparison with falsity, truth becomes clearer and gains the "greater Power" of belief. This is not to say that men are infallible, only that this is a reason to open, not to censor, the press, since licensers may be wrong, and ultimately men must discuss and argue for the truth to prevail.[51]

But if Tindal gave priority to religious reasons centering on the truth's power to emerge from debate, he did so not because he thought there were no convincing "civil reasons" for wider press liberty. For starters, Tindal concurred with the radicals of an earlier day in maintaining "That once [Liberty of the Press] falls, nothing we hold dear or precious is safe." Royal prerogatives would surely know no bounds. But, more than that, even "*Westminster-Hall*" would prove arbitrary if there were no press to "warn the people of their Danger."[52]

This notion that Parliament, the people's traditional defenders against royal power, could be a danger to the people flew in the face of the assumptions of the age. But Tindal would prove more radical still. After blandly maintaining that "the People retain a right to offer their Advise to their Representatives," Tindal remarked that, since the Commons "thought fit to publish their proceedings to prevent being misrepresented [as they recently had in the Occasional Conformity Act], why should they deny those they represent the Liberty?"[53]

Here, then, we find Tindal "claiming the Commoners right" and suggesting—if only obliquely—the grant-of-power logic first seen in Walwyn. He again echoed Leveller arguments in reasoning that the people should be allowed to criticize those in power; the powerful could not be injured by criticism, "since they have a number of dependents, ready upon all occasions to write in justification of their measures."[54] This argument went a long way toward undermining the concept of seditious libel, and it certainly contradicted the contemporary claim that press attacks are "irremediable."

Tindal responded to some of the most widely accepted claims of his day by renewing and refining arguments that had first flourished in the 1640s. Significantly, Tindal did more than this, he further developed his "civil" and "religious" arguments and demonstrated how they are ultimately intertwined. This unity results in part from the fact that "Priestcraft and Slavery go hand in hand." But, in fact, it goes much deeper than that. Everyone, Tindal explained, "has a natural Right in all matters of Learning and Knowledge" to say and hear what can be said on all sides of all issues, even extending to the criticism of government.[55] With this argument, Tindal went well beyond responding to any argument in support of a return to licensing. He provided a broader, more secular, and more reason-centered body of argument than had been hitherto available.

Cato and the Emergence of the Free and Open Press

With the writings of John Trenchard and Thomas Gordon, we witness the emergence of the ambivalent body of thought I have called the free and open press. The narrowing of the myriad arguments that exploded onto the scene in the 1640s concludes with the two general strains of thought developed by Trenchard and Gordon under the pseudonym "Cato." This narrowing was not entirely of their own doing, of course. Broad cultural, political, and philosophical changes contributed to the falling away of other concerns and arguments. For example, by 1720, a secular approach to political argument was far more the norm than it had been even at the turn of the century. Trenchard and Gordon's work contributed to this secularism, not merely in the anticlerical attitude of their *Independent Whig* essays, but, more significantly, in their reliance on reason and ancient history for their sources and arguments.

Cato's arguments had not only different sources but also different subjects. With licensing gone for more than a quarter of a century, Cato's press liberty concerns were primarily libel law and subsequent punishment. Stamp taxes had been introduced several years earlier by Queen Anne on Bolingbroke's advice but had proven ineffective due to readily exploited loopholes, making them gratuitous targets.[56]

The issues, too, had changed somewhat. Freedom of conscience was primarily a starting point for Cato.[57] And, while the common man's inability to reason had been disputed by Trenchard and Gordon's colleague Anthony Collins back in 1713, Cato saw fit to ignore this issue.[58] Finally, since Cato forthrightly maintained that press liberty was a natural right, he did not need to claim it as a commoner or derive it retroactively from the grant-of-power argument.

One strain of argument that Cato did employ was what I have been calling open press doctrine.[59] An open press supported the right of every man to voice his own views on any subject, whereupon others would decide for themselves whether these views had any merit. But, as modern as this formulation may sound, the reader searches in vain in Cato's works for a claim of some absolute, inherent human right to free expression. Rather, this doctrine was an elaboration and reworking of the "truth-shall-prevail" argument first stressed in the radical tracts of the 1640s.

In Cato's able hands, the argument was based less on radical Protestant notions of a continuous reformation than on logic and historical lessons. We find, for example, remarkably few recourses to the traditional phrasing and no reliance on Scripture. Using a much more secular, rational approach, Trenchard and Gordon cited recent history and ancient examples.[60] Further, these examples were more likely to show a "virtuous Administration" exalted than God's truth revealed.

Cato's secular and historical rationalization of the "truth-shall-prevail" logic served to place the argument on a new footing; moreover, it brought the argument explicitly into the realm of government, defying Tindal's rigid categorization of this notion as a "religious" reason for press liberty. Perhaps more important for open press doctrine was Cato's emphasis on and development of the other side of the well-worn "truth-shall-prevail" coin: "it is Error and Imposture alone, which dread a fair Enquiry, as being conscious of their own Weakness." Thus, it is "Knavery and Deformity alone" that need "Disguise."[61]

Why is it that knavery seeks disguise and shuns a fair enquiry? Because, Cato reasoned, "misrepresentation of publick Measures is easily overthrown, by representing publick Measures truly." The same is true of an honest man's "clear Reputation," which even "foul Mouths cannot hurt." The rationale was that "Truth has so many Advantages above Error, that she wants only to be shown, to gain Admiration and Esteem."[62]

Cato, then, had no fear that the people would be unable or unwilling to examine and perceive the truth once the press was open. In fact, "certain Experience shews us" that when great men simply "despise" the libels against them, "then [the libels] always lose their force." Recent history confirmed this, Trenchard and Gordon pointed out, when good ministers "knew very well that [a wild] Calumny could make no Impression upon any judicious Man, and they laugh'd at the simplicity and malice" of their attackers.[63]

Others, of course, were less sanguine than Cato about the ability of an open press to permit the common people to separate knavery from virtue. Recognizing this, Cato conceded that an open press occasions abuses; yet "it is an Evil arising out of a much greater Good." Press liberty is a life-sustaining force, like the Sun or the Nile, which may unavoidably produce "Monsters" on occasion but remain "general Blessings."[64] The "bad tendency" of the press was at once conceded and minimized by comparison with its virtues.

Thus, Trenchard and Gordon stressed and made explicit the notion of an open press's net advantage. This view had been implicit all along, for even the religious radicals of the 1640s knew that reformation was an uneven struggle, rather than a sweeping and immediate conquest. For Cato, however, this was a secular axiom proven by Tacitus's histories of Rome, wherein we learn that during three centuries of open debate "not Five publick Ministers suffered unjustly." And here again we also see that Cato's open press logic was aimed not so much at truth's revelation as at the virtuous administration of government. "Slander is certainly a very base and mean Thing: But surely it cannot be more pernicious to calumniate even good Men, than not to be able to accuse ill ones."[65]

We should note that, even as he defended the individual's right to free expression, Cato was more concerned with public liberty, despite the fact that a few individuals may have to sacrifice a prized possession, their good reputation. Moreover, Cato, here as elsewhere, was clearly blending philosophical fundamentals and practical methods. This certainly cautions us against an interpretation that stresses an ends/means distinction and Cato's Lockean liberalism.[66] More important, with these claims, the role of the open press in acting as a check on government and possible defender of the people's liberties is made evident. And, in fact, the peculiar coherence in Cato's thought between open press doctrine and these other, longstanding defenses of press freedom later proved to be a pivotal piece of the American colonists' ideological inheritance. But, to understand fully the unity of this tradition, we must first understand how these other traditional defenses of press liberty coalesced into free press doctrine.

Free press doctrine claims that the paramount role of the press is to serve as a bulwark against governmental power and, thus, to act as the essential defender of all of the people's other liberties. With an entrenched and expanding Whig oligarchy in power and the government tied into the ill-fated speculation scheme known as the South Sea Bubble, Cato saw a dire need for a free press. Trenchard and Gordon, along with other radical, "independent" Whigs, saw in the politics of the 1720s a critical juncture in the relentless struggle between the people's liberty and the government's power.

The fundamental opposition between the relentless, aggressive power of government and the ever-vulnerable liberties of the people was, for Cato, a matter of historical fact: His letter on "The encroaching Nature of Power, ever to be watched and checked" draws heavily on Roman history.[67] But it was also an aspect of simple, natural reality: "Power is naturally active, vigilant, and distrustful. . . . Now, because Liberty chastises and shortens Power, therefore Power would extinguish Liberty; and consequently Liberty has too much Cause to be exceeding jealous, and always upon her Defence. Power has many Advantages over her."[68]

Given this stark view of the vulnerability of the people's liberties, it is not surprising that free press doctrine provides the second thrust to Cato's philosophy of press liberty. While various formulations of this doctrine were ubiquitous in *Cato's Letters,* it received its classic expression in his first letter on the subject, "Of Freedom of Speech: That the same is inseparable from Publick Liberty." In this letter, Trenchard and Gordon declared succinctly that "Freedom of Speech is the great Bulwark of Liberty; they prosper and die together: And it is the Terror of Traytors and Oppressors, and a Barrier against them."[69]

Statements like these, advancing free press doctrine, appear again and again in the *Letters,* but this emphasis alone does not explain their importance. Rather, Cato's significance here lies in his having taken the boundaries of free press doctrine to radical extremes and having explicitly defended them. Whereas other authors were cautiously abstract about precisely what can or cannot be said about public men and measures, Cato expressly defended a broad view of press liberty and an exceedingly slender concept of seditious libel.

None of this is to say that Cato did not make some moderate statements. In one of his later essays on libel, he defined libel in a mainstream way and concluded by approving of the current laws "when prudently and honestly executed."[70] Some scholars claim that these comments are best understood as mere "face-saving gestures," while others maintain that passages like these betray Cato's acceptance of the legal status quo.[71] Perhaps Cato's claim that an unrecognized type of libels, those against the people, is at least as bad as all other types betrays his essential radicalism.[72] In any event, this question is not crucial for us here: Trenchard and Gordon's own intentions aside, they were read by many in England, and especially later in America, as ardent defenders of the people's liberties who placed few if any bounds on criticism of public men and measures. There is much to recommend this reading.

Trenchard and Gordon's earliest and most popular essay on libel appeared in June 1721, only two months before its vehicle, the *London Journal,* would peak its circulation at more than 10,000 copies.[73] This *Letter,* in turn, was one of those most often reprinted in America. In it, Cato immediately defined a libel as "a Sort of Writing that hurts particular Persons, without doing Good to the Publick." And, while he acceded in the traditional notion that the truth may still be libelous, he restricted this doctrine to "private and personal Failings," for "it is quite otherwise when the Crimes of Men come to affect the Publick."[74]

The "exposing of Publick Wickedness" Cato further maintained, is a publick "Duty," and this is true even of exposing a public man's "private Ignorance," as this may well cause "publick Confusion." For support of this radical narrowing of seditious libel, Cato cited Machiavelli to the effect that it is beneficial to a state that the people can accuse magistrates who are criminals, or merely "thought to be so." Calumny, Cato conceded, is an evil, but it is better that even good men be maligned falsely and maliciously than that bad magistrates not be accused.[75]

Cato insisted on this radical latitude in tolerating even false and malicious attacks on public men and measures in part because, as we saw earlier, even "foul Mouthes" cannot hurt an honest man's reputation, and in part out of jealousy for the people's ever-threatened liberty. Ultimately, for Cato, "it is certainly of much less Consequence to Mankind, that an innocent Man should be now and then aspersed, than that all Men should be enslaved."[76]

Once again, then, we find Cato appealing to the advantages of press liberty and combining free press doctrine and open press doctrine. For Trenchard and Gordon, both truth *and* the people's good may sometimes be slightly set back by press liberty, but they will ultimately prevail—and usually in short order and with little effort. Conversely, without a broad freedom of the press, even one permitting seditious libel, "the World must soon be over-run with . . . Tyranny, and the most stupid ignorance."[77]

How is it, then, that these competing doctrines, though distinguishable for us, remained indistinct for Cato? Trenchard and Gordon could see the two doctrines, what I call the free press and the open press, as complementary simply because history showed them that they were. On this point Cato could turn to ancient history or even the history of Christianity, since both demonstrate that a press open to the people frees the people. The early Christians, Cato noted, could not regulate discourse to hamper their opponents; indeed, their enemies had all the advantages, "yet Christianity spread." And, more significant—at least for Cato, who would belabor the point—ancient history clearly proved that when discussion was open to all, it was the champions of the public good and the people's liberties, not the corrupt advocates of superstition and tyranny, who prevailed.[78]

Cato, then, could and did see a coherent, harmonious, practical, as well as theoretical, basis for his radical understanding of press liberty. In fact, the consistency of the free and open press is apparent from the very first line of the first *Letter* devoted to the subject. "Without Freedom of Thought," Cato declared, "there can be no such Thing as Wisdom; and no such Thing as publick Liberty, without Freedom of Speech: Which is the Right of every Man, as far as by it he does not hurt and controul the Right of another; and this is the only Check which it ought to suffer, the only Bounds which it ought to know."[79] During the first half of the eighteenth century, British colonists in the New World would repeat these ideas and reprint these very words again and again, all the while maintaining a similar coherence, though in a different context and for different reasons.

2

The Coming of the Crisis

The first half of the eighteenth century witnessed a period of considerable change for the British colonists in America in matters political, social, demographic, economic, and religious. Against this backdrop of change, the discourse of press liberty seemed rather more stable and continuous. As one measure, *Cato's Letters* remained nearly as popular in the 1750s as in the 1720s. Accordingly, one of the primary themes of this chapter is the remarkable continuity of the free and open press tradition throughout this period. Reflecting on this marked rhetorical continuity, some scholars see little development at all in colonial press liberty. Yet, within the enduring bounds of the free and open press tradition, important if subtle transformations were taking place. As political life became more secular and more popular, the early American public sphere emerged and expanded, and the meaning of press liberty was broadened and refined. Though the terms of debate scarcely changed, new tensions emerged.

To make sense of the subtle shifts in the discourse of press liberty, we need to examine a number of controversies over press liberty that challenged the colonists to explore the tradition of press liberty that they had brought with them from England. Though many of these changes grew out of the increasing popularization and secularization of government, these forces created their own tensions, as the conflicts between legislative privilege and press liberty demonstrate. To begin, however, we would do well to establish the context of the colonial world to which *Cato's Letters* and other English tracts were imported. Accordingly, this chapter opens with an overview of changing views of press liberty in seventeenth-century colonial America and then examines some challenges that strained even the growing leniency of that early period. Then, we briefly return to Cato to establish his central place in early- to mid-eighteenth-century America. Next, we turn to the celebrated seditious libel trial of John Peter Zenger. This case receives extensive analysis not only because it heralded the end of seditious libel as a serious restraint on press liberty in the colonies but also because the controversy produced some of the richest discourse over press liberty in this period. The next section examines the subtle but significant developments within the free and open press tradition occasioned by the increasingly popular nature of government in the 1740s and 1750s. Finally, the chapter closes by considering nascent tensions between press liberty and legislative privilege that grew out of these same alterations in the nature of colonial government.

Press Liberty in Seventeenth-Century America

The British colonies in America, like far-off Great Britain itself, were ruled by a monarch. This monarchical background is crucial to understanding the suppression of free expression in early colonial America. Admittedly, the immediacy of monarchical authority varied: In some colonies, the king appointed both the governor and his Council; in others he appointed no officers at all. But everywhere, colonial governors traditionally received the same "Instructions" from the king:

> Forasmuch as great inconvenience may arise by the liberty of printing within our said province[s], you are to provide by all necessary orders, that no person keep any press for printing; nor that any book, pamphlet, or other matters whatsoever, be printed without your especial leave and license first obtained.[1]

Colonial governors were usually willing to comply, as they too were suspicious of press liberty. Sir William Berkeley, Governor of Virginia, makes this clear in his much-quoted letter to the Lords Commissioners of Foreign Plantations in which he thanks God that there is yet no printing in his colony.[2] This, however, did not mean that elites had no use for the press; Berkeley himself had Virginia's statutes printed in London in 1662 and scribal (i.e., hand-written) production was used for a variety of colonial publications.[3] What Berkeley and his successor, Lord Culpeper, wanted most was to maintain order through control of public discourse.

After the arrival of North America's first printing press in 1638, governors of Massachusetts Bay would likewise see to it that the press was adequately supervised. Indeed, the way Massachusetts Bay approached press liberty is of considerable importance, not only because it had the first press, the first newspapers, and the first newspaper controversy but also because the Puritan theocracy's notoriously restricted view of free expression reveals the crucial role of religion in early understandings of press liberty.

The Puritans' belief in their uniqueness in history as the founders of a "new Israel" required that they keep their covenant with God by maintaining an especially pious community. One aspect of this covenant was tracking God's unfolding providence, and the very first newspaper in the colonies opened by declaring its primary aim was to ensure "That *Memorable Occurences* of *Divine Providence* may not be neglected or forgotten."[4] Another requirement of the covenant was that all means be taken to avoid God's wrath. The theocracy's leaders felt it their duty to God to punish pernicious authors.[5] Thus, both Anne Hutchinson and Roger Williams were banished from the Bay colony, and the very same newspaper that aimed to relate God's providence was suppressed after its first issue appeared in 1690. Indeed, one might well wonder why Benjamin Harris thought his paper had any chance of surviving beyond its first issue. Though a respectable publisher for some of Boston's elite, Harris must have known that the newspaper's political comments would displease magistrates who had the law on their side.[6] A licensing system had been in place since the 1660s that continued uninterrupted through the early 1690s, despite the temporary expiration of licensing acts in the mother country.[7] Censorship and the Puritans' broader approach to hierarchical information diffusion served to maintain their political, social, and cultural system, as Richard D. Brown's study of the Boston merchant, judge, and sometime press censor Samuel Sewall (1676–1729) makes clear.[8] Nevertheless, Harris was right to sense an increasingly permissive approach to the press at the turn of the seventeenth century.[9]

In a recent comprehensive study of seditious expression prosecutions in seventeenth-century America, the historian Larry D. Eldridge has revealed the striking expansion of the freedom to criticize government and its officials.[10] This transformation must be understood in comparison to an approach to liberty of expression that was so repressive in some cases as to mete out "bodily correction," such as whipping, tongue boring, or ear cropping. The paramount reason for this sort of control of expression was understood throughout the century: The state had to be preserved, and this in turn required keeping the peace as well as maintaining social, political, and moral institutions.[11] Also, in the small, cohesive communities of early America, the good reputation of any individual, public or private, was critical to his practical ability to interact with anyone else in that community, and thus the practice of vehemently contradicting "false aspersions" continued well into the subsequent century.[12] Nevertheless, "the gulf between theory and practice, between statute and enforcement, was substantial."[13] Though the legal historian Leonard Levy saw the practice of freedom of expression as irrelevant to understanding the emergence of press liberty, in fact the nascent defenses and distinctions that contributed to a new leniency in regard to seditious libel foreshadowed some of the early challenges of the next century.[14]

Some of this leniency was merely the result of a new stress on technicalities in seditious libel cases. But these technicalities could now seize on emerging, if unofficial, notions about legitimate expression. For one thing, toward the end of the century, people were less likely to attack the authority of government in general and more likely to criticize a particular official or measure, an act less threatening to state preservation. Further, these criticisms would increasingly be punished only if the claims were found to be groundless. This period also saw an augmented reverence for, and success with, jury trials, though some judges would occasionally still overrule these acquitting juries.[15] Finally, Eldridge notes that, by 1700, harsh punishments were "reserved for words that posed a genuine . . . danger to the government"; the bad tendency of words alone brought little if any punishment.[16]

With these unofficial shifts in the approach to seditious expression and the expiration of the British licensing law in 1694, it is perhaps not surprising that the early eighteenth century saw state censorship end in the colonies. By 1700, men debated in sworn depositions whether or not licensing was a "new thing," and soon there were "numerous" controversial but unlicensed pamphlets.[17] In 1704, Boston's first (sustained) newspaper appeared; the second arrived in 1719. Finally, in 1721, Governor Samuel Shute appealed to the Massachusetts General Court for a licensing law, thus conceding that, though his royal Instructions had not changed, they had become irrelevant. The House refused to enact any such law, noting "the innumerable inconveniences and dangerous Circumstances the People might Labour under" if the governor were to control the press.[18]

Early Challenges

With the practical end of licensing as a restraint on liberty of expression and an increasing leniency toward seditious libel, one might imagine that the early eighteenth century would experience a relative lull in the theoretical development of press liberty. To the contrary, however, the early 1720s saw one of the most important controversies over freedom of the press. The dispute over James Franklin's *New-England Courant* not only signaled the arrival of a genuine public sphere and heralded the arrival of Cato in America but also established the coherence between the free press and the open press that characterized the first half of the eighteenth century in America.

The *Courant* entered the Boston printing scene just as a dispute over the merits of smallpox inoculation was animating the town's public discussions. Dr. William Douglass opposed the policy on the grounds that the cure was worse than the disease, but his original medium for publication, the staid *Boston News-Letter,* was effectively closed to him when its printer learned that Increase and Cotton Mather, the politically powerful theologians and inoculation supporters, disapproved of allowing Douglass to make his case. (The government's paper, the *Boston Gazette,* was certainly closed to such a skeptic, as well.) Franklin, having recently returned from training in London, applied the vigorous printing practices of the imperial capital to Boston's new controversy. Having first given Douglass a new outlet, the "Hell-Fire Club" of Franklin and his colleagues took to printing controversial pieces and mocking local authorities such as the Mathers. But when the *Courant* insinuated that the provincial government was only lamely attempting to capture a nearby pirate vessel, it went too far.[19]

Reacting to this "high Affront," the Massachusetts General Court imprisoned Franklin under its powers of legislative privilege, a provincial version of the parliamentary privilege recognized in the English Bill of Rights (1689), which mandated that legislators not be questioned in any other place for their actions in the legislature. Accordingly, Franklin was imprisoned for the remaining month of the General Court's session. The *Courant* continued to ridicule the local elite, and, by the following January, the General Court had once again censured Franklin, though this time it voted to forbid Franklin to print a paper without a license. Franklin continued to publish—though now under his younger brother Benjamin's name—and the General Court had him arrested again.[20] But the ruse worked, for when the case came to the grand jury, it returned the bill *ignoramus,* rejecting it as ungrounded due to lack of evidence.[21]

The case of the *Courant* is significant in the development of colonial press liberty for a number of reasons. First, it conclusively buried licensing in the colonies. Even at the height of displeasure with Franklin, the House refused to reinstate prior censorship, despite the Council's attempt to attach this provision to a compromise bill placing Franklin under a "good behavior" bond. More significant, the case advanced the role of the jury in the development of colonial press liberty. While this aspect of controversies over freedom of expression has generally been overlooked or dismissed, it is crucial to understanding the conceptual evolution that is our central concern here.[22]

As noted, juries had played a role in the growing leniency of the previous century. Two trials for seditious libel in the 1690s are particularly relevant. Both in the case of William Bradford, in Philadelphia, and in that of Thomas Maule, in Salem, the trial juries were allowed to find a "general" verdict; that is, they ruled not only on the *fact* of publication but also on the *law* as to whether or not the published words amounted to seditious libel.[23] Similarly, in 1707, a New York jury issued a general verdict in an odd case involving unlicensed preaching.[24] These expanded jury powers were a marked deviation from standard English practice.[25] And a Massachusetts jury chose to enter a "special" verdict —on the facts only—as late as 1724, giving a "hard-earned victory" to the colonial government and permitting the conviction of John Checkley for a "scandalous Libel" defending Episcopacy.[26] Yet, expanding jury power to include use of general verdicts complemented and advanced existing facets of colonial political discourse.

Juries had long been part of the radical Whig ideology that was so well received in colonial America. In *English Liberties, or the Freeborn Subject's Inheritance,* Henry Care popularized the freedoms inherent in the "Great Charter" and other authoritative sources. In this familiar book, reprinted in its entirety by Franklin as well as excerpted in the *Courant,* Care maintained that juries, along with Parliament, were "the two Grand Pillars of *English* Liberties," with the jury trial being the "great jewel of liberty." The reasoning was that the people, through the jury, thus played a role in the executive power of government.[27] Colonial charters echoed these sentiments in favor of the protection provided by "twelve men of the neighborhood."[28] By midcentury, Samuel Adams would equate juries with the judgment of the people as a whole.[29] Indeed, the notion that the jury embodied the public voice would reappear throughout the century.[30]

Juries, then, had an important place in colonial political thought. Yet, the significance of jury power went deeper still. The well-worn distinction between liberty and licentiousness centered on the notion that genuine liberty existed in accordance with the law. The rule of law was the countervailing force that moderated the popular components of government.[31] Expanded jury powers, therefore, weakened the conservative element that otherwise defended unpopular, usually elite, individuals and minority groups. The resulting vulnerability of unpopular authors, while inconsequential in the 1720s, proved more important as popular power grew. For the moment, though, it was the liberating potential of increased jury powers that was most conspicuous.

The shift from restricted "special verdicts" on the matter of publication only to "general verdicts" concerning culpability for seditious libel thus entailed a shift in the origins of the authoritative definition of the society's most threatening restraint on press liberty. Juries, of course, do not set legally binding precedents, nor does the popular voice always defend the freedom of expression for the unpopular. Nevertheless, when the grand jury returned Franklin's indictment *ignoramus* (thus precluding a jury trial), they participated—no doubt consciously, if not intentionally—in the expansion of the effective understanding of permissible press liberty in the colonies.

Juries, however, rarely explain their findings. We are thus at a loss to uncover a detailed explanation for any conceptual change afoot. We may speculate, however, that the free and open press notions available in *Cato's Letters* played a role in the jurymen's thinking. They certainly had access to them; Franklin shrewdly had seen to that. In only its sixth issue, the *Courant* rushed into print Cato's most popular letter on press liberty, "Reflections upon Libelling" (#32), only ninety-three days after its appearance in London (115 days was more typical). The "Hell-Fire Club" also reprinted other *Letters* espousing "free and open" press liberty, as well as offering its own similar statements.[32]

The appearance of free and open press notions in the colonies, when taken together with the end of licensing and the marked expansion of practical press freedom due to increased jury powers, made for unmistakable signs of a transformation of the colonial newspaper culture, and even of the political culture more generally. These signs of growing leniency were certainly not lost on Increase Mather. Calling the *Courant* a "*Wicked Libel,*" he complained in the *Boston Gazette* that, having been in New England since its early days, he could "well remember when the Civil Government could have taken an effectual Course to suppress such a *Cursed Libel!*" Were this not done, Increase continued, he feared "the *Wrath of* GOD *will arise and there will be no Remedy.*"[33]

That a religious minister would invoke the wrath of God amid a civil controversy was entirely in keeping with longstanding New England tradition. Indeed, prior to the arrival of the *Courant,* most Bostonians would have heard such subjects discussed only in the form of Puritan sermons: "The sermon was the sole form of legitimate public address." Until the early eighteenth century, information regarding public affairs was spread orally, through a closed network of the colony's elite, including the Rev. Mather and his friend Judge Samuel Sewall. News of public relevance was shared with the vast majority of common folks on what we call a "need-to-know" basis—and, in elite eyes, commoners most certainly did *not* need to know much. Indeed, it was seen as the duty of the leading people to use their authority to screen out reports about things that might cause a panic, such as a smallpox epidemic.[34] However, "the issue of clerical authority was in large measure what the inoculation controversy was all about."[35]

The *Courant* not only undermined traditional deference to elites but also elevated the role of ordinary people, thereby ultimately legitimating and expanding an inchoate colonial "public sphere." Such a public sphere entails two profoundly significant assumptions. First, legitimate authority is not embodied by special individuals, such as Increase Mather, Judge Sewall, or King James I; rather, the only legitimate authority is "the authority of the better argument" that emerged from public debate. Second, the public sphere must be, in principle, open to all.[36] The Hell-Fire Club was making government policies such as smallpox inoculation the focus of ongoing public debate. It was also criticizing the exclusivity of the public sphere, even if it was using the "genteel" idiom of satire to do it.[37] Whereas Franklin's London forerunners Richard Steele (*The Tatler*) and Joseph Addison (*The Spectator*) presented themselves to their readers from a social position beyond reproach, happy to provide the particulars of their backgrounds, the *Courant* was introduced with a voice that aggressively criticized readers' desire to know anything about the social distinctions of the author:

It's an Hard Case, that a Man can't appear in Print now a Days, unless he'll undergo the Mortification of Answering to ten thousand senseless and Impertinent Questions like these, Pray Sir, from whence came you? And what Age may you be of, may I be so bold? Was you bred at Colledge Sir?[38]

Thus, the *Courant*'s very first words in the emergent public sphere of Puritan Boston maintained that it was "imperrinent" to inquire after the breeding of the author. The author's age was soon disclosed, with the hopes that *"no One will hereafter object against my soaring now and then with the* grave Wits *of the Age."* But all other questions were postponed until the next issue, and in fact no such answers ever appeared, sending the message that the authority of the author was unimportant. From this first issue on, the *Courant* would repeatedly accuse the local elite of asserting its own view solely on the basis of its authority, "on the Merits of their Characters, and for no other reason."[39] This used to be reason enough, but no longer.

A similar transformation was beginning to take place in the Chesapeake, where an anonymous "Freeholder" responded to a letter in the *Virginia Gazette* because he agreed with the correspondent "that it is the indispensable Duty of every Man" to publish his thoughts on important public matters, such as a proposed tobacco law. Furthermore, "not being Master of a correct Stile, or Propriety of Expression, is no Excuse for being silent on so important and pressing an Occasion."[40] Clearly, this "Freeholder" saw authority as resting in a public sphere that extended beyond a gentlemen's elite. Indeed, the very printedness that the press makes possible allowed for an anonymity that sought to remove personal authority, leaving only the "authority of the better argument," as Michael Warner has shrewdly observed.[41] The colonial public sphere was beginning a profound upheaval.[42]

These transformations in the political culture of early America laid important groundwork for the expansion of the public sphere and the ultimate advance of popular sovereignty; indeed, they were a critical part of that expansion. More immediately relevant here is the role played by the first colonial opposition press in supporting the coherence of free and open press discourse. Franklin did this by advocating, and in fact pursuing, an open press policy that was also clearly aimed at the free press purposes of checking government's power and defending the people's liberties.

Not that Franklin had much choice in the matter. On a practical level, the Mathers and other members of Boston's elite were far too powerful to be restricted in any way from press access by the likes of the Hell-Fire Club. Theoretically, Franklin would have had to break with the most recent and radical thinking on the subject, since even the *Letters* of Cato he was reprinting in no way questioned the government's right to make its case in the press. This would have required critical political insight beyond even the celebrated capabilities of his brother Benjamin.

But if it is true that James Franklin would have been exceedingly hard pressed to legitimize press constraints on the Mathers and their ilk, it is also true he did not have to. In fact, while he was reprinting the free and open press thinking of Cato, Franklin himself stressed the open press ideal of impartiality. Only days after the first issue of the *Courant* appeared, he not only printed but published the Matherian retort, *The Anti-Courant*.[43] Three months later, Franklin printed a *pro*-inoculation letter in the *Courant* with the hope that "our Readers (Anti-Inoculators) will bear with [us], since they have been promis'd, and are welcome to the same Liberty of speaking their Minds in this Paper."[44]

Franklin was appealing to the seemingly more reasonable and less radical half of the increasingly mainstream "free and open press" tradition to justify an opposition press culture that undermined elite authority and provided a new public voice for marginalized people. Of course, this novel understanding of press liberty was not well received by the *ancien régime* of Puritan theocrats and crown officers: "Such discourses and arguings before the People do but make us grow weaker and weaker."[45] For a society in which elites generally hid their disputes from simple folks, opening the press to opposing arguments from gentlemen and artisans alike was a profound threat to deferential politics. Nevertheless, thanks to a sympathetic and empowered grand jury, Franklin lost only one month's freedom while expanding the nascent American public sphere and effectively demonstrating the colonial coherence of the inherited tradition of press liberty.

Cato in America

Franklin's immediate recourse to the persuasive philosophy of free expression available in *Cato's Letters* would prove an omen of things to come. Early Americans again and again appealed to the ideals espoused in the *Letters*. Indeed, before we proceed any further in analyzing the evolution of press liberty discourse in America, it is crucial that we appreciate the extent to which Cato provided the very terms of the debate, thus in large measure establishing both the limits and the potentials of colonial discussions of freedom of the press.

The limitations of Cato's rhetoric were real, and they proved influential in the conceptual shifts that we examine later in this chapter. But, for the colonists of the 1720s, 1730s, and 1740s, it was the liberating potential of Cato's press discourse that was most remarkable. To be sure, there were other sources to which the colonists could refer for explanation and legitimation of their expanding view of permissible political expression. The Bible, of course, was a familiar touchstone. But, despite its frequent use by Civil War radicals, the Bible was rarely cited explicitly concerning eighteenth-century colonial press liberty.[46] Extreme Whig interpreters of traditional legal sources, such as Coke and Hawkins, and even the Magna Carta itself, were often appealed to; witness Franklin's reprinting and excerpting of Henry Care. And the "immortal Milton" would prove more and more relevant as a political thinker, especially after *Areopagitica* was reprinted in the aftermath of the seditious libel case against John Peter Zenger in 1735. The *Discourses* of Sidney, the "republican martyr," were also important, though they rarely spoke directly on freedom of the press. Further, Sidney's famous passage on the "Character of a Good and of an Evil Magistrate" was available in one of Cato's oft-reprinted *Letters,* as were other important excerpts.[47] Finally, Locke's *Treatises* were also influential, but, as Clinton Rossiter long ago aptly remarked, "no one can spend any time in the newspapers, library inventories, and pamphlets of colonial America without realizing that *Cato's Letters* rather than Locke's *Civil Government* was the most popular, quotable, esteemed source of political ideas in the colonial period."[48] If this was true for political ideas in general, it was true in spades for ideas of free political expression.

It was not only the more controversial opposition papers such as the *Courant* and Zenger's *New-York Weekly Journal,* that took to reprinting Cato on free expression, either with or without attribution.[49] More important, the colonists were shaping Cato's free and open press ideas and language into original statements, thereby quite literally making his discourse their own. Thus, Thomas Fleet, of the *Boston Evening*

Post, defended his press first by noting that those who want to shut the press "are of tyranical Principles, and Enemies to *Liberty* . . . , and would be glad to keep the People in the most abject Slavery." He continued by observing that "all Men [should] have an Opportunity to judge for themselves," for "no good [Cause] . . . ever yet suffered by being examined."[50] And when colonial Americans were not championing both halves of the free and open press in the same breath, one author would advance one logic, while another author would posit the other, with no apparent incongruity; sometimes the very same author would stress the different strains of thought on different occasions.[51]

The early Americans saw no inconsistency in all this, of course, since for them the free press's defense of public liberty and the open press's appeal to the power of truth were merely two sides of the same coin, inherited from their radical Whig forebears back home in England. In turn, this tradition of press liberty dovetailed perfectly with the broader Whig view of politics that saw the struggle between liberty and power as ending, if ever, in liberty's inevitable demise. To reinforce this point and its critical relation to press liberty, Benjamin Franklin's *Pennsylvania Gazette* hurried into print a letter from Bolingbroke's *Craftsman* that declared that, should "the Artifices of *Men in Power*" meet with "the Silence of the *Advocates for Liberty,*" the results would be disastrous for "the LIBERTY OF THE PRESS." Speaking in its own voice, the *Gazette* went further to specify the unity required of a people hoping to defend their liberties: The balance of powers in government is "*Nonsense,* when applied to a *Democratical* Government. If the people are *Equally* divided, you may easily enslave both parties."[52]

Finally, not only did the colonists increasingly assume Cato's conception of press liberty and of politics more generally; they even began to perceive the grander coherence between the free press and the open press, between liberty and truth. For Cato, a classic example of this coherence was the Protestant Reformation, in which the separation of God's Truth from papist superstition advanced the people's liberties. For midcentury colonists, this coherence was more civic. Part of this consistency rested on the belief that only evil magistrates could suffer from even the most malicious libels, for a good character was "above the reach of ignorance, envy, or malice." Or, as Poor Richard epigrammatically put it, "Dirt may stick to a Mud Wall, but not to polish'd Marble."[53]

One also had to presume that the Truth would always lead directly to the realization of the people's liberty. An open press could never be perverted to the detriment of free press objectives, since "altho' *Publick Virtue* cannot be affected by the Indulgence of the most *unlimited* Freedom of speaking or writing, yet *Oppression* and *Tyranny* as it derives all its Influence from its secrecy may be extremely benefited by the *reverse*."[54]

Thus, in the decades after James Franklin demonstrated in the colonies the practical consonance of the free and open press—provided that the press was open to opposition voices—some colonists began to reveal this logic on a more abstract, philosophical level. This conceptual development, however, advanced no further. The arrival of the crisis in imperial relations in the 1760s brought these vague ideals down to the sullied and imperfect level of specificity and pragmatism. The struggle for control of the colonies was the long-expected battle between power and liberty. And, as we shall see in the next chapter, the ambiguous unity of free and open press tradition would not survive unscathed.

In the first half of the eighteenth century, however, the vague language of the free and open press tradition was one of its greatest strengths. As we shall see presently, in press controversies it was not uncommon for all sides to concede the authority of Cato. But this very ambiguity means that to find many of the real developments in press liberty discourse, we must take recourse to actual debates that forced to the fore the specific issues of the extent and purpose of freedom of the press. In this regard, no dispute over press liberty is as fertile as the celebrated case of John Peter Zenger.

Zenger and the End of Seditious Libel

As a locus of historical significance, the trial of John Peter Zenger for seditious libel published in his *New-York Weekly Journal* has hit on hard times. Once lionized as a turning point for American liberty, the past few decades have seen the trial minimized and Zenger marginalized. The editor of the most recent edition of the *Brief Narrative* of the trial maintains that Zenger's associates were "a somewhat narrow-minded political faction seeking immediate political gain rather than long-term governmental or legal reform."[55]

This recent reinterpretation is correct as far as it goes. Zenger himself was little more than a pawn in the struggle between the faction supporting former Chief Justice Lewis Morris against the recently appointed New York governor, William Cosby. And the primary objective of the Morrisite faction was surely to have Cosby removed and to elevate Morris to his former political prominence. Furthermore, as many have hastened to point out, Zenger's trial failed to produce a valid legal precedent that formally overruled the common law of seditious libel.[56]

Nevertheless, it is a mistake to minimize the significance of the Zenger case. Political motives, no matter how low or particular, sometimes yield consequences much loftier and more general. The motives at work surrounding Zenger forced the competing camps to debate issues of press liberty in more explicit terms than would be the case at any other time in the first half of the century. The results demand our attention for the richness of the political discourse and the significant elaborations of the received tradition of the free and open press. Finally, the results did not make law, but they proved "better than law."[57]

With the mounting opposition to Governor Cosby yielding few substantive gains, the Morrisite faction sought to redirect its pamphlet attacks to the more timely and more widely available, not to mention anonymous, vehicle of newspaper articles. The only paper in New York at the time was William Bradford's *New-York Gazette*. Bradford had moved from Philadelphia after the seditious libel trial discussed earlier. Since that time, he had been "the King's Printer" for New York and by 1733 was "known to be under the direction of the government" thanks to an annual salary of £50.[58] James Alexander, the leading mind of the Morrisite faction, therefore enlisted Zenger, heretofore an obscure printer and a former apprentice and partner of Bradford's, to print the *Journal*. It soon became apparent that the paper "had been deliberately created as an instrument of propaganda" against Cosby and his circle of supporters; in a word, "the *Journal* was looking for trouble."[59]

And trouble it quickly found. After only two months, Cosby had Chief Justice James DeLancey, whom he had recently promoted after unseating Morris, lecture the January 1734 grand jury on the traditional interpretation of libel law. Under the usual common law understanding, any "reflections" on the government or its officers were illegal, and the truth of the matter was at best immaterial and at worse an aggravation of the offense. The jurymen surely knew what DeLancey wanted but did nothing. When DeLancey tried again in October, the grand jury presented two *"Scandalous Songs"* but insisted that it could find no one responsible, though everyone knew the songs were the work of Zenger's press.

Cosby and his Council then had Zenger arrested and jailed on their own authority, though without support of the Provincial Assembly, which refused to concur. They then optimistically attempted to have charges brought against Zenger by yet another grand jury, though this time they appointed a new sheriff, confident he would seat sympathetic jurors. But even these jurors refused to act.

Not to be disappointed, Cosby had Zenger charged by way of an "information," which avoided grand juries altogether and was thus widely seen as a tyrannical legal instrument. Next, the Cosbyites tried to pack the trial jury, but the Morrisites exposed this plan. In response, DeLancey publicly threatened to charge any jury that acquitted Zenger with perjury, and he had the defense counsel, Alexander and William Smith, disbarred. These actions may have stacked the deck, but the Cosbyites also clearly had the law on their side. As one scholar observes, "The trial itself seemed destined to uphold the governor."[60] Yet, on the day of the trial the jury recessed for only ten minutes before acquitting Zenger, ending the eight months he had spent in jail awaiting trial.[61] How could this be? By what manner of argument could "twelve men out of the neighborhood" find him innocent?

One searches in vain through DeLancey's grand jury charges, the *Gazette,* or the prosecution's case to find some draconian new discourse that would severely restrict free expression and thus understandably engender the jury's ire. The Cosbyites, their heavyhanded political moves notwithstanding, actually made their case on very solid ground.

Zenger's enemies made their case on established, traditional lines, and the divergence from the *Journal's* approach was immediately apparent. The first *Gazette* article defending DeLancey's view of libel even reprinted a former Chief Justice's grand jury charge claiming that reflections on government were highly punishable because "Government is that sacred Institution appointed by GOD to restrain the irregular Appetites and Passions of Men."[62] Though this might have been unassailable logic in 1716, it was a far cry from the natural-right rhetoric and social-contract ideas New Yorkers were now reading in *Cato's Letters* and the *Journal.*

For the most part, though, the Cosbyites appealed to the conventional distinctions between liberty and licentiousness and between the use and the abuse of the press. These well-worn distinctions rested on the "direct Tendency" of abusive expressions to break the peace and cause sedition. One could freely use one's press, just as one could one's sword, but if one breaks the peace, the law must punish.[63]

In fact, libels were traditionally understood to be more dangerous than swords. Certainly, a society that holds duels on the "field of honor"—as eighteenth-century America occasionally did—clearly prefers bodily wounds to reputational ones. But there was more to it than that. Libels were "the Arrows that fly by Night," the "small Sparks" easily blown into a flame but *not easily to be extinguished.*[64] Or, to use the most common metaphor, libels were poison, the more dangerous because their secrecy meant "none can defend himself against it."[65] To be sure, the rhetoric of "poison" had been employed metaphorically in regard to libel and sedition since at least the 1650s,[66] though its counterconcept, "antidote," was notably absent in the traditional, conservative argument. Instead, seditious libel was likened to a *"Scorpeon's Bite,"* the only remedy for which were Chinese "snake stones" or other such useless quackery.[67]

Because libels were so dangerous, the truth of the libel was held to be no defense. This claim had its origins in the Star Chamber of Stuart England, but DeLancey aptly cited Coke to the effect that in a stable government there were other, proper channels of redress. Press liberty was not the safeguard of the people's liberty, the *Gazette* declared; "Magna Carta, and such other wholesome Laws . . . were rather the Bulwark."[68]

Recognizing that even these tried and true principles might prove too moderate and traditional for the times, the Cosbyites could take heart in the fact that some of their number spoke the increasingly popular language of the free and open press. Understandably stressing open press logic, an anonymous contributor to Bradford's *Gazette* even praised Gordon as a "great Author" and hoped that the press "may be always open, to defend the Innocent, and shame the Guilty." Another unnamed correspondent went so far as to borrow his definition of press liberty from Zenger's *Journal.* Prior to Zenger's arrest, at least one Cosbyite consoled himself with the open press confidence that "the more Outragious and bitter the Invectives are, the more they will redound to the advantage of [Cosby's] character."[69]

Given these solid if moderate arguments, it must have seemed to many of Cosby's supporters that they had played their rhetorical hand well. Actually, they had; but the rules of press liberty discourse were changing without their noticing. To begin with, *Cato's Letters* and the free and open press thinking were now too widespread for a few weak gestures to suffice. In response to DeLancey's first grand jury charge, Alexander and the rest of the Morrisite faction began exposing New Yorkers to the *Letters*, especially those on free expression.[70] More importantly, Alexander himself took to theorizing about press liberty, elaborating on Cato's arguments and adapting them to the very sorts of legal attacks Zenger would soon encounter.

In only the second issue of the *Journal*, Alexander defended his approach to press liberty in terms clearly borrowed from Trenchard and Gordon, even maintaining the vague yet provocative rhetoric. Calling himself "Cato," Alexander claimed to "communicate . . . the Sentiments of a late excellent Writer," and his phrasing and arguments betrayed his debt to the English "Cato." Should anyone still wonder about the origins of Alexander's thinking, he closed with a quotation from Gordon's popular translation of Tacitus's *Discourses*. With the first legal challenge still a couple of months off, Alexander ignored the issue of libel, stressing only the dangers of "any restraint" of free expression.[71]

Alexander's indefinite arguments were no longer tenable after DeLancey's first grand jury charge and the ensuing *Gazette* letters supporting him. Alexander had Zenger reprint Cato in response, but his own writings took on a new radical specificity.[72] Observing that libel's definition changed with the times and that this flexibility was often exploited to suppress government critics, Alexander went so far as to suggest that the only way to define libels fairly was to "have the Readers [be] Judges." In practice, this meant that the "twelve good Men" of the jury would define the boundaries of permissible political expression.[73]

Another extreme interpretation of the free and open press tradition attacked the very notion of "libelling the Government" as unintelligible and insisted that libels could harm only individuals, and even then the libel "must descend to particulars," naming individuals in no uncertain terms. This understanding had something in common with Cato's insistence that public men's private doings were legitimate subjects of public discussion, though Alexander seemed to be attacking the whole notion of seditious libel. The *Journal* soon made its interpretation unmistakably clear when it reprinted a free press declaration that condemned all restraints on the press, *"but what is just sufficient to prevent Men from writing either* Blasphemy *or* Treason."[74]

With the transfer of the dispute to a criminal trial, the Cosbyites had succeeded in shifting the context to a legal one seemingly less open to radical interpretation than the relatively vague public discourse of the free and open press tradition. But the disbarring of Alexander and Smith brought the celebrated Philadelphia lawyer Andrew Hamilton to Zenger's defense. Hamilton recognized that the conservatism of the law's dependence on precedent and authoritative commentary left Zenger with hardly a legal leg to stand on, despite the strong support offered by public opinion. But, of course, the Anglo-American tradition brought the public into the case through one powerful institution, the jury. Hamilton accordingly admitted Zenger's guilt as far as printing the alleged libels and spent the rest of the trial arguing two points: (1) the jury's right, even duty, to issue a general, rather than a special, verdict, and (2) that "*Truth* ought to govern the whole affair of libels."[75]

Both of these claims had precedents in the evolving tradition of the free and open press, if not in the law, and Hamilton succeeded largely by appealing directly to the jury in these terms. Of course, the appeal to truth resonated with open press logic. Furthermore, the claim that truth should be a valid defense was a successful legal move, in part because Cosby's dictatorial behavior made the prospect of witnesses being called to testify about the governor's conduct an unwelcome one for the prosecution. Why DeLancey let Hamilton make his case at such length remains a mystery, though his inexperience (and Hamilton's commanding presence) may well explain it. In any event, the jury's acquittal clearly demonstrated its general verdict powers and put the effective determination of permissible political expression in the public's hands.

In fact, when the controversy was revisited in print in 1737, the most trenchant legal critic of Hamilton's defense arguments readily conceded the jury's power to find a general verdict.[76] The issue of using truth as a defense was much more complicated, and "Anglo-Americanus" makes clear that the law made truth immaterial and opinions still libelous. James Alexander responded in a long essay spread over four issues of Benjamin Franklin's *Pennsylvania Gazette*. Despite this generous allotment of print, Alexander rehearsed free and open press arguments and largely ignored the many legal issues presented. When he did attempt to address the legality of truth as a defense, Alexander was forced to retreat to civil law, a system of jurisprudence largely alien to the British system of statute and common law. Alexander was trying to find legal support for the view that only direct assertions of demonstrably false facts could be libelous. Ultimately, Alexander found it easier and more persuasive to argue that liberty of the press as it was now understood would be "wholly abolished" if one could punish truth.[77]

This late exchange proved to be the Zenger case's denouement. The partisan dispute itself was short-lived, and the *Journal* soon became an ordinary opposition newspaper. And, in a few years, with a change of political fortunes, Zenger even became the colony's public printer. The Zenger case itself never became a legitimate legal precedent. His proved to be the last seditious libel trial to appear before a colonial jury, however. In an America where "Custom and Usage are the best Expositors of every Law," the Zenger case served as an effective deterrent to seditious libel charges. Few cases would even appear before a grand jury.[78]

The role of juries, and through them the people, was one of the primary facets of the controversy, and herein lies its predominant influence. In colonial political discourse, juries had long been lionized as the "great bulwark" or "principal pillar" of liberty.[79] In practice, colonial juries had some experience exonerating those guilty of breaking laws the juries found unfair, a practice that increased in frequency during the imperial crisis of the 1760s.[80] With the Zenger case, this jury power in seditious libel cases was permanently established in the colonies. This was a marked divergence from practice in the mother country. Only a few years before the Zenger case, Richard Francklin, printer of Bolingbroke's *Craftsman,* was found guilty of seditious libel in a case in which the jury was restricted to a special verdict and the defense counsel did not even object.[81] It would be almost two decades before an English jury would similarly presume the power to determine the extent of press liberty.[82]

In the colonies, press liberty was effectively broadened by the jury power established in the Zenger case. For example, in 1747, a South Carolina grand jury refused to indict the printer Peter Timothy for printing two attacks on the governor in the *South-Carolina Gazette.* The Charleston grand jury could have simply ignored the request to indict Timothy or pretended it could not find anyone responsible, thus following the lead of the first two Zenger grand juries. Instead, it publicly declared that indicting Timothy for these caustic criticisms would be "*destructive* of THE LIBERTY OF THE PRESS."[83]

The Zengerian appeal to the power of the jury had its roots in a developing colonial practice. The move to truth as a defense, to the contrary, had antecedents in *Cato's Letters.* Yet it was taken further in the colonies than in the mother country. Twice in the 1740s, printers were charged for factual assertions made in their newspapers. In both cases, the available records suggest that the charges were dropped when the printers proved the veracity of their claims.[84] More than that, one suspects that the prospects of allowing zealous critics to debate the truth of their claims in the public eye had what we would now call a "chilling effect"—in reverse—on government prosecutions. In practice, then, as well as in theory, the appeal to truth as a defense against seditious libel charges was instituted in the wake of the Zenger controversy. Indeed, when the Federalists fashioned the Sedition Act (1798) to muzzle their vociferous Jeffersonian critics, they made sure to respect the two Zengerian principles of the jury's general verdict power and truth as a defense.

The Zenger controversy brought about changes in press discourse and practice that elaborated on and expanded the existing concept of press liberty. Ultimately, one could now say whatever public opinion, through the jury, would allow, and one could appeal to the truth of the matter to make one's case. As we shall see shortly, this did not exhaust all threats to press liberty in the colonies. Nevertheless, the removal of seditious libel as a real threat in the colonies advanced and made explicit the inherited free and open press tradition.

Post-Zenger Developments

The Zenger trial left the press a far cry from the theocratic control of seventeenth-century Puritanism or even the monarchical worldview that was predominant in England and was still commonplace in the colonies. The colonial public sphere was expanding, as the *Journal*, like the *Courant* before it, had made a powerful and largely successful claim of legitimacy for debate between authorities and opposing voices.[85] Further, the jury had demonstrated its role as defender of the free and open press, advancing a conception of the press as open to all, including the free-press voices that sought to advance public liberty and opposed governmental power.[86] With the rise of the discourse of the free and open press and the end of seditious libel as an effective threat, free-expression theory might have seemed on the brink of real philosophical shifts. Certainly the decades of the 1740s and 1750s did not lack for profound transformations in colonial America. Demographic and economic growth in the ever-expanding colonies brought a surge in the number of (often competing) newspapers. More significant, the religious and political upheaval of the Great Awakening sparked the expansion of the public sphere, introducing public affairs to many who had previously been excluded. But, despite these important changes in colonial life, few serious challenges emerged to the increasingly mainstream press liberty tradition.

Open press logic had thrived in the colonies through the 1720s and 1730s in part because of its roots in the inherited radical Whig philosophy. The prevailing economic context also contributed to its saliency. Simply put, the economic realities of running a printing shop in the colonies tended to promote open press doctrine.[87] At least early on, "each urban area, until the population expanded adequately, could support but one newspaper, usually an official one that depended on government contracts for economic survival."[88] Even with the arrival of opposition papers, maintaining a press open to all sides was partially a matter of economic necessity in the first half of the century.[89] Perhaps Benjamin Franklin's classic "An Apology for Printers" best captures the complementary logics that informed the colonists' open press doctrine:

> Printers are educated in the Belief, that when Men differ in Opinion, both Sides ought equally to have the Advantage of being heard by the Publick; and that when Truth and Error have fair Play, the former is always an overmatch for the latter: Hence they chearfully serve all contending Writers that pay them well, without regarding on which side they are of the Question in Dispute.[90]

Franklin is a bit wishful here; "there is no evidence to suggest that in practice printers of colonial newspapers routinely received payments from contributors." Still, maintaining a press open to all sides generally brought the largest possible subscribership.[91]

But how open should one's press be? Printing *every* piece of malicious scurrility sent to a printer would serve neither truth nor the printer's pocketbook, as someone would surely be offended. Franklin saw this clearly; the "Apology" itself was responding to some disgruntled readers. Franklin made much of open press logic and insisted that "Printers naturally acquire a vast Unconcernedness as to the right or wrong Opinions contain'd in what they print." Nevertheless, printers must "continually discourage the Printing of . . . bad things."[92] Later, Franklin would be more forthright about a printer's duty to judge, even when open press doctrine dictated that a criticized person be allowed to respond.

> I think there is a good deal of Difference between a *Vindication* and an *Invective*: and that, whatever Obligations a Printer may be under to publish Things of the former kind, he can be under none with Regard to the latter.[93]

Other printers would also insist on the propriety of exercising their judgment, "the Censure of the most snarling Critick" notwithstanding.[94]

This insistence that a printer's judgment could temper an open press would fade as the turbulent 1740s and 1750s wore on. Indeed, in 1740, shortly after dictating the distinction between a vindication and an invective reproduced here, Franklin himself printed a vindicating letter that contained, by his own admission, "Invectives" and "personal Reflections."[95] When presented with criticism of his press, Thomas Fleet appealed to open press notions and further maintained that he was simply a printer trying to make a living. While his language was clearly reminiscent of Franklin's "Apology," Fleet's apology contained no discussion of the duty of judgment that had moderated Franklin's reasoning only a decade earlier.[96]

By the mid-1750s, many would qualify this duty of judgment, insisting that the printer have "some very substantial Reason for his Refusal." The reason that the printer had to "justify him[self] to the world," James Holt explained, was that the press belonged to "the *Publick*" as much as to the printer.[97] Holt further maintained that the liberty of the press did not require even the "least restraint," because an open press inherently "carries the Means of restraining or reducing itself to its proper Boundaries" by way of a critical response.[98] When Hugh Gaine set himself up as "sole Judge" of what to print and closed his *Mercury* to William Livingston, William Smith, Jr., and their radical Whig associates in New York, they went so far as to wonder whether "a Press . . . inaccessible to every Antagonist, be not more dangerous to the civil and religious Rights of the People, than the total Suppression of Printing." Upon reflection, they decided total suppression would be better than a partisan press.[99]

The popular upheaval of the Great Awakening increased the confidence of many that the reading public could sift through the excessive scurrility of a wide open press. It also occasioned an expanding appreciation of an open press as a *right*. Cato, of course, had spoken broadly of rights that included the liberty of free expression. Some colonists, however, now took to explaining press liberty as necessary to popular government. In a little-remembered passage, Samuel Adams's *Independent Advertiser* implied something remarkably reminiscent of our modern notion of "the right to know" when it discussed legitimate restrictions on free expression for reasons of military security. "There are indeed some Things which require Secrecy, NOT BECAUSE THE PEOPLE HAVE NOT A RIGHT TO KNOW THEM, but because the Promulgation of them will necessarily defeat them: But such instances are extremely rare," perhaps found only "in a Time of War."[100]

Why exactly do people have a "right to know"? With the *Mercury* again open to him, Livingston explained that, "if no Law can be binding upon the Subject without his Consent, he has surely a Right to divulge his Sentiments" on men's conduct and measures.[101] This principle, it should be noted, is a far cry from the claim that the press must be open because the truth will prevail in a fair fight, though it is not necessarily contradictory to it. But might not truth be hurt by mistaken persons exercising their open press rights? In a sermon that otherwise repeatedly echoed Milton's *Areopagitica*, Jonathan Mayhew conceded this threat but insisted that this was no ground on which to deny citizens the right that comes from "*God and nature, and the gospel of Christ.*" "We may as well pick our neighbour's pocket," Mayhew explained, "for fear he should spend his money in debauchery."[102]

It is perhaps not surprising that Mayhew, as a minister, so thoroughly intertwined natural law and religious principle. Nevertheless, his expansive understanding of free expression increasingly fell on sympathetic ears. And, whereas Mayhew was careful to remind his congregation and his readers that the gospel instructs all to follow their civil leaders, others would see in an augmented conception of press liberty an opportunity to reinterpret many of the traditional restrictions on free press activities.

As always, it was the radical challengers of the established powers, and not the traditional elites, who were likely to be excluded by a printer's judgment.[103] So, as the duty of judgment began to fade from view, it was opposition press forces that explained how free press logic required a wide-open press. During the Great Awakening, the "New Light" forces of religious evangelism turned to the press, to the alarm of the "Old Light" elites. The "New Light" minister and former Yale rector Elisha Williams defined press liberty not only as "*the Right* that *everyone* has *to speak his Sentiments openly*" on all public matters but also the duty of each to "give notice of the danger" he sees. Leaders, in turn, must not suppress his warning or punish him, even if they think him in error.[104] This obligation to alert the public of dangers to the community, though the alarms may well prove false, was a considerable extension of the Zengerian principle of the right to publish truth.

Zenger's *Journal* had declared that press liberty allowed everything but blasphemy and treason. The letter to the *Independent Advertiser* maintaining that "*the Liberty of the Press, perhaps, is exempted from nothing, but Blasphemy and Treason*" might therefore appear redundant or uninteresting. Indeed, existing histories of press liberty ignore the passage, for it seems to do no more than to provide ethical approbation for the practical fact of seditious libel's demise. But contemporary readers would have understood the claim in light of Samuel Adams's redefinition of "loyalty" a few months prior. "Loyalty," Adams asserted, was no more than "a firm . . . attachment to a legal Constitution." "Sedition," accordingly, was best understood as "all Tendencies, Machinations, and Attempts to overset a *Legal* Constitution."[105] Since the *Advertiser* had often insisted that a free press was sacred to the British Constitution, the implication was clear to all: Those who attempted to restrict the opposition press were the seditious ones.

With his essay of 1748, Adams was only beginning his career as a leading propagandist for the Whig cause; indeed, his bold attempt at conceptual redefinition of "loyalty" was part of emerging changes in the meaning of "patriotism."[106] But it is the attempt to transform the concept of "sedition" that is most significant for this study. Adams's statement not only undermined the authority of the prevailing legal definition of sedition (and thus seditious libel) but also shifted the burden of justification from radical Whigs to ministerial elites.

William Smith, William Livingston, and their colleagues in New York would soon elaborate these claims and make them explicit. The authors of the *Independent Reflector* were excellent students of Cato's works, and their essay, "*Of the Use, Abuse, and* LIBERTY OF THE PRESS," elaborates on Cato's notion of "treason against the people." Turning the well-worn distinction between liberty and license on its head, the *Reflector* argued that press liberty "is always to be restricted from becoming a Prejudice to the public Weal." Printing "any Thing injurious to his Country . . . is criminal,—It is high Treason against the State." Conversely, refusing to print "any Thing, not repugnant to the Prosperity of the State, is an unjustifiable and tyrannical Usurpation."[107]

If treason was no longer an attack on the king or his ministers but anything "injurious" to the country, then it was corrupt "government" papers, not the opposition press, that were radically endangering the public peace. With the free and open press tradition firmly established as the predominant colonial understanding of press liberty, the more radical forces of the 1750s thus began to hint that a press open to ministerial forces could be "Enemies to the *Press* and the *Public*."[108]

These conceptual shifts occasioned by the Great Awakening, like those that contributed to the Zenger controversy, did not go unnoticed by a contemporary audience that would have recognized the significance of even the subtlest reinterpretation of the established discourse of free expression.[109] Indeed, midcentury radicals were not altogether rebuilding the received tradition, but they were shifting its center of gravity. With the printing world now wide-"open," opposition forces seized on the ambivalent character of the now-dominant press tradition to stress both the primary importance of the free press defense of public liberty and the dangers of a press open to a power-hungry ministry "disloyal" to the people.

In retrospect, however, what is perhaps most remarkable—and yet is often ignored—is the extent to which the upheaval of the 1740s and 1750s left the inherited tradition of press liberty fundamentally unaltered. From the meager beginnings of three newspapers in 1720, the burgeoning colonies could claim twenty-two active papers by 1760.[110] This economic and demographic expansion, did *not* translate into an expanded exploration of the theoretical foundations of press liberty, however. The growth of multinewspaper towns could conceivably have led to a bold new discourse concerning press liberty that permitted or even encouraged a system of avowedly partisan presses, each representing a leading faction; significantly, no such discourse emerged.

The religious and political upheavals of the 1740s and 1750s were even more thoroughgoing than the demographic and economic ones. In the face of an established, Old Light ministry and a genteel political culture, both of which stressed learnedness, New Light ministers emphasized the transparency of the Word, reaching out to the previously excluded "rabble."[111] With traditional religious institutions undermined, the political establishment was seriously challenged.[112] The newspaper culture itself was also reshaped in accord with the Great Awakening; the newspapers' local focus and controversial character were solidified.[113] Moreover, the newspaper audience grew hand-in-hand with the expansion of the public sphere, which now included most white men and many white women.[114] William Livingston made this connection clear when, in a "Watchtower" essay exalting the press, he affirmed that it is "highly commendable" for "every member of the Community" to study subjects which concern his well-being, such as government and religion. That this "community" of citizens and readers was expanding is evident from the *Independent Advertiser*'s first issue. The colophon hinted at this new audience in its simple note that "all Gentlemen and others may be supplied with this Paper" at the printing shop. The modest status of these "others" was indicated by the introductory preface. The editors promised that "for the Benefit of those who are unacquainted with the Geography of foreign Parts, we may insert such Descriptions as may enlighten them therein."[115]

Despite the expansion of the public sphere and the popularization of the political and print cultures, the free and open press tradition that the colonists avidly imported from England remained fundamentally unchanged. There were novel and more extreme interpretations of the inherited discourse, but the foundation of the concept of press liberty endured. Indeed, the very coherence of the free and open press persisted, though now in more practical terms and in a new context. A newspaper's policy of impartiality effectively opened a forum for public debate, which in turn allowed radicals to challenge all manner of authority, religious or otherwise.[116] A press increasingly open to constant, vigorous, even scandalous attacks on public men and measures tended to undermine elite power and exalt public liberty. The open press was a free press.

Or was it?

Legislative Privilege and Press Liberty

During the first half of the eighteenth century, colonial political thought had become increasingly popular, or, as the colonists would have put it, republican. This is evident in the expanding popular participation in government and in the growing expectation that it was not the people's duty to serve the government, but the government's duty to serve the people.[117] Press liberty discourse was also republican. The free and open press tradition embodied in *Cato's Letters* was "classically republican," not only in its reliance on the likes of Tacitus and

Machiavelli but also in its faith that only public virtue and vigilance could delay the inevitable decline into governmental tyranny. Most significant, the consistency of the free and open press in the colonies rested on the fact that an increasingly open press permitted free press forces to defend the people's liberty and the public good from the menacing "designs" of the government and its "ministerial tools."

But what if one who made use of a wide-open press to assail public liberty was not merely another ministerial "placeman"? What if, in the process of defending public liberty, a defender of the people should criticize the institutional protectors of that liberty, the popular legislature? For the seventeenth century generally, this was not a problem. Since the political elite was relatively homogeneous, one part of the government or another would punish improper expression as either sedition or contempt; sometimes, the Assembly and the governor would combine to bring offenders to justice.[118] However, this sort of cooperation would be rare in the eighteenth century as the Assembly began to represent the people's interests more directly. The popularly elected Assemblies developed into defenders of the people's liberty against the governor and his Council.

This shift was not without its complications. James Franklin, let us recall, was imprisoned for a month under the legislature's power of legislative privilege. Under the radical Whig understanding of politics, the Assembly was the people's key weapon in the struggle to combat royal or ministerial power. Accordingly, any criticism that undermined the people's faith in it was a threat to this crucial bulwark of the people's liberty. Of course, in Franklin's case, the Assembly was in general agreement with Governor Shute and his Council, whereas Franklin echoed the sentiments of many previously marginalized people. Yet, Franklin, consistent with the opposition thinking he had picked up in London and was still reading in *Cato's Letters*, only once—and then fleetingly and obliquely—addressed legislative privilege, despite all the ink he spilled in his defense.[119] In fact, this potential contradiction in the received tradition of press liberty would remain in the background until the 1750s.

With the spread of radical Whig ideas and the popularization of government in the 1740s and 1750s, the struggle of liberty versus power, the people versus the ministry, was increasingly evident in theory and in practice. Cato himself had explained the representatives' critical role in the defense of public liberty when he wrote that "the

Representatives . . . will always act for their Country's Interest; their own being so interwoven with the People's Happiness, that they must stand and fall together."[120] Like so much radical Whig thinking, these burgeoning notions found much more fertile land in the colonies than in the mother country. The close relationships that naturally developed between citizens and their assemblymen in the small communities of colonial America led to the view that the people's rights should emulate, rather than be subordinate to, Assembly privilege.

The equating of Assembly rights with popular rights often reappears in the political literature of midcentury America, but the Pennsylvania Assembly may have put it most succinctly when it matter-of-factly agreed that criticizing the Assembly was a "high breach of privilege, and an invasion of the liberties of the freemen of the province."[121] This privilege gave the Assembly an upper hand vis-à-vis the governor that was not lost on Governor William Denny. He complained that though the Assembly could scream "Breach of Privileges" should it be criticized, he would have to bear the brunt of its "unbounded Freedom in calumniating" him.[122]

The ability to punish individual critics of an Assembly for breach of legislative privilege left colonial legislatures in a stronger, more unified position from which to defend public liberty against the governor and his minions. Dozens of times in the first half of the century, a particularly outspoken opponent was dragged before the bar of the House to answer for written or spoken affronts.[123] Usually the accused would ask to be pardoned and would receive a reprimand, a small fine, and at most a brief imprisonment.[124] But generally, in these cases, as James Franklin's virtual silence on the issue suggests, no conflict between legislative privilege and free press logic was alleged. Two controversies in the 1750s, however, put colonists in a position to begin exploring the limits and tensions inherent in the received tradition.

When preliminary skirmishes of the Seven Years War (1756–63) between Britain and France threatened Pennsylvania's western frontier, opponents of the Quaker-run Assembly criticized the weak half-measures that were the most the Friends' pacifist consciences would permit. William Smith, provost of the nascent University of Pennsylvania, was perhaps the Quakers' most acerbic critic. As Quakers, however, the assemblymen were not only pacifists but also firmly wedded to the ideal of freedom of conscience. The Assembly therefore refused to dignify

Smith's scurrilous pamphlets with a response. But, when Smith's vitriolic letter to London's *Evening Advertiser* was forwarded by Friends there, Assembly members could abide no more. They called Smith before the bar of the House and found him guilty of "libelous, false, and seditious Assertions."[125]

The Pennsylvania Assembly postponed further proceedings against Smith, however, and never got back to the case. Smith, for his part, insisted that his case was a matter of freedom of "Writing and Preaching."[126] That Smith included an appeal to religious freedom was no accident, since his criticisms were primarily aimed at Quaker influence in government. More important, the existence of Quaker ministers—and their scruples about freedom of conscience—in the Assembly proved his saving grace. But Quaker ministers and assemblymen had withdrawn from politics by early 1758, when the county magistrate William Moore, with Smith's editorship, condemned the defunct 1756–57 Assembly. With the religious ministers absent, the issue was now clearly one of press liberty versus Assembly privilege. The Assembly imprisoned the men for three months, but, after his release during a legislative recess, Moore sailed to England to appeal to the Privy Council. The Privy Council found in Smith's and Moore's favor, *not* because their press liberty had been violated but on the grounds that an Assembly could not punish criticisms of an earlier and now defunct Assembly.

The right of the assembly to imprison for breach of privilege survived the test of the Privy Council. And though Smith and Moore technically won on the issue of criticizing *former* Assemblies, the Assembly had succeeded in imprisoning them for three months, thus demonstrating its practical power. Most important for this study, little was said in this case that revealed any contradiction between press liberty and legislative privilege.[127] For the first significant discussion that undermined the equation of Assembly rights with popular rights, we must look to the case of Daniel Fowle, in Massachusetts.

When Fowle was dragged from his dinner one night in 1754 to appear before the Massachusetts House of Representatives on suspicion of having printed *The Monster of Monsters,* a satirical assault on the House, Fowle declared that it was not his printing. After some beating about the bush, Fowle admitted that he had sold it, having bought some copies from Royall Tyler's apprentice. Fowle was then imprisoned, whereas Tyler was committed only briefly for contempt, having refused to answer any questions. Tyler's partner, Daniel's brother Zechariah Fowle, was not imprisoned due to illness. After six days of harsh imprisonment, Fowle had won public sympathy, and the House wisely freed him on his own recognizance. It then let the prosecution drop.[128]

Fowle did not let the matter drop, however. After writing *A Total Eclipse of Liberty* to tell his side of the story, he sued the Speaker of the House and the arresting messenger for illegal imprisonment. By the time the suits and appeals were settled in 1757, Fowle had been printing in New Hampshire for a year. From Portsmouth, Fowle simply ignored the Court's ruling against him, and he neglected to pay the assessed court costs. After five years, he was finally sued for the money. Fowle petitioned the Massachusetts General Court several times in the mid-1760s, eventually having his own legal costs paid and a damage award paid for his suffering.

The fact that the only person ever seriously punished for *The Monster of Monsters* was later paid damages for his trouble is of some significance for the development of press liberty in America. The House had called it a "false scandalous libel" that was a "Breach of the Privileges" of its members, yet Fowle was £50 richer by 1767.[129] Much more important for this study, however, is the manner in which Fowle censured the House for its behavior. The House, confident that Fowle was culpable, defended itself in traditional terms, maintaining that its members alone were the "indisputable Judges" of a breach of privilege and declaring that Fowle's suit was "an Attempt against the Rights of the People." Furthermore, much of Fowle's response was traditional, for he complained that his personal freedom had been violated and his right to trial ignored. He cited such conventional Whig sources as Magna Carta and Care's *English Liberties*.

Fowle's use of standard arguments and his failure to discuss press liberty specifically has led some scholars to slight his case, and the literature has generally ignored it.[130] But Fowle's peculiar situation led him to reconsider the traditional equation of Assembly rights with the people's rights. In *A Total Eclipse of Liberty*, Fowle appealed to the people *and* their representatives. Anticipating that some would call this redundant on the grounds that "the Representatives are the People," Fowle admitted that this was true, but only "in a qualified Sense, i.e., when they act according to the Laws of the Land . . . and their Conduct is agreable to the Constitution of a free People; and . . . consequently will be approved by the *Voice of the People*."[131]

Applying this rupture between the people and their representatives more boldly to his own case, Fowle explained that representatives have "no more than a *delegated* Power," so that when the "common Rights of this Community [are] trampled upon, or only the Liberty of *one* is attempted against," the trust is broken and representatives at "that Moment forfeit all the Power committed to them." "For if but one Member suffers unjustly," Fowle continued, "the *whole* Community is wounded *through his* Sides."[132] Here, then, was one harassed person, defending the people's liberty against its erstwhile defender, the popular Assembly. Fowle would reiterate this theme in his final petition to the General Assembly, hoping that "the Loss of Liberty may be thought equally distressing to an innocent Individual, as to the whole Community."[133]

As we have seen, there had been occasional references to press liberty as an individual, natural right that existed apart from the "ancient" Constitution, Parliament, or colonial assemblies. But Fowle's case, despite its silence on press liberty as such, explicitly calls into question not only the equation of the Assembly's liberty with the people's liberty but also the central notion that animated much of colonial political thought: the simple yet unavoidable opposition between the people's liberty and the ministry's power. Could not a popularly elected legislature use its powers to silence a single, liberty-minded elector? If so, who was defending liberty? More to the point, was liberty the community's, or the community's through individuals?

This sort of sophisticated thinking evinces a tension in early American political thought between republican discourse and emerging liberal ideas. More specifically, it presents a contradiction in the colonists' free and open press tradition. If the press was open to a number of individuals—none of them "ministerial tools"—who differed over fundamental questions of how the public good was best served, it was no longer clear who was defending public liberty. Juries, popularly chosen representatives, and the free press were all intended to protect the people's liberty. But now that the community's liberty could be "wounded" through one person, it was no longer entirely clear whose liberty was at stake. These strains on the received tradition were being felt more strongly as the popularization of government proceeded in the 1740s and 1750s. But, with the arrival of the pre-Revolutionary crisis in the 1760s, these complicated issues were marginalized by a political context that unambiguously appealed to midcentury America's polarized logic of the ministry versus the people.

Conclusion

Though often overlooked, Fowle's tempered reconsiderations about Assembly rights are a far cry from the traditional appeal to parliaments as one of the main pillars of the people's liberty. In many respects, the first half of the eighteenth century had taken Americans a long way. The practice of press liberty had changed significantly. The end of licensing (legally) and seditious libel (effectively), the increased authority of juries, and the expansion of the common person's role in the print and political cultures had brought the colonists a great distance from even the most lenient proceedings of the previous century.

The discourse of press liberty had also changed considerably, often evolving hand-in-hand with the practical innovations. First, the radical Whig discourse of the 1720s in England became midcentury America's dominant alternative to conservative notions of seditious libel. Second, the range of permissible expression had been expanded. Most observers now accepted the arguments that the press should be free to criticize public men and measures, that the truth—or even honest error—was allowable, and that only private and particular libels were illegal. Furthermore, the role of the jury as the finder of law as well as fact, and thus as the final arbiter of lawful expression, had been theoretically established. Finally, a more meaningful function for the public and public opinion had been philosophically advanced. Others—not just Gentlemen—now had a right, even a duty, to participate in the public sphere.

Yet, despite all these changes, both theoretical and practical, the free and open press tradition received from Cato and other radical Whigs remained fundamentally intact. The structure of argumentation and the conceptual arsenal endured. The inherited tradition endured because the biggest, most significant change took place *within* that tradition. This profound transformation was not merely the mainstream acceptance of a previously radical discourse; that acceptance was part and parcel of the popularization of the print and political cultures. More than that, the growth of the public sphere complemented a pivotal shift in the very center of gravity within the "free and open" press tradition: If in 1720 radicals stressed the need for an open press in an effort to force open the narrow window of permissible expression to justify their subtlest and soundest insinuations, by 1760 radicals stressed free press arguments to legitimate even dubious and vitriolic accusations, while beginning to cast a suspicious eye at presses open to seemingly corrupt ministerial forces. This, then, was a shift of emphasis that made the most of the radical potential inherent in an ambiguous and ambivalent tradition.

Though midcentury Whigs made a great deal of the promise of the vague yet unified free and open press tradition, its limitations were no less real. A discourse fashioned in a time and place where Parliament was the sole institutional defender of the people's liberty was bound to experience philosophical and conceptual strain in a period when legislative privilege had replaced seditious libel as the only real threat to press liberty. By 1760, the emerging notion of an individual's natural right to free expression and the tension immanent in Daniel Fowle's qualifications of Assembly rights presented complications for the inherited press liberty tradition. These potential contradictions might have been explored given enough time and attention. But the uncompromising political context of the 1760s and 1770s would leave little time for such nuances.

3

The Pre-Revolutionary Crisis

If the 1740s and 1750s brought about a shift in the center of gravity within the free and open press tradition, the fifteen years prior to the Revolution proved to be the crucible in which that conceptual tradition was broken down and analyzed. As a result, many of the elements remained, but the theoretical structure and ideological weights were permanently transformed.

It is not at first surprising that the period immediately before a war should be given to increasing tensions and great changes; we have come to expect such rumblings in antebellum periods. But the American colonists of the 1760s had little reason to expect grand innovations, least of all in the concept of press liberty. The publication, beginning in 1765, of *Commentaries on the Laws of England* by the distinguished Tory jurist and Oxford law professor William Blackstone might well have been expected to solidify at least the legal conceptualization of press liberty. Certainly, Blackstone's *Commentaries* served as the standard legal resource for decades to come on both sides of the Atlantic. More to the point, this enormously influential work codified the traditional legal understanding of press liberty with a great deal of authority.

Blackstone in America

Formally, the law of seditious libel, and press liberty more generally, had changed little since the expiration of the Licensing Act in 1694. For example, neither the Zenger case nor its later English analogue, the Owen case, were legitimate precedents. Reflecting this legal conservatism, Blackstone maintained that

> the liberty of the press is indeed essential to the nature of a free state: but this consists in laying no *previous* restraints upon publications, and not in freedom from censure for criminal matter when published. . . . To pun-

ish (as the law does at present) any dangerous or offensive writings…is necessary for the preservation of peace and good order, of government and religion, the only solid foundations of civil liberty.[1]

Blackstone's endorsement of subsequent punishment and his concern for preserving government is further evident in his definition of "libels" as

> malicious defamations of any person, and especially a magistrate, made public by either printing, writing, signs, or pictures, in order to provoke him to wrath, or expose him to public hatred, contempt, and ridicule. The direct tendency of these libels is the breach of the public peace.

The direct-tendency contention is a familiar conservative argument, as is Blackstone's insistence that "it is immaterial with respect to the essence of a libel, whether the matter of it be true or false; since the provocation, and not the falsity, is the thing to be punished criminally."[2]

Though there is nothing novel here, and certainly nothing colonial Whigs could applaud, Blackstone's monumental work was widely admired for codifying and simplifying the otherwise byzantine common law. Indeed, even the radical Whig *Boston Gazette* reprinted a piece that praised Blackstone as "a sensible, judicious author." What Whigs appreciated most about Blackstone, however, was his praise for juries, "the most transcendent privilege."[3] Blackstone went so far as to maintain that it was up to each jury to decide whether it would find a general verdict (on the law and the facts) or a special verdict (on the facts only). This is important for press liberty, as we have seen, because government supporters often attempted to extract special verdicts on the fact of publishing only, thus taking the effective definition of seditious libel out of the jury's hands. But even this allowance on Blackstone's part was not enough for Whiggish colonists, for he considered it a hazardous right to exercise, since misapplying the law would put the jury in breach of their oaths.[4] Opposition forces in colonial America instead argued that returning anything but a general verdict was a violation of the jurors' oaths.[5]

Differences over jury power aside, the colonial Whigs broke from Blackstone most notably over his view of press liberty. Especially egregious, in their view, was his claim that truth could still be seditious libel. This classic Tory argument was perhaps the most memorable part of the Zenger case for colonists, and, in fact, the pamphlet account of the trial was reprinted in 1770.[6] When only a small part of Andrew Hamilton's lengthy defense would fit in the moderate *Boston Evening-*

Post, the newspaper naturally excerpted Hamilton's closing argument that only falsity could be libelous.[7] The continuing disagreement between lawyers over whether truth could be libelous was a license for printers to do as they wish, the *Boston Gazette* suggested. More important, if truth could actually be libelous, the vaunted English Constitution was simply tyrannical.[8]

Despite Blackstone's influence, then, Whiggish Americans of the 1760s and 1770s maintained their contrary stance on a number of issues concerning press liberty. The most radical response to the *Commentaries* printed in America, however, was that of an Englishman, the Dissenting minister and theologian Philip Furneaux. Rebutting Blackstone's reading of religious freedom laws, Furneaux wrote letters to the jurist that were included in two pamphlet collections of responses to the *Commentaries.* The colonists had access to this debate, for just as the Philadelphia printer Robert Bell busied himself with an American edition of Blackstone, he also took to reprinting *An Interesting Appendix to Sir William Blackstone's "Commentaries on the Laws of England"* and *The Palladium of Conscience.*[9]

Furneaux's chief concern was to preserve a generous interpretation of Dissenters' rights, especially freedom from punishment for religious sentiments. This concern led Furneaux to argue that the laws should punish overt acts only, leaving professed religious principles and their "tendency" beyond the reach of the magistrate. Yet, in one revealing passage, Furneaux not only applied this logic to the civil realm but actually drew his doctrine from it.

> The distinction between the tendency of principles, and the overt acts arising from them is, and cannot but be, observed in many cases of a *civil* nature; in order to determine the bounds of the magistrate's power, or at least to limit the exercise of it, in such cases. It would not be difficult to mention customs and manners, as well as principles, which have a tendency unfavourable to society; and which, nevertheless, cannot be restrained by penal laws, except with the total destruction of civil liberty. And here, the magistrate must be contented with pointing his penal laws against the evil overt acts resulting from them. In the same manner he should act in regard to men's professing or rejecting, religious principles or systems.[10]

Furneaux's overt-acts doctrine, here fleetingly drawn from his expansive view of civil liberty, was not entirely without precedent: As we have seen, Walwyn and Williams had made similar assertions more than a century before. Still, these were startling claims that confuted not only Blackstone but the vast majority of previous Anglophone discourse over press liberty. Most significant, this passage does not argue *for* the civil overt-acts doctrine; Furneaux apparently did not think he had to. Instead, he *presumed* its general acceptance as the standard for free political expression and sought to use it as the unexceptionable premise in arguing for a religious overt-acts doctrine.[11] These views might well have expressed many radical colonists' unspoken practical ideal of press freedom. But we will never know. Furneaux's overt-acts doctrine grew out of an obscure controversy over English laws that concerned religious freedom. As promising as the argument was, the American colonists of the early 1770s had no time and little need to pursue such speculative disputes.

Legislative Privilege

Another press liberty issue that would not receive its due in the turbulent prewar years was legislative privilege. It was not until the mid-1760s that the Massachusetts Assembly awarded Daniel Fowle damages for his punishment for breach of legislative privilege. This belated reversal points to a theoretical change afoot. Most likely, other factors weighed into the Assembly's decisions. As we shall see more fully, the Stamp Act certainly had the effect of making the colonists more alive to the smallest infringement on press liberty. In that charged ideological context, remunerating Fowle for his damages amounted to a symbolic vote in favor of free expression. Also, the popular uproar in favor of the beleaguered English politician John Wilkes probably contributed to this change of heart.[12] Wilkes was the author of the notorious *North Briton,* No. 45, which defamed the king and began a series of legal attacks that made Wilkes a martyr to liberty, especially press liberty.[13]

Even if these factors contributed to the Assembly's reversal in Fowle's case, popular understanding of legislative privilege was, in fact, undergoing a limited change. The theoretical shift was limited in that not once did a popularly elected lower house unreservedly renounce its contempt[14] powers in a case where they were the targets of vituperation. Still, the notion of legislative privilege as a curb on press liberty was weakened considerably.

About a year after awarding Fowle the last of his damages, the

Massachusetts lower house refused to exercise its legislative privilege and instead praised liberty of the press. When the opposition *Boston Gazette* printed a vicious attack on Governor Bernard, the governor duly sent it to the legislature for action. The Council, acting as the upper house, was quite willing to go along, but the House of Representatives preferred to take recourse in legal niceties. It skirted the issue by noting that no particular person had been named, despite the fact that Joseph Warren, writing as "A True Patriot," made it unmistakable that Bernard was his quarry. Equally unmistakable was the rebuke evident in the free press language of one passage in the popular branch's response.

> The Liberty of the Press is a great Bulwark of the Liberty of the people: It is therefore the incumbent Duty of those who are constituted the Guardians of the People's Rights to defend and maintain it. This House however . . . are ready to discountenance an Abuse of this Privilege, whenever there shall be Occasion for it: Should the proper Bounds of it be at any Time transgressed, to the Prejudice of Individuals or the Publick.[15]

The House insisted it was ready to use its contempt powers if ever "any extraordinary Aid shall become needful." But since there was no emergency at the moment, it told the governor to pursue the issue in the courts. Bernard did take the *Gazette*'s printers to court; despite a lecture from Chief Justice Thomas Hutchinson, the grand jury refused to find against them.[16]

Less than two years later, after Hutchinson had been elevated to governor, the Massachusetts upper house again had its claims to legislative privilege foiled. Writing as "Mucius Scaevola," Joseph Greenleaf brazenly attacked Hutchinson as "a usurper" in the pages of Isaiah Thomas's *Massachusetts Spy*.[17] The Council members debated for more than a day before deciding to order Thomas to appear before them. They should have debated longer. Three times they sent for Thomas, and three times he defied their authority on the advice of a "distinguished law character" who informed him that only a sheriff could "serve such a process upon him."[18] The subsequent motion to imprison him for contempt "did not obtain." And, though the reason for this remains unclear, there is no question that at least one councilman argued that the Council had "no legal authority" to commit him.[19] When a grand jury was presented with the alleged seditious libel, it returned the bill *ignoramus*. The government soon thereafter dropped the matter entirely.[20]

The upper chamber's right to legislative privilege was denied outright in a South Carolina case in 1773. When Thomas Powell printed, in his *South-Carolina Gazette*, Councilman William Henry Drayton's dissent to the Council's decision not to send £1,500 to help support John Wilkes, the Council had Powell arrested for breach of legislative privilege. In their roles as justices of the peace, the Speaker and another member of the lower house freed Powell by issuing a writ of habeas corpus. The Council then found the two assemblymen guilty of a "Breach of Privilege and Contempt" against the upper house, though the Council dared not have them arrested. The Speaker presented his reasons for the writ to his colleagues, concluding "that it would be dangerous to countenance such a Usurpation of Power in the Council, [and] would render the Liberty of the Subject precarious." The lower house unanimously found this reasoning "extremely satisfactory."[21] In an effort to avoid utter defeat, the Council sent the case to England, but the war soon preempted the issue.[22]

Upper houses, then, had an increasingly precarious hold on their power to punish what they took to be licentious expression as a breach of legislative privilege. But what of the lower houses? These were the popularly elected branches of the legislatures, and so it is precisely here that the people's liberty and an individual's freedom would mostly readily come into conflict. And conflict they did when Alexander McDougall assailed the New York Assembly for approving provisions for the king's troops late in 1769. The affronted Assembly stopped at nothing to get the author's name, and soon the printer, James Parker, had been pressured into identifying McDougall. McDougall refused to admit his guilt and accepted martyrdom in jail, rather than post bail. America had its own Wilkes.

With the government united against him, and a packed grand jury in place,[23] McDougall became the first man indicted for seditious libel in more than a quarter century. This only endeared him further to his growing throng of Whiggish supporters. Then, only days before the trial, James Parker, who had long regretted giving up McDougall, saved him at last: Parker died. The loss of the only eyewitness brought the indefinite postponement of the criminal case.

Not to be outdone, the Assembly had McDougall arrested and brought before it. Charged with writing the offending essay, McDougall refused to plead, arguing on the grounds of freedom from self-incrimination and double jeopardy. When the mere assertion of the latter reasoning was held to be "a Breach of Privilege," Assemblyman

George Clinton argued that the house was scorning "Justice" and "straining its Authority." The question was put to a vote, and only Clinton and four others refused to find McDougall in breach of legislative privilege; he spent the remaining three months of the legislative session in jail.

Ultimately, the issue of legislative privilege as a threat to press liberty had been broached, but not substantially addressed. Indeed, the change suggested by these episodes might best be understood as a shift in the political, rather than the ideological, context. The antagonism between the people and the ministry reached its zenith in the pre-Revolutionary crisis, empowering the popularly elected branches of the legislature to challenge the contempt power of the upper houses in cases where the governor or the Council itself had been maligned. Such cases thus undermined the upper houses' privileges without confronting the conflict between an individual's liberty and the people's liberty as embodied in their chosen representatives. This tension, revealed in Daniel Fowle's case, was revisited in the prewar period only in the controversy over America's Wilkes, Alexander McDougall. Then, only five New York assemblymen would agree with McDougall and his supporters that such use of a legislature's contempt powers undermined the freedom of expression, "the peculiar Right and Privilege of Freemen."[24] This, however, should not surprise us. For, as we will see, the escalating struggle between the people and the ministry put a premium on unity and made every attack on the people's representatives, the traditional guardians of public liberty, an attack on the people themselves.

Increasing Division

It was not Blackstone's *Commentaries* or debates over legislative privilege but a remarkable transformation in the general political context that brought the issue of press liberty to a head in the 1760s and 1770s. As we observed in the previous chapter, the expanding public sphere in midcentury America occasioned a significant shift but no great restructuring of the free and open press legacy. To be sure, mounting partisanship and the increased number of newspapers in the 1740s and 1750s led to many disputes over the extent of press liberty. But these economic strains and political quarrels did not force a wholesale re-examination of the existing press liberty tradition.

The larger political changes after the Seven Years War (1756–63), in contrast, altered drastically the relationship between Britain and its colonies, ultimately revealing the ambivalence and inconsistencies in the inherited free and open press discourse. No individual political change was compelling in itself. Rather, it was the cumulative effect of these events that forced things onto an entirely different footing. The acts of the British Ministry again and again fit into what Bernard Bailyn has called the colonists' "logic of rebellion." That is, they believed that it was no accident that new policies increasingly endangered basic pillars of freedom; rather, they became conscious of an intentional, covert attack on English liberties.[25] The colonists had long known about the dangers ministerial power presented for the people's liberty. True to their English heritage, they now turned a suspicious eye to government.

In 1763, at the end of the war, some regiments of British army regulars were left in the colonies. These regiments bore alarming similarities to the sort of "standing armies" that John Trenchard, Robert Molesworth, and others had taught the colonists were a presage of arbitrary power and therefore a threat to the people's liberty. But, as these troops were left out in the newly won territories, far from any population centers, they were seen as a minimal threat. Following this controversy came the introduction of the Revenue or Sugar Act, in the spring of 1764, which presented an undue burden during hard economic times.

George Grenville, first minister to the young King George III, was simply trying to raise some funds to help defray the costs of defending the colonies from the French in the recently concluded Seven Years War. And, in fact, the Sugar Act cut the duty on foreign molasses in half. Grenville's idea was to put an end to the rampant smuggling that characterized the giant sugar market. To that end, he expanded the jurisdiction of the jury-less vice-admiralty courts and increased the number of customs personnel. All this had the effect of raising the duty, as smuggling merchants were now less likely to go undetected or to be acquitted by a local jury. More important, these changes presented the vigilant colonists with convincing evidence of a ministerial conspiracy: The vice-admiralty courts were despised for circumventing juries, one of the traditional "pillars" of the people's liberty, and the customs officials seemed to be ministerial lackeys or "placemen." Later that spring, the Stamp Act was tentatively announced for passage the following year.

When the Stamp Act was passed on 22 March 1765, to become effective in November, it cut right at the heart of the press. Admittedly, wartime stamp duties had been established in Massachusetts in 1755 and in New York in 1757; yet they were temporary and relatively inexpensive and were enacted by local authorities.[26] These new taxes were different. First, the duties were considerably higher than either of the earlier provincial duties, especially given the postwar recession and the myriad paper products to which they applied. Second and more important, these duties, combined with the difficulty of getting stamped paper, seemed a type of censorship particularly aimed at those newspapers not governmentally supported. The Stamp Act also brought up even larger issues, such as the very real fear of more "taxation without representation." And, as with the Sugar Act, Stamp Act violations were supposed to be handled by vice-admiralty courts. Taken together, these new elements seemed to reveal an unfolding conspiracy for arbitrary power.

Even with the news of the repeal of the Stamp Act in May 1766, relations failed to return to normal. Parliament had simultaneously maintained its complete authority over the colonies in the Declaratory Act. Making good on this declaration, the Townshend Duties arrived a year later and imposed taxes on a wide variety of commodities. To this the colonists responded by raising the stakes. They undertook to establish and maintain a nonimportation agreement. These and myriad other smaller political controversies led to a heightened sense of tension. Then, on 1 October 1768, two regiments of British regulars, complete with artillery, arrived in Boston. These troops, soon to number four full regiments, were the very sort of "standing army" the colonists had long feared. The ministerial design for arbitrary power had never been more evident.

These developments, and especially how they were viewed by the colonists, are significant for this analysis because the political dispute and the escalating polarization undermined the practical consonance between open press doctrine and free press doctrine. While there had long been successful opposition newspapers, the power of the Ministry and the government side more generally would never have allowed such papers if there had been no government press open to ministerial voices. Shifting political power meant that the opposition presses could exist while placing increasing pressure and public scorn on the government printers. More important, developing public attitude held that a press open to ministerial arguments was now a considerable threat to the people's liberties. The open press was no longer consonant in practice with the free press.

The developments of the 1760s brought increasing political division to the colonies. Admittedly, the Stamp Act crisis itself brought a great deal of heat but little new light to the issue of press liberty. For example, when the famous "Tombstone Edition" of the *Pennsylvania Journal* protested the imminent enforcement of the Stamp Act, it failed to augment the discourse of press liberty. Within thick black borders and amid ominous crossbones and coffins, the editors merely reprinted a 1756 essay from the *Boston Gazette*, itself a reprint of an earlier piece in the *Independent Advertiser*.[27] In fact, the Stamp Act was such a blunt weapon, affecting all newspapers and numerous other goods, that opposition printers were successful simply by rehearsing the traditional rhetoric of free and open press discourse. Nevertheless, events after the Act's repeal induced the more Whiggish printers and their Tory adversaries to reconsider and even recast the free and open press. The polarized politics of the day did not force them to abandon their press liberty tradition; it did, however, lead them to begin to identify distinct logics and to examine differing consequences.

In 1766, after the Stamp Act had been repealed, William and Thomas Bradford, of the *Pennsylvania Gazette,* printed some letters of a former stamp distributor, John Hughes, which indicated that he had supported the Stamp Act and had hoped to be able to help enforce it. Hughes denied the letters' authenticity and began a suit against the Bradfords. In retrospect, the Bradfords' response demonstrates the ambivalence of Whig printers who wanted to have it both ways, wanting to espouse both a free press and an open press:

> We are only the printers of a free and impartial paper. . . . We can appeal to North-America not only for our impartiality as printers, but also for the real advantages derived to us very lately from the unrestrained liberty, which every Britain claims of communicating his sentiments to the public thro' the channel of the press. What would have become of the liberties of the British Colonies in North-America, if Mr. Hughes's calls on Great-Britain had been heard, to restrain printers here from publishing, what he is pleased to stile *inflammatory pieces,* and if every prostitute scribler, and enemy to his country had been suffered, without controul from the pens of true patriots, to rack their distempered brains, to find out arguments to gull a free-born people into a tame submission to perpetual slavery, and to impose their flimsey cobwebs upon us, instead of solid and substantial reasoning.[28]

Though Leonard Levy finds the Bradfords' essay hardly worth quoting and reads in it a "complacency," we should not ignore its inherent tension.[29] The Bradfords here appeal to open as well as to free press doctrine, in that they laud the right of each man to print his sentiments and also point out the danger to the people's general liberty when this right is exercised by those with tyrannical principles. Ultimately, the weight of the piece stresses the free press fear of curtailed liberties. The passage evinces little confidence that the "truth will prevail." The fear was that the ministerial party would muster its strength to restrain the opposition presses, thus jeopardizing public liberty. Most important, the Bradfords' response provides an early suggestion of the practical tension between free press and open press logic.

Part of the Bradfords' concern stemmed from a fear that the open press backed by the ministerial party was open especially to those who intended "to impose their flimsey cobwebs" upon the public. Since, as Cato had long taught, "power has so many advantages," a press open to ministerial "tools" might very well defraud the people of their liberties. Despite this logic, even the more Whiggish printers could not abruptly break with the long-established concept of the free and open press. Rather, the rupture was a gradual process.

The Whigs' first step was to implicate the Tory printers in the unfolding ministerial conspiracy while at the same time maintaining their faith in the open press notions inherent in their press liberty tradition. The very first edition of William Rind's *Virginia Gazette* bore the following motto on its masthead: "Open to ALL PARTIES, but Influenced by NONE." The immediate intention was to suggest, as all would have understood, that Alexander Purdie's rival *Virginia Gazette* was "influenced," perhaps even bribed, by the ministerial side, particularly the governor. This claim was credible in part because of the British government's earlier practice of bribing opposition editors into supporting the government. This happened even in the case of the *London Journal*, where the earliest of *Cato's Letters* originally appeared.[30] Rind's insinuation, therefore, fit both relatively recent British history and the colonists' conspiratorial "logic of rebellion." Indeed, the slogan captured the new sentiment of the opposition presses throughout the colonies; many would soon pick up the phrase either as their own motto or simply as an argumentative refrain.[31]

Having implicated the Tories' open press, the Whigs' next rhetorical move was to qualify the demands of "openness" on their own free and open presses. William Goddard, of the *Pennsylvania Chronicle,* was perhaps the first to put a Whig cast on the impartiality of open press doctrine. He maintained that press freedom did *not* require the printer to forfeit all judgment. Goddard thus resurrected an argument we saw fade in the 1740s: Open press doctrine allowed, even required, the printer to use his own judgment in deciding what to print. Press liberty, Goddard thus insisted, does not "consist in publishing all the Trash which every rancorous, illiberal, anonymous Scribbler may take it into his Head to send him."[32] But, if the printer had to judge what to print, the principles underlying that judgment would provide new specificity to the previously nebulous open press tenet. A month later Goddard would defend his judgment, maintaining that it had "never been bias'd, in the least degree, to the injury of the Public, or the poorest individual."[33] By specifying the "Public, or the poorest individual," Goddard shifted his concerns away from the Tories, who were generally more affluent and who were not, in any case, what the Whigs thought of as defenders of the "Public" in the struggle between ministerial power and the people's liberty. Although these shifts may not at first appear radical, they were a far cry from Franklin's simple claim that printers would "chearfully serve all contending Writers."[34]

These subtle changes regarding the "openness" of the free and open press were unmistakable to the Tories. "A Constant Customer" of Purdie's *Gazette* saw all too clearly that Rind's "weekly declaration" provided him with "an easy screen" to close his press to pieces of which he disapproved. "He can, at any time, want [i.e., lack] room to do what he has not a mind to do." With such ambiguous principles, this contributor wondered whether Rind "may be quite so open to all parties" as he claimed to be.[35]

But, while the Whigs were implicating the open Tory press and were tinkering with the "openness" of their own, the Tory *Boston Chronicle* glaringly demonstrated that a truly open press can cut both ways. After the introduction of the Townshend Duties, John Hancock and other members of the Committee of Merchants in Boston took to imposing the nonimportation agreement by exposing alleged violators to public derision by printing their names in the opposition press. John Mein and John Fleeming responded by alleging, in their *Chronicle* and in widely available pamphlets, that certain of the "well disposed" members of the Committee of Merchants were violating the spirit, if not the letter, of the nonimportation agreement, as well as publishing false accounts of imports and importers. After making these claims, from November 1769 on, the *Chronicle* began each edition with the question, "Is not the detection of the 'WELL DISPOSED' owing to the Glorious LIBERTY of the PRESS?"[36]

The Tories were partially correct. This was precisely the sort of exchange that open press notions supported. However, it was not, as was becoming increasingly clear, the Whigs' practical ideal of press liberty. Harbottle Dorr, an ordinary shopkeeper and a Whig, noted contemptuously in the margins of his bound collection of Boston newspapers that Mein had "attempted to ridicule the Characters of the most respectable men."[37] Others clearly concurred, for during the riots over the nonimportation controversy Mein and Fleeming's printing shop was vandalized. Mein was then personally threatened, and, after the first revelations concerning the Committee of Merchants, he and Fleeming were attacked by a mob. Amid the pandemonium, a wounded Mein escaped to the safety of a royal guardhouse. Soon thereafter, he fled to London. Fleeming, however, continued printing until Hancock managed to act on behalf of Mein's creditors and shut down their press.[38] In this way, the patriots closed down the most active Tory vehicle to date and gave practical evidence of their increasing disdain and suspicion of the Tories' use of the open press. The Whigs clearly knew what they were doing, for when Mein had assaulted the opposition printer John Gill the year before, the Whigs called it an attack on press liberty.[39] Nevertheless, assaulting Mein and closing down the *Chronicle* was as yet scarcely justified by free press doctrine.

Isaiah Thomas, of the avidly Whig *Massachusetts Spy,* took free press notions further than anyone had hitherto taken them. In December 1770, Thomas enlarged the *Spy* and used this opportunity to reaffirm his principles. He made the briefest nod to open press doctrine and then spelled out in some detail his extreme free press logic. Beginning with the now-common masthead motto "OPEN TO ALL Parties, but *Influenced* by NONE," Thomas made but one other reference to his "*Impartiality of Conduct*" and spent the rest of the statement extolling the free press. Considering himself a faithful "FRIEND to TRUE LIBERTY," Thomas declared that

> the *Free* Use of the PRESS has ever been acknowledged one of the greatest Blessings of Mankind, especially when its PRODUCTIONS tend to defend the GLORIOUS CAUSE OF LIBERTY; and to point out to the

world those base and wicked arts of designing men, who fain would set nations together by the ears, and involve whole kingdoms in slavery.

Hoping to expose such "miscreants," the printer promised that "a great regard will always be paid to such political pieces as tend to secure to us our invaluable rights and privileges."[40]

The significance of Thomas's ardent declaration of press liberty was not in implicating the Tories' open press or in qualifying the demands of "openness" on the patriot press. Rather, Thomas's pronouncements served to shift the balance between the increasingly contradictory demands of a free and open press, ultimately relegating open press doctrine to a very subordinate position. In so doing, he placed himself at the very forefront of Whig free press doctrine.[41] Indeed, Thomas's assertions, when taken together with the attack on Mein, foreshadow the violently exclusionary "press of freedom" that would achieve dominance only after a more substantial bifurcation of the inherited tradition of press liberty.

Bifurcation

The increasing division between Tory and Whig, both ideological and political, reached a peak in 1770. Violent exchanges in January and February led to the "Boston Massacre" of early March. These events exacerbated the colonists' fears about the standing army that was occupying Boston. Further, these events provided more evidence, if any were needed, that the people must redouble their efforts to defend themselves from the "arbitrary designs" of ministerial forces.

In contrast to the heightened tensions evident in 1770, the period after 1770 constituted something of a détente. The repeal of the Townshend Duties in March 1770, the removal of troops from Boston, and the absence of any new provocative events afforded a period of eased tensions.[42] The détente was sometimes strained, as it was by the arson of the *Gaspee,* a customs ship, in Providence Harbor in June 1772. Still, something of a calm did exist. The storm, however, arrived with the Tea Act in the autumn of 1773. The so-called Tea Party of that December and the introduction of the "Intolerable" or "Coercive" Acts the following May spurred on the renewed, intensified political tumult.

With the intensifying polarization of the political crisis, the ideological debate over press freedom evinced a similar cleavage. A virtually complete philosophical bifurcation set in as the Tories, more and more defensive politically, began an ideological offensive. Capitalizing on the introduction of a new, ardently Tory newspaper, they continued to defend, even advance, their open press doctrine, while attacking the Whigs' free press logic. In response, the nascent Patriots further entrenched themselves in this free press doctrine, distancing themselves from open press doctrine and all but abandoning its practice. Although the political dispute was ultimately resolved through force of arms, the free press debate would not find permanent resolution even then. Nevertheless, as the ideological crisis reached its most intense stage, the inherent tensions of an ambivalent tradition were at last unmistakably revealed.

The Tories Make Their Case

With the forced closing of the *Boston Chronicle,* the Tories lost their premier vehicle for propaganda. Indeed, they lacked such a leading voice until the founding of the *New-York Gazetteer* in 1773. Its printer, James Rivington, proved a shrewd editor and a trenchant defender of open press doctrine. As a result, the *Gazetteer* soon maintained the largest circulation of any paper in the colonies; it had subscribers from Portsmouth to Charleston and beyond. Further, its articles were often printed in other papers throughout the colonies, making it the Tories' "political bible."[43]

Given the indictments of "influence" or bribery that had become common in the Patriot press, the Tories took up defending themselves and their open press. First, though the Patriots' "trick" of labeling all adversaries "ministerial minions" was "now worn threadbare," Tories frequently denied the charges.[44] Second, seeking to fight motto with motto, Rivington emblazoned his masthead with the simple retort "PRINTED at his EVER OPEN & UNINFLUENCED PRESS." Making only a passing gesture to free press logic, he insisted "the Printer has, without reserve, inserted every piece sent to him relative to the liberties and interests of America; his press has been equally open to the sons of freedom, and to those who have differed in sentiment from them."[45] While his claim to complete "openness" was not strictly true, this press philosophy did lead Rivington to open his press to more opposing views than could be found in the Patriot press.[46] More important, Rivington was pushing open press notions to their extreme, discarding the Patriot claim that the printer must exercise some judgment. Later, when defending himself from criticisms about his press, Rivington would spell out this extreme open press doctrine at length (cleverly using the term "free press"):[47]

> It is worthy to remark, that in this, and many other charges of the like nature, no attempt has been made to convict [the Printer] of *partiality*. His crime then is neither more or less, than the keeping a *free press*, in a land of Liberty: For if this news-paper is not *impartial*, it is the fault of his correspondents. He does not arrogantly set himself up as a judge, of every piece that is offered for publication, by selecting *this*, and rejecting *that*, he is content to lay them before a more respectable tribunal, to have their merits tried, as they ought to be, by the public voice.[48]

Shrewdly, Rivington deflected any criticisms of the partisan bent of his paper by simply claiming his contributors were partial. More important, gifted rhetorician that he was, Rivington expropriated the term "free press" and emphasized it. This, however, was not likely to fool anyone. Indeed, as free press doctrine became increasing rare in the Tories' pronouncements on press liberty, the rhetoric of the free press also disappeared.

Rather than expropriate the language of their enemies, the Tories more often took to ridiculing the freedom of the Patriots' free press, thus further expanding the theoretical divide. The vicious, partisan slant of the Patriot press made criticizing their free press an easy business. Rivington sometimes made spirit of it, publishing poems and satirical dialogues. These were often lengthy pieces, but excerpts from one oft-cited poem suggest the character of these barbs. Lambasting the Patriots, one amateur poet wrote,

> THEY tremble at an equal press,
> for reasons any dunce can guess,
> . . . Dares the poor man impartial be,
> He's doomed to want and infamy
> . . . [he] Sees all he loves a sacrifice,
> If he dares publish aught—but lies
> . . . Alas vain men, how blind, how weak;
> Is this the liberty we seek[?]![49]

The Continental Congress's "Address to Quebec" provided material for more serious reflections on the Patriots' evolving view of press liberty.

In this famous appeal to their French-Canadian brethren, members of Congress enumerated the rights they were defending, including freedom of the press.

> The importance of this consists, besides the advancement of truth, science, morality and arts in general, in its diffusion of liberal sentiments on the administration of government, its ready communication of thoughts between subjects, and its consequential promotion of union among them, whereby oppresive officals are shamed or intimidated into more honorable and just modes of conducting affairs.[50]

This traditional free and open press rhetoric was meant for uncontroversial consumption beyond the colonies, but the ministerial side made the most of the ambivalent language. "A Sailor" actually quoted the entirety of the Address and then asked "whether the Congress meant to encourage liberal and free sentiments concerning every other *administration of government*. but not to tolerate them when they relate to their *own*?" But, if such a question did not make the increasing conceptual tensions clear enough, a fellow loyalist, "T.W.," sought to distinguish sharply between their own open and the Patriots' free press. While these "men of dangerous designs, dark purposes, and foul deeds" sought to "destroy the productions of the press," the "ears of a genuine son of liberty are ever open to all doctrines, it is his glory to hear them, to examine them, to adopt them if they are true, to confute them if they are false."[51]

With a sharp distinction drawn, an extreme open press defended, and the free press mocked, it remained only for the Tories to contend outright that the Patriot press was *not*, in fact, free. As the "republican press" became more and more extreme, it was, naturally, Rivington himself who most sharply took the Tory attack to its outermost bounds, turning the free press's underlying logic on its head. Rivington simply insisted that, "while his enemies make *liberty* the prostituted pretense of their illiberal persecution of him, their aim is to establish a *most cruel tyranny*," the tyranny of the Whig majority.[52] And, with this contention, the bifurcation of the received tradition, at least from the Tory side, was complete; the only truly free press, as far as they were concerned, was the open press. But, even as Rivington's words were being printed, the news of Lexington and Concord was racing to New York. Increasingly, the Patriots' free press would become the extreme and exclusive "press of freedom," and Rivington's words would become treasonous.

The Patriots Respond

In response to the end of détente in 1773 and the multiplying Tory assaults on their press, the Patriots further explored their increasingly extreme free press doctrine. This shift and the deepening bifurcation are evident even in the emergence of a new motto. At Williamsburg, the home of Rind's "open and uninfluenced press," Alexander Purdie, now an unequivocal Patriot, eschewed this motto and introduced his new paper with the masthead exclamation "ALWAYS FOR LIBERTY AND THE PUBLICK GOOD."[53]

Just what did liberty and the public good require from the press? "A Customer" of the *Maryland Gazette* spoke for many Patriots when he spelled out free press logic, insisting that press liberty was subordinate to the general cause of the people's liberty: "the liberty of the press is the most powerful adversary to slavery, ambition, and faction; but it is repugnant to the principles of honor and general liberty, that it should not be totally at the devotion of the *professed* friends of the people [i.e., the Patriots]."[54]

The more cautious Bradfords felt it best not to dispense completely with open press rhetoric. Still, their response to an attack on their press evinces an adherence to free press doctrine where there had been strained ambivalence only eight years before. Under their new "Unite or Die" masthead, the Bradfords now insisted they supported liberty of the press,

> but will any say that this requires the publishing [of] . . . every piece that may be sent to a printer? It has ever been . . . our fixed resolution to keep *our Journal* free and open . . . yet we do not mean that it should be a vehicle of . . . inflammatory declaration. —In the present unhappy controversy between G.B. and these colonies, which so nearly concerns the freedom not only of our country, but of all the British Empire, we defy any one of those pretended advocates for ministerial measures, to say they were denied a place for their pieces in our paper; yet, at the same time, we look on it as a right to judge and have always followed our own judgement.[55]

This judgment, the Bradfords continued, would ensure the omission of anything "calculated to inflame and divide."

This obscure passage suggests much about the polarization of free press doctrine. Despite the claim that their paper was "open," the

Bradfords qualified that "openness" beyond recognition. Whereas Rivington claimed that he would not "arrogantly" judge but would print all pieces, the Bradfords explicitly disagreed, specifying that they *would* judge in an effort to maintain the people's unity in the "present unhappy controversy." In so doing, the Bradfords subordinated the demands of the open press to the free press imperatives of the general freedom of the country.

With the political crisis deepening, it was becoming more and more obvious, to most Patriots at least, that the underlying concerns of the free press greatly outweighed those of the open press.[56] But, with the Tories continually appealing to open press doctrine to justify their practices, the Patriots still needed to undermine these claims entirely. John Holt, of the *New-York Journal,* was that city's foremost Patriot printer and a frequent victim of Rivington's barbs. Going far beyond mere claims of influence or bribery, Holt maintained that a "fair" contest would be impossible with the "devious" ministerial supporters.

> My paper is sacred to the cause of truth and justice, and I have preferred the pieces, that in my opinion, are the most necessary to the support of that cause; and yet, if I could see anything on the opposite side that had the least degree of plausibility, truth and commonsense to recommend it,—I would endeavor to find a place and give a fair hearing to such a performance,—but when I see every thing on that side to be no better than barefaced attempts to deceive and impose upon the ignorant, and imprudently overbear and brazen them out of their reason, their liberty and their property—I disdain such publications, but yet will meet any of them upon fair ground.[57]

Given the political crisis and the designs of the Tories, Holt was implying, a fair hearing for truth was not to be had. Thus, with an open press the truth might *not* prevail, and general liberty was at risk of being stolen forever. This was a risk that Holt and other Patriots were increasingly unwilling to accept.[58]

Their concept of press liberty no longer told them they had to accept this risk. The loyalist press was perceived to be influenced, unfair, deceitful, and divisive; meanwhile, the very cause of liberty hung precariously in the balance. Once the Patriots established, at least in their own minds, their right, even the need, to judge what was deceitful and divisive, a thoroughly distinct free press emerged.

The Free Press Becomes the "Press of Freedom"

The Patriots had scarcely distinguished and developed their free press doctrine when the political crisis deepened irrevocably and gave rise to the most extreme manifestation of free press logic. With the commencement of hostilities on Lexington Green on 19 April 1775, the dire threat to the people's liberties from ministerial forces became dramatically apparent. The free press doctrine of the Patriot party was further polarized, and an extreme, active formulation of the free press emerged. Rather than maintain that the press ought to be "sacred to liberty," this new militant view consisted of an active program of threats, public exposure, financial sanctions, and, ultimately, physical violence. The aim was to ensure that all presses were free *only* for the speech of freedom.[59] The Patriots' free press was becoming the exclusive "press of freedom."

It is true that there was intimidation prior to Lexington. The emergence of what I identify as the "press of freedom" was gradual, foreshadowed by extreme moments in the development of free press doctrine. The accusations of ministerial bribes, when tied to specific Tory printers, were certainly early efforts at intimidation. And the riotous attack on Mein and Fleeming, as well as the *Chronicle*'s coerced downfall, were omens of what was to come. Shortly before Lexington itself, Rivington was condemned by town meetings up and down the coast; and on 13 April a mob in New Brunswick, New Jersey, hung him in effigy.

It was only after Lexington and Concord had drastically altered the political context that the exclusive, repressive "press of freedom" truly flourished. The pro-British side almost immediately lost two of its papers due to shifting public sentiment. A third loss poignantly symbolized the end of the free and open press discourse as the colonists had known it. Thomas and John Fleet were Patriots who, true to the inherited legacy of press liberty, maintained an open press, the only press acknowledged by all sides to be truly neutral. Even a unique Patriot-owned paper such as the Fleet's *Boston Evening-Post* could no longer maintain a free and open press in the face of the emerging "press of freedom." The paper closed immediately after Lexington.

These losses were replaced by avidly Whig papers that contributed to the atmosphere of verbal and, increasingly, physical attacks on Tories. For example, Rivington's printing shop was vandalized by a mob of seventy-five horsemen less than three weeks after news of Lexington reached New York. In late autumn, the repressive extremity of the free press burgeoned. By then, most Patriots could agree with an earlier *South-Carolina Gazette* contributor who baldly maintained that it was "no *Loss of Liberty,* that court-minions can complain of, when they are silenced. No man has a right to say a word, which may lame the liberties of his country."[60] On 23 November, the "press of freedom" incarnate visited Rivington's printing shop a second time. A mob led by the militant New York Patriot Isaac Sears had marched three days, all the way from New Haven, in order to destroy his press and steal the type. This time, Rivington understandably fled to a British ship, and the *New-York Gazetteer,* the Tories' most powerful voice, went silent. Without that leadership, the remaining pro-British presses in Patriot-held America became more and more tame. In March 1776, when the British abandoned Boston, the "only outspoken Tory organ then left," the *Massachusetts Gazette and Boston Newsletter,* expired.[61]

With the establishment of hostilities and the solidification of opposing sides, propaganda became one of many weapons of war. As "A Tory" observed in Philadelphia, "amongst the other implements of war, the *pen* and the *printing-press* are not the least important." "By influencing the minds of the multitude, [they] can perhaps do more towards gaining a point than the best rifle gun or the sharpest bayonet."[62] As a result, forthright suppression of the enemy became the practice on both sides of the dispute. The Patriots, as we have seen, had been intimidating Tory printers for some time in their struggle for freedom. Virginia's governor, however, made it clear that both sides could play that game. Lord Dunmore simply had his soldiers confiscate the Patriot printer John Hunter Holt's press. Shortly thereafter, in early 1776, Dunmore was publishing his own *Virginia Gazette* from a ship off the coast.

Patriots, for their part, took to instituting oaths of allegiance and other wartime restrictions on freedom of expression.[63] Pennsylvania, for example, initiated penalties for those who refused to swear a Patriot oath; they consisted of exclusion from jury duty, public office, and voting. The so-called nonjurors also had their taxes doubled. Since Quakers rejected oaths on religious grounds, they, too, were penalized by these laws. Printing presses were closed to Quakers, as well as to Tories, since the former's pacific beliefs were suspect in wartime. Though these practices hardly bespeak an open press, we should bear in mind the context. Sedition was a very real threat. One Revolutionary committee went beyond sedition ordinances to set up rewards for catching deserters because some Tories had been "exceedingly industrious in sowing the seeds of sedition in the minds of the militia."[64]

It was because of the genuine danger presented to the people's liberty that the "press of freedom" had such support on the Patriot side. Even a young James Madison could snarl, "I wish most heartily we had Rivington & his ministerial Gazetteers for 24 hours in this place. Execrable as their designs are, they would meet with adequate punishment."[65] The Philadelphia Committee of Inspection and Observation preferred official, authorized punishment of such "ministerial enemies," and justified its repressive resolves by explaining the "press of freedom."

> The rights which all men are entitled to, of speaking their sentiments candidly, so far as is consistent with the peace and welfare of society, they hold to be sacred, and that it ought to be inviolate. But when this privilege is used for the purpose of raising jealousies among the people, distracting their councils, and counteracting their virtuous exertions against injury and oppression, all laws, human and divine, justify the punishment of such licentiousness.[66]

Notwithstanding these pronouncements at the locus of power, the "press of freedom" was in fact retreating.

Beyond the "Press of Freedom"

The spreading hostilities brought about the suppression of Tory voices. In one sense, the threat that the ministry would attack the people and their liberties was more dangerous than ever. But in another sense, the danger was now external and overt. Thus, the logic of the free press, while held in the extreme for Tories, no longer made sense within the Patriot circle. Gradually, a refined open press replaced the "press of freedom."

As early as 1776, the open press was beginning to return to Patriot America. Not surprisingly, there were overzealous moments. Daniel Fowle once again got in trouble with his legislature when his *New-Hampshire Gazette* ran an anti-independence piece in January 1776; this position concurred with the Continental Congress's view at the time, but the Provincial Congress reprimanded him. Samuel Loudon, of the *New-York Packet*, agreed to print some anti-independence pamphlets in March.

Despite his pledge to hold up publication, a mob stole the whole run of 1,500 copies and burned them on New York Common. Still, the open press was in fact returning, and Patriot authorities from the New York Committee of Safety put Loudon on the payroll.[67]

The Continental Congress certainly endorsed an open press approach. It recommended that the various Revolutionary committees presume that all "erroneous opinions" proceeded "rather from want of information than want of virtue or public spirit." The delegates were convinced that "the more our right to the enjoyment of our ancient liberties and privileges be examined, the more just and necessary our present opposition to ministerial tyranny will appear." Congress therefore advocated a policy of publication and persuasion, not repression and intimidation, for all but the ostensibly dangerous.[68] Soon, even the Philadelphia Committee of Inspection was toning down its rhetoric.[69] Though many were penalized for refusing the oath or were imprisoned as dangerous Tories, there was only one conviction for seditious speech under Pennsylvania's misprision of treason laws: a man had advised someone to supply the enemy with a stolen horse.[70]

Treason aside, the "press of freedom" was soon both practically restricted and theoretically criticized. In practice, with a war on, it was generally quite clear who could talk and what could be said; *within* a given side, then, an open press prevailed, even flourished.[71] William Smith, provost of the College of Philadelphia, thus had no trouble getting his attacks on *Common Sense* into the *Pennsylvania Packet.*[72] In a more theoretical vein, Robert Bell, the publisher of *Common Sense,* used an appendix to a now rare pamphlet to defend his printing of *Plain Truth* and other anti-independence pieces on the sole basis of the "AUTHORITY [OF] THE LIBERTY OF THE PRESS."[73] Adding "a few more words," Bell criticized those who argued for limiting the press "under the specious pretence of there being a necessity at some trying exigence for a temporary restriction of the FREEDOM OF THE PRESS" and argued that if "their foolish advice should at any one time be adopted, we may then bid final adieu to everything pertaining to Liberty." To substantiate his point, Bell reminded his readers of Parliament's switch, in 1716, from triennial to septennial parliaments on the dubious grounds that "there were too many Jacobites in the Nation." The point of the analogy was to demonstrate that, in times of crisis, seemingly temporary, repressive moves made ostensibly to protect general liberty can set tyrannical precedents.[74]

This history lesson notwithstanding, not everyone would conform with Bell's open press standard, especially when it came to heated, personal matters. The mercurial Thomas Paine threatened the Tory-leaning printer Benjamin Towne with a "halter" [i.e., noose] in order to get the name of an anonymous critic. When a mob went after Paine's antagonist, Whitehead Humphreys, it was Humphreys who got the better of the incident, "several gentlemen having explained the liberty of the press, and clearly demonstrated that it ought not to be restrained."[75] Even after the war was over and the Treaty of Paris signed, James Rivington's old enemy Isaac Sears raided the printer's shop as he had in 1775, this time ending Rivington's printing career forever.[76]

Two more notorious episodes provide a clearer window into understandings of freedom of political expression. William Goddard's active insistence on the liberty of his press occasioned two revealing clashes between an individual's open press and a community's free press. A satirical piece in Goddard's *Maryland Journal* praised some terms of peace allegedly offered by Britain; the same issue also carried a spirited caution against any terms offered by the corrupt British government. The satire, however, was lost on the zealous Whig Club of Baltimore, and the caveat was ignored. Taking the first piece to be genuinely dangerous, the Whig Club dragged Goddard before it and demanded the author's name. When Goddard refused, he was banished from Baltimore. The printer left, but only to appeal to the authorities in Annapolis. A committee of the Assembly found the Whig Club's proceedings in "manifest violation of the Constitution, [and] directly contrary to the Declaration of Rights."[77] The Maryland Declaration held simply "that the liberty of the press ought to be inviolably preserved."[78]

The Whig Club incident demonstrates that, at least in Maryland, press liberty was officially understood to permit expression of an individual's sentiments ostensibly in favor of submission to the enemy, even if those sentiments seemed to undermine the fight for public liberty. But, if Goddard "was thought severe, and . . . little friendly to the American Cause" for the views he published in 1777, we can be sure the "Queries" he published in 1779 made him extremely unpopular.[79] General Charles Lee had already published a lengthy response to his court-martial when he sought to publish "Some Queries, Political and Military." The "Queries" were as much an attack on General George Washington as they were a defense of Lee; Philadelphia printers wanted nothing to do with them, despite that city's factious and unrestrained press. Indeed, the exalted Washington was just about the only public figure safe from vilification in the Pennsylvania papers; the printers there feared the "Queries" would raise mobs.[80] As Goddard soon found out, these fears were well founded.

Again a mob came after Goddard, and this time they forced him to sign a statement in which he begged the people's pardon and made him promise to publish it in the *Journal*. Goddard did publish it, but he again went to Annapolis to plead his case.[81] The subsequent hearing has left no record, but Goddard was apparently satisfied, for in the next day's *Journal* he recanted his apology. A week later, he printed both a response to Lee's "Queries" and an anonymous letter insisting that no country is free where "restraints on the Press in any Cases, except Libels and Treason" are tolerated.[82] These episodes involving Goddard, the people of Baltimore, and the Maryland authorities demonstrate that open press notions were returning—in fits and starts—to patriot America. More important, they suggest that new, deeper understandings of the relationship between public liberty and individual liberty were emerging in the Revolutionary era.

A more sophisticated open press dominated the colonies. The Tories had no access to the press and increasingly few sympathizers, but within Whig circles all were allowed fair play. When the debate raged over independence, this toleration led not only to serious debate but to exaggeration, invective, and misrepresentation. Notably, reunionists used many old Tory arguments; yet they were allowed to take their case to the people, since, as Whigs, they all agreed that the current British rule was unjust, arbitrary, and deserving of opposition. Moreover, this toleration held, even though disunionists such as Samuel Adams took to calling the reunionists "disguised Tories."[83]

In 1775, the free press arguments of the Patriots, newly distinguished and developed, took their most extreme form, the "press of freedom." Still, "the great and honorable exception to this reign of intolerance" was the "free and open debate within the Whig party" over independence.[84] With the threat to the people's liberty predominantly external, the "press of freedom" began to give way to a renewed, yet better defined and better understood, open press.

4

The Making of the First
Amendment

The pre-Revolutionary crisis had broken down the free and open press tradition and exposed its contradictions. Patriots had taken free press doctrine to its extreme and then seen it become largely immaterial as the threat to the people's liberty was limited to the guns and pens of Tory-held towns. In the debates over independence, and later over how to conduct the war, fellow Whigs could be trusted to make their sentiments known through an open press. But it is one thing to practice, even justify an open press, quite another to institutionalize it. That, however, was only one of the challenges facing a war-torn America.

Revolutionary Shifts in American Society

Like so many of the revolutions that followed it, the American Revolution was not only a radical turning point but also an intentionally transformative event.[1] Yet, like all human action, the Revolution was also fraught with a number of unintentional consequences and many repercussions that were at best dimly perceived. For some of the most radical colonists, of course, the Revolutionary War was indeed a matter of fundamental political, economic, and social transformation. But, for the great mass of the people, even independence from Britain was not clearly a goal until the war was more than a year old. Nevertheless, the ramifications of the war were such that major forces of change were unleashed that would reverberate throughout colonial society.

The war, as we have seen, brought the marginalization, even persecution, of outright loyalists and suspected Tories. This was obvious and clearly perceived at the time. The implications of this reality, however, were less distinctly comprehended. The Tories had made up a large portion of the colonial elite, and even conservative Patriots were slow to take command of the remarkably fluid mid-1770s. The net result was a void at the top layer of the emerging Revolutionary society.

The political vacuum created by these changes was both exploited and exacerbated by the continuing development of revolutionary committees, conventions, and militias. From the early 1770s on, as Tories maintained a tight grip on the conventional reigns of power and other traditional colonial elites vacillated, political outsiders bypassed these authority structures to create their own. Once independence was declared and these new institutions were formally adopted, many more people, from a wider swath of American society, were involved in political power. And drawing more deeply into the well of Revolutionary America was only part of the political reformation. More important still was the nature of the authority these political parvenus held. The role of the middling and lower classes "out of doors"—in crowds, protests, and mobs—had long been a quasi-institutional aspect of British politics.[2] Yet "the difference was very real," as the historian Edward Countryman aptly observes: "a crowd could act, but a committee could set and execute a policy; a crowd would dissolve, but a committee could adjourn."[3]

No less significant for our understanding of American political thinking in the 1770s and 1780s is the economic void that was created by the marginalization of the conservative and moderate portions of the traditional elite. Add to that the war itself, which accelerated economic development in America, and the consequence, intentional or not, was a profound shift in the emerging nation's economy.[4] The rise of new merchants and consumers was certainly significant, since wealth had long been the most significant determinant of social status. The wartime stress on local manufactures was perhaps even more critical, since the resulting boon for the artisan class hastened the spread of nascent liberal ideas in the middle classes.

Another momentous transformation of colonial society expedited by the war was the development of distinct public and private spheres, which in turn led to a decoupling of individual status and public power. As we have seen, this evolution had been under way since early in the century, when the "sharp modern distinction between private and public was as yet scarcely visible."[5] The rise of republicanism during the century had entailed a population that could distinguish public good from private interest, even in weighing its own decisions.[6] Thus, whereas an individual's status and his public role traditionally had gone hand-in-hand, now public power was a separate entity granted provisionally by a less deferential people to the individual who proved he deserved it.[7] For example, in 1770s Virginia, a man's learned cosmopolitanism still defined him as a "gentleman," but it no longer ensured public power: "now emotional, popular rhetorical skills which could bond white people of all classes together—as exemplified by Patrick Henry—were more important."[8] This shift meant that, whereas prior to the War a person's station in life encompassed public and private attributes, in the 1770s and 1780s a person's office, not his status or reputation, was increasingly the source of his authority. While mid-century officials knew "that their ability to govern rested on their personal reputations," public men of the 1780s increasingly drew a distinction between their public characters and their private reputations.[9] To be sure, one's reputation was still sacred and to be defended at all costs, but it was now increasingly a separate, unofficial asset.

Finally, the watershed of the Revolution marks the establishment of a practical distinction between private, individual liberty and the communal, public liberty that had long been the focus of Whig political theory. The Tories had occasionally appealed to individual rights even in the early 1770s. They had little choice, since an appeal to public liberty would have been considered thoroughly unpersuasive by those who were convinced the Tories were part of the "ministerial design" to destroy American (public) liberty.

As we shall see more fully, with the arrival of the war, even Patriot America would see signs of the rise of notions of individual liberty. Merchants, for example, often claimed the right to withhold goods in order to reap higher profits when the commodities were scarce. These merchants, however, would often be reminded of the traditional dominance of communal priorities over individual liberty: Crowds—sometimes with committee orders—would raid a warehouse, leaving behind the "just" price. These conflicts between sections of "the people" were not easily explained by the radical Whig philosophy that dominated Patriot America. A "democratic despotism," John Adams insisted in 1776, "is a contradiction in terms."[10] Yet it was becoming less clear that public liberty would guarantee private liberty. Rather, as one prickly army colonel-turned-printer maintained as early as 1778, "he that will not contend for his own rights, as an Individual, will never defend the Rights of the Community."[11]

Press Liberty and the First American Constitutions

The various, interrelated, and momentous Revolutionary transformations in American political, economic, and social thought can perhaps be most readily appreciated in the early state constitutions and declarations of rights. More specifically, the press clauses provide a promising starting point for a conceptual history of press liberty in the decade and a half leading up to the First Amendment. The rhetoric of these passages clearly draws from the free and open press tradition. The first press clause written in Revolutionary America is found in George Mason's *Declaration of Rights* for Virginia (1776) and employs the traditional free press vernacular: "That the freedom of the Press is one of the greatest bulwarks of liberty, and can never by restrained but by despotick Governments."[12] Not only does this declaration exhibit the free press fear of despotic government, but it borrows Trenchard and Gordon's classic rhetoric of the "bulwark of liberty."

The language of open press doctrine is no less evident in the early constitutions. Vermont (1777) quoted almost verbatim from Pennsylvania's *Declaration* (1776) in proclaiming "that the people have a right to freedom of speech, and of writing and publishing their sentiments; therefore, the freedom of the press ought not be restrained."[13] Here one finds the conventional open press notion that people have a right to air sentiments, presumably on any side of an issue. But it is Pennsylvania's radical convention that best exemplifies the free and open press tradition of eighteenth-century America. In keeping with the ambivalent nature of that tradition, the Convention enacted the open press language borrowed by Vermont, while also incorporating unequivocal free press thinking in the accompanying *Plan or Frame of Government*: "The printing presses shall be free to every person who undertakes to examine the proceedings of the legislature, or any part of government."[14]

Several of America's first constitutions, then, employ the language of the free and open press tradition. Nevertheless, it remains to be seen just what they meant by these pronouncements. Could one speak one's mind with complete immunity? Scholars such as Leonard Levy have long maintained that eighteenth-century Americans followed William Blackstone in claiming that the "liberty of the press is indeed essential to the nature of a free state; but this consists in laying no *previous* restraint [such as licensing] upon publication, and not in freedom from censure for criminal matter [such as seditious libel] when published."[15]

As we have seen, Americans admired Blackstone's *Commentaries*. Yet its appeal lay in its comprehensive derivation of fundamental principles from the jumble of English common law, not in some flawless interpretation of specific laws.[16]

The later state constitutions demonstrate the colonists' willingness to revise Blackstone on particular issues. Thomas Jefferson, who would later dismiss the *Commentaries* as "honeyed Mansfieldism,"[17] made clear in his own drafts for a Virginia constitution (1776) that the only permissible subsequent punishment is for *private* defamation: "Printing presses shall be free, except so far as by commission of private injury cause may be given of private action."[18] The later constitutions of Massachusetts (1780) and New Hampshire (1783) are at once less explicit and more anti-Blackstonian. Both states' clauses began by virtually quoting Blackstone: "The liberty of the press is essential to the security of freedom in a state." But where the eminent jurist went on to allow subsequent punishment, these later American constitutions simply declared that press liberty "ought not be restrained" and "ought, therefore, to be inviolably preserved."[19] The French, to the contrary, in writing their *Declaration of the Rights of Man and Citizen* (1789), did not quote Blackstone, though they did explicitly include the Blackstonian notion of subsequent responsibility for "abuse" of press liberty.[20]

Though suggestive, this analysis of parallel texts can at best provide the foundation for speculation. What would help us draw accurate conclusions about these declarations is some record of discourse concerning the value, meaning, and limits of the "liberty of the press." In fact, such a record exists in the proceedings of the various town meetings called throughout Massachusetts to debate the proposed Constitution of 1780. Contra Levy, this evidence demonstrates that the townspeople across Massachusetts read the press clause to warrant no subsequent legal responsibility whatsoever. It was this understanding that led a number of towns to resolve that the clause should be explicitly amended to provide legal damages for defamation of private individuals.[21] The distinction found in these debates between private reputations and public characters, along with the occasional references to the people's right to comment regularly on public men and measures, suggests that there were more thoroughgoing changes afoot than merely the decreasing influence of Blackstonian notions. But even these animated debates over press liberty were bound, like most constitutional discussions, by the constraints of time and the burden of countless fundamental issues. By expanding our sights to include the vast newspaper, broadside, and pamphlet literature of the Revolutionary and Confederation periods, we can more fully analyze the metamorphosis of the free and open press tradition. In the wake of these changes, the concepts "free" and "open" lost their distinctive meanings and critical power; the terms came to be used much more interchangeably. More significant, both strains of argument were theoretically transformed.

A Sovereign People, a Sovereign Press

An extensive analysis of the press liberty discourse of the decade following independence reveals a comprehensive reworking of free press doctrine. This doctrine had been elucidated when the pre-Revolutionary crisis occasioned the bifurcation of the vague and ambivalent free and open press tradition. A free press was seen as an essential bulwark in the seemingly continual struggle between the people's liberty and ministerial power. Another key safeguard, as Whig theory had it, was Parliament. As we have seen, for Cato and for midcentury Americans, the legislature's rights were equivalent to the people's rights.[22] And, while there were some few hints of doubt about this equation prior to the 1760s, it was in large part because of Parliament's patent failure to defend the colonists' popular rights (at least as they saw them) that some Patriots were led to question the conventional wisdom.

Masters, Servants, and Legislative Tyranny

Perhaps the most significant democratic development of the Revolutionary era—more important even than the expansion of electoral offices or the widening of suffrage—was the devolution of the bulk of political power into the hands of popular legislatures.[23] But, given Parliament's recent behavior, several Patriots and their philosophical friends back in England reminded all who cared to listen about the threat of legislative betrayal. According to John Adams, James Burgh had "exhausted the subject" in his *Political Disquisitions* (1775).[24] Not all Americans would be so wary or critical, however, and as late as 1785 we find "Lucius" admonishing those who "think that nothing, that is done by our own legislature, the representatives of ourselves, can be wrong." "As freemen," Lucius continued, "let us...[not] pay so great a deference to our legislature, as to suppose, that they cannot err."[25] Others took a different tack by criticizing the notion that the legislature, not the people, was the supreme power; on this matter, as on others, Blackstone was simply wrong.[26] For "the only definition of a free government is, *security of person and property*; and when these essentials depend on the *will* of even a *republican legislature, it is absolute tyranny.*"[27]

The notion that "the people" were the ultimate source of political power and authority had roots in the English Civil War and was a staple of radical Whig theory. But this idea of popular sovereignty not only became more widespread in the Revolutionary era but also took on a new cast. Public officials were now "servants" and the people their "masters." More important, one begins to find suggestions of the manner of oversight implied by such a relationship. Virginia's *Declaration of Rights,* for example, proclaims in its second clause "that all power is vested in, and consequently derived from, the People; that magistrates are their trustees and servants, and at all times amenable [i.e., answerable] to them." Benjamin Church (writing as "Leonidas") certainly thought he had the right to supervise and guide the actions of the Continental Congress; his article severely criticizing Congress's monetary policy demonstrates this. More important, Church wrote that he would be overwhelmed with the thought of addressing Congress

> did I not consider myself at the same time as one of the people from whom you derive your authority. Let the subjects of monarchs tremble at the feet of their sovereigns . . . the citizens of America . . . invert the systems of government which are now established in Europe, and instead of addressing you as *masters*, I presume in the name of all the honest Whigs in America to address you as the SERVANTS of the public.

The Massachusetts Constitution (1780) declared simply that "all power residing originally in the people," all government officials "are their substitutes and agents, and are at all times accountable to them."[28]

Electoral accountability, at the very least, was stipulated by the constitutional rhetoric and newspaper discourse of the Revolutionary era. But this power, as Rousseau's famous observation would have it, left Englishmen slaves on every day save election day.[29] What further safeguards could be instituted against the threat of legislative tyranny? The representative assembly, John Adams explained in 1776, "should be in miniature an exact portrait of the people at large."[30] The movement to larger legislatures that characterizes America's first constitutions can thus be recognized as an attempt to draw from a broader public sphere and to cast a wider, more representative net.

Another effort to contain legislative power can be seen in the augmentation, both qualitative and quantitative, of the instructing power. The practice of instructing representatives was by no means new to Revolutionary America. Yet the more frequent use and application of instruction beyond parochial issues to more general concerns signals a greater effort to check the popular assemblies. Indeed, instructions were not at all controversial in the late 1770s.[31] The declarations of rights for Pennsylvania, North Carolina, and Massachusetts all expressly protect the people's right to instruct.[32] With the emergence of the later constitutions of Massachusetts (1780) and New Hampshire (1783), one detects a sharpened distrust of representative legislatures. "There is scarcely a newspaper, pamphlet, or sermon of the 1780s that does not dwell on this breakdown of confidence between the people-at-large and their representative governments."[33]

The Press of Sovereignty

The threat of legislative tyranny and the attendant need to check even the most representative government is but one part, the negative part, of the Revolutionary change that affected the press. Conventional Whig thought considered the press, like the popular assembly, primarily a bulwark against ministerial or royal tyranny. Or, more precisely, the press was seen as a last resort should the more moderate, more continuous safeguard provided by the representative legislature fail. Pamphlets, broadsides, and, especially, newspapers were the place for dire warnings rallying the troops against an imminent assault on the people's liberties. This role for the press would certainly continue, but with the advent of broad-based, annual elections for larger, more representative, and more powerful legislatures, the people's duty and the press's role now centered on *maintaining*, rather than simply *defending*, the republics they had established. This transformation of the press and the public sphere had roots in the more radical strains of Whig theory, but its realization required the practical experience of committee rule and the complete saturation of society with the public concerns of the war.

These forces were perhaps most pressing in Pennsylvania, and so it is no surprise that the Pennsylvania Constitution of 1776 is both the most radical state constitution and the one most clearly demonstrative of these new understandings. In this constitution, for example, we find frequent elections and rotation in office established not only as precautions but because "by this mode . . . more men will be trained to public office." And it is this very "frame of government" that most clearly stipulated the incipient role of the press. As we have seen, in addition to declaring that "the people have a right to freedom of speech, and of writing, and publishing their sentiments," the Pennsylvania Convention further established that "the printing presses shall be free to every person who undertakes to examine the proceedings of the legislature, or any part of government."[34] What we might call the "press of sovereignty," the press of a sovereign people, must foster the continuous examination of every aspect and branch of government.

As is frequently the case with constitutional pronouncements, one is left wondering what exactly they meant, or were taken to mean. The printer allied with Pennsylvania's conservative "Republican" faction—those who opposed the radical 1776 Constitution—maintained "that the public, whose right it is, may know every thing for and against their servants." Indeed, Francis Bailey went further, maintaining that a printer had a public duty to print everything that was sent to him, excepting only private libel.[35]

Further hints that the people were taking on a more active role in politics and in the press can be seen in the conservative responses. Some conservatives began to view the prospect of instructions, constant oversight, and the "master-servant" relationship as subversive. It was in radical Pennsylvania that this reaction first appeared. "It has been said often . . . that 'all power is *derived* from the people,' but it has never yet been said, that all power is *seated* in the people. Government supposes and requires a delegation of power."[36] And this view was by no means restricted to Pennsylvania. Judge Alexander Contee Hanson, of Maryland, writing as "Aristides," allowed that "all power indeed flows from the people, but the doctrine that the power, actually, at all times, resides in the people, is subversive of all government and law."[37]

Perhaps the best way to appreciate the new understanding of the role of a sovereign people and their relationship with the press is to examine the little-known debates over the Massachusetts stamp act (1785) and its replacement, the advertisement tax.[38] Admittedly, printers had a stake in both of these taxes, but we are less concerned with the purity of their motives than with the nature of their arguments. And the arguments surrounding this issue are particularly revealing for the "press of sovereignty" because the taxes were a *modest* restriction on the press. To be sure, many—and printers especially—cast the situation in the most dire terms, predicting (wrongly) that numerous newspapers would fold. But the resulting price increases did not undermine the traditional role of the press, for elites could still afford the papers and the press would remain sufficiently free to raise the alarm in a crisis; rather, it was the press of sovereignty that was at stake, for the common people would be less able to purchase "those necessary vehicles of public Information" and discourse. If "it is the right and duty of every sober, considerate citizen, to speak his mind, and to communicate what has but a probability of being serviceable," then newspaper taxes of any sort were likely to come between the common people and their duties as political masters.[39]

One of the printers' most common refrains was that the taxes would make it more difficult for their papers to circulate "among all ranks of the people, even among those of the lowest fortune," and would "prevent the circulation of that political Intelligence, which is manifestly necessary to the virtue, freedom and happiness of the people."[40] It was not only printers who feared that the duties would undermine the sovereignty of the common people, however. Recognizing that the tax would "fall on the midling and poorer classes" most heavily, one correspondent maintained that "the consequences that will ensue from clogging this channel of information, must be obvious to every person of common sense, and painful for every lover of his country to reflect on."[41] Indeed, some would even blame Shays's Rebellion on the lack of political information resulting from the taxes.[42]

This oft-ignored discourse concerning a modest stamp tax proposal, then, reveals a conception of the public sphere as at least in principle, and increasingly in practice, open to all white men, regardless of rank. Further, a new norm of "supervision" was instituted here in which the term "public servant" took on a new literalness, entailing continual oversight by—and accountability to—the people. But if the press of sovereignty required a significantly more active, informed, and broad-based citizenry than ever before, it remains to be seen just how far the common people could—or should—go in reviewing and criticizing the characters and policies of their public officers. The seditious libel charge brought against the Philadelphia printer Eleazor Oswald by Pennsylvania's Chief Justice, Thomas McKean, presents perhaps the most unadulterated dispute over the limits of a sovereign people's press. There were other episodes, of course. The seditious libel charges stemming from Shays's Rebellion seem promising, but only one case ever made it to trial. Moreover, the breach-of-peace aspect—understandably a significant aspect—obfuscates the episode for our analysis of free political expression insofar as the case focused on direct and effective incitement to violence. In another legal action, Chief Justice McKean won a libel ruling against General Charles Thompson, but it was private matter. The only public angle was Thompson's memorial to Congress in which he criticized the Chief Justice (also a congressman for Delaware); Congress found him in breach of privilege but did nothing more. By 1784, even the threat of reprimanding someone for insulting a representative would be renounced as an abuse of legislative privilege.[43]

In comparison to these episodes, the Oswald/McKean controversy of 1782–83 presents a rich and unambiguous case.[44] Oswald's *Independent Gazetteer* carried two denunciations of two separate fines handed down by a court over which McKean presided. McKean arranged to have charges of seditious libel presented to the next grand jury. The grand jury, which considered itself a "bulwark of our civil liberties" and which others considered "a kind of representation of the people at large," examined a number of witnesses, both for and against; it returned the first bill of indictment *ignoramus,* by a vote of sixteen to three.[45] Then McKean, who was still presiding over the court, told the jurymen to reconsider and sent a second bill (for the second article). This time the jurors voted seventeen to two against indicting and returned both bills.

The jurymen, in the memorial they published to complain of McKean's handling of the case, maintained their abhorrence of wanton defamations, public or private.[46] "Adrian" (George Bryan, one of the presiding judges), in turn, criticized them for examining extra witnesses and suggested that they had refused to indict Oswald on the presumption that he was merely misinformed about the facts of the two cases criticized in the original articles.[47] "Aristides" defended the jurors and asked Adrian, "cannot you suppose, that some amongst them may have been averse to the introduction of that accursed engine of tyranny, the doctrine of criminal libels to our courts, where it has been hitherto unknown?"[48] What was beyond question was that one grand jury in the early 1780s, despite its "abhorrence of defamatory publications," refused to indict a printer for pointed criticism of public men and measures. Though the jury's memorial concentrates on the role of juries, rather than on press liberty, the broader debate occasioned by the controversy provides us with a uniquely rich and extensive discourse on press freedom—and evidence of an emerging conceptual refinement.

The Public/Private Distinction

As we had an opportunity to observe earlier, the Revolutionary and Confederation periods were significant eras for the developing bifurcation of the public and private spheres. The republican principles that colonists had long mouthed and now increasingly lived encouraged and required the ability to differentiate "disinterested" public good and private interests, thus enabling a distinction between one's public office and one's private identity.[49] But if personal reputation lost much of its import as a source for political authority, it retained its sacred value for the private individual. One result of these contending social forces was to place the nascent press of sovereignty in a precarious situation. It soon became clear that if the people are to use the press not merely as a bulwark against tyrannical government but also as a medium for active, continual, and spirited contribution to the public sphere, then some acceptable and relatively distinct dividing line must be fashioned between a people that exercises its sovereignty and an individual who scandalizes his enemies.

Thomas Jefferson, as we noted earlier, made it clear as early as 1776 that he understood press liberty to permit only private actions for private injuries; but it was not only visionary thinkers who expressed this distinction. In 1778, the printers of the *Independent Chronicle* apologized for unintentionally defaming someone in their press: "And we beg leave to assure the Public, that while we shall preserve our Press free for Animadversions on public Characters, we shall, in future, guard against Attacks on private Reputations."[50] By the time the towns of Massachusetts met to debate the proposed Constitution of 1780, their primary concern regarding the press clause was that the immunity to censure public men and measures not be construed as an opportunity for private defamation.[51] This public/private distinction would appear again and again during the Confederation period.[52]

The public/private distinction provided some means of allowing criticism of public men and measures while protecting solely private reputations, but it begged the question of what was permissible discussion of public men's private characters. Some insisted that attacks on the private affairs of public officials went beyond the constitutional provisions of Massachusetts, while others went so far as to maintain that even purely private characters were assailable insofar as they had a tendency to injure the community.[53] But it was in Philadelphia, in the midst of the Oswald trial, that the outer limits of a sovereign people's press liberty were most thoroughly debated.

"Junius Wilkes," writing in defense of Oswald and combining the names of England's two most notorious public critics, maintained a distinction between "circumstances . . . entirely of a *private* and malicious dye, with which the *public* have no business, *quasi* public," and public affairs. Comments regarding "public servants . . . when they even appear false and groundless, [are] rather an inconvenience upon the occasion, a kind of *damnum absque injuria* [a harm without legal injury]." Government officers understood that the public might "stain a fair character."[54] Others went further, insisting that the "private vices of our governors" or even candidates for office were to be scrutinized. One final correspondent in the Oswald controversy admitted private attacks on all who were merely eligible for public office, though he, like many others, left false and malicious attacks to the jury in civil suits for private defamation.[55] Perhaps in response to discussions such as these, by 1786 Thomas Jefferson contended that personal attacks of public men are "an evil for which there is no remedy." A public servant simply had to prepare to sacrifice, among other valuable things, his reputation.[56] And this from a man who thought slander "worse than assassination, theft, suicide or robbery."[57]

Despite all this, some conservatives held fast to Blackstone's contention that press liberty meant no more that a freedom from prior restraint. Once one published, one was criminally liable. In the Confederation period, however, even conservatives ignored Blackstone's claim that truth merely exacerbated seditious libel; true discussions of public men and measures were deemed permissible. By early 1791, both sides of a private libel case brought by a Massachusetts representative conceded that the public characters and measures of public figures were, in the words of the maligned legislator, "proper subjects of discussion for a free press."[58] If the people were to be sovereign masters of their public servants, they required a more active, positive, and continuously scrutinizing press liberty: a press of sovereignty.

The Advantage of an Open Press

The free press doctrine that had made up half of the free and open press tradition of midcentury America was not the only part of that tradition to undergo major conceptual and theoretical change in the run-up to the First Amendment. The primary claim of open press doctrine had always been that the truth would prevail over falsehood in an open encounter. Yet the related, fail-safe argument was never far behind: Even if the press permitted some objectionable or even untrue things to be printed, the benefits of an open press far outweighed the costs. This auxiliary postulate, however, became a much more prominent fixture of press liberty discourse in the decade preceding the debates over the federal constitution. We find, in fact, a more sophisticated version of the open press argument. The implication was largely the same—let individuals print what they please—but the shift in argument to a more pessimistic and provisional view of the open press was at once subtle and portentous.

From our retrospective position, what is perhaps most remarkable about the Confederation period is that continuing open press notions did not give way to a system of avowedly partisan presses, each representing a particular faction, providing truth through confrontation. There were some signs of partisan presses, especially in Pennsylvania, where the competing political factions were most thoroughly established. The demographic and economic contexts were conducive to such a development, since by 1784 there were two or more papers in each of the ten major cities.[59] Nevertheless, factionalism was still seen as a threat to republican government, and press norms continued to require that each printing press remain open to sentiments on every side of an issue.

What we do find emerging even in the Revolutionary period is a new skepticism regarding the positive potential of an open press. This increased skepticism combined with the developing reality of noncommunal, interest-based politics. The result, at its most extreme, was the first signs that the identity of authors should be made known, not necessarily to punish them but, rather, to provide the single best way to overthrow their ideas: not a truer, more compelling argument, but the public knowledge of their character and interests. "Many good people have been lately mislead," the Albemarle Instructions (1776) noted. "Had [the authors'] names been published, their Characters would have been the antidote to their own poison."[60]

The more general diffusion of this individualized, interest-based logic lay a few years in the future; the skepticism on which it was founded, however, was already broadly dispersed. There was, in fact, good reason to be dubious about the notion that truth would best false-hood, given the functioning of the newspaper exchange system of the 1780s. As newspapers were widely exchanged, free of charge, between printers, so, too, were errors, half-truths, and misprints; these inaccuracies were often further distorted in the transmission. In part this resulted from the expansion of the public sphere: more universal access to (mis)information and the end of the elite filtering that had taken place frequently during the previous century.[61] Now, as many in the new nation observed, nothing—certainly not retractions—traveled faster than erroneous rumors.[62]

As the war wound down, faith that the truth would prevail was waning. Many, to be sure, still praised a press open to all sides, despite the occasional abuses. "Where," they asked, "is that blessing of life that may not be abused!"[63] Those abuses, went the familiar phrase, were only a "partial evil for universal good." The ambivalence over the power of truth to prevail is most clearly evident in the statement on press liberty that introduces the premier issue of Eleazer Oswald's *Independent Gazetteer*. Against those who maintained that an open press would allow truth and justice to prevail, Oswald replied:

> Tho' this should be true, on a full Discussion, yet so much might be said to misrepresent and disguise the Truth; and such a long Train of Argumentation be necessary to make it apparent, that few People would have Leisure or Opportunity, Inclination or Ability, to go thro it, and form a right Judgement of its Merits. And thus the Liberty of the Press might be controverted to the worst Purposes, and occasion much more Evil than Good.

But, in concluding the same article, Oswald's vacillation is apparent.

> Let the Press be but free, and that Freedom will sufficiently check its Extravagacies—He that has Truth, Reason and Justice on his Side, will always be an Overmatch for his Adversaries of equal Abilities, and it will be in the power of one sensible Man, armed with those divine Weapons, to put a thousand of his most formidable Adversaries to right.[64]

As the 1780s progressed, many would be less and less ambiguous about the dangers of abused press liberty. That is not to say that there was a movement to restrict the press; quite the opposite, as we have seen. But citizens of the new states had a heightened appreciation of the disadvantages, as well as the advantages, of press liberty. "Honestus" was hyperbolic, but at least he was succinct: "Popular licentiousness will ever destroy the efforts of the most wise Governours."[65]

A contributor to the *Massachusetts Centinel* echoed Honestus's view but posited the advantage of press liberty.

> It must be owned that the *press* is sometimes applied to an ill use, and is made the channel through which falsehoods and scurilities flow in too violent a torrent; yet, however injurious the unlimited licence of printing may prove to particular persons, the liberty itself is of too great a benefit to the publick in general, to be abolished, or restrained.[66]

These "private inconveniences" were the "disadvantages" of public office.[67] The *Independent Chronicle* reprinted a statement by the Englishman Richard Price, in which he argued that more mischief came from restraint of the press, even when its freedom led to violence; thus, only the overt acts ought to be punished.[68]

Nor was it only anonymous newspaper correspondents and distant English philosophers that held these views. John Jay, reflecting on some newspaper defamations against his own private character, agreed with Jefferson that there was no remedy. "The Liberty of the Press," Jay explained,

> is certainly too important to the public, to be restrained for the sake of personal Considerations; especially as it is in every man's power to frustrate Calumny, by not deserving censure; for altho Slander may prevail for a while, yet Truth and consistent Rectitude will ultimately enjoy their rights.[69]

Jay and Jefferson, like other men of the Confederation period, were much less sanguine about the power of truth than their predecessors had been only two decades before. Press liberty could impose a heavy price on certain individuals. Yet, with a bloody war for liberty behind them, they were not likely to dicker about the cost. Later, others would see things differently.

Anti-Federalists and Federalists

The debate between proponents of the new federal Constitution and their adversaries provides an opportunity to deepen our analysis of press liberty. It has the preponderance of abstract rhetoric typical of constitutional debates, but there is considerable relevant discourse, I have found, when one sifts through the mountain of primary literature. The secondary literature, however, has only recently become helpful. Although there is plenty written about the victors, the Federalists themselves had every political incentive to ignore the issue of press liberty as much as possible, and the secondary works have tended to reflect this paucity of discussion. Concerning the Anti-Federalists, who discussed press liberty frequently if not exhaustively, most of what has been written is dismissive or distorted. Long before Cecilia Kenyon labeled them "men of little faith," the Anti-Federalists were being belittled from a perspective sympathetic to the Federalists.[70]

Fortunately, the Anti-Federalists have enjoyed a resurgence recently. Herbert Storing's *What the Antifederalists Were For* takes the Anti-Federalists seriously, examining and explaining their views sympathetically. Michael Lienesch's "In Defense of the Antifederalists" makes sense of Anti-Federalist views by placing those views within the conventional wisdom of the 1780s. And Christopher M. Duncan has placed the Anti-Federalists within a "communitarian" tradition dating back to the Puritans.[71] Most recently—and most significantly—Saul Cornell has provided an exhaustive study of the "Other Founders." Cornell has revealed and investigated different varieties of Anti-Federalism, including elite, middling, and radical strains.[72] Our analysis stresses the thought of the radicals, as they happened to make most of the novel contributions to the evolution of the concept of press liberty. And this may well be a more accurate picture of the Anti-Federalist landscape than previous scholarship has provided, since, as Cornell points out, "plebeian ideas were generally underrepresented in print," and radical authors like Centinel were among the most influential and widely reprinted authors.[73] All in all, Cornell's outstanding book affords us a richer picture of the dissenting tradition and provides an excellent platform for recovering an Anti-Federalist view of liberty of the press.

The literature concerning the history of press liberty has been less kind to the Anti-Federalists. Leonard Levy minimizes their arguments as mere political manipulation in his most recent book on the subject; his recently reissued collection of primary sources on press liberty all but ignores the Anti-Federalists.[74] David Rabban, in a much-needed rejoinder to Levy, marginalizes the Anti-Federalists in favor of their ideological descendants, the Democratic-Republicans of the 1790s.[75] The resurgence of Anti-Federalist studies has only begun to bridge this lacuna in the literature. Focusing on broader issues, Lienesch and Duncan understandably do not descend to the necessary level of specificity,[76] and Storing simply presumes that the "general view" was the Blackstonian belief "that freedom of the press meant a prohibition against prior restraint."[77] Here, again, Cornell's work furnishes an important corrective.

The People and a Declaration of Rights

Levy dismisses much of the Anti-Federalist discourse as originating in "ulterior party purposes." The lack of a bill of rights became a "mace with which to smash the Constitution." Ultimately, he concludes, the Anti-Federalists' "prime loyalty belonged to states' rights, not civil rights."[78] But this sort of distinction owes more to the twentieth century—or the nineteenth—than the eighteenth. "While many Anti-Federalists . . . wanted to guard the rights of states," Saul Cornell explains, "[they] were equally committed to the idea of limited government and natural rights." Indeed, this localist, states' rights view "was closely tied to their own egalitarian defense of the 'republic of letters.'"[79]

Levy is on more solid ground in observing that the lack of a declaration of rights in the proposed federal constitution was a powerful political argument for the Anti-Federalists. This, however, is no reason to dismiss their arguments. Rather, the magnitude of the issue demonstrates a deep and widespread concern for declaring and defending certain rights, press liberty chief among them. The difference between Anti-Federalists and Federalists can be most readily seen in the Anti-Federalist suspicion of the Federalists' novel claim that the new national government would only have those powers expressly given to it; all other powers and rights would implicitly be reserved to the people and the states.[80] Press liberty, Federalists repeatedly insisted, was thus beyond federal authority.[81] Many Anti-Federalists—especially elite figures and plebeian radicals—maintained the conventional Whig view that governmental power continuously and inexorably struggles to expand. This logic led them to see potential threats to press liberty in several clauses of the Constitution, even in the federal government's role in observing the law of nations.[82] But, beyond their differences over the Constitution and the lack of a declaration of rights, Federalists and Anti-Federalists generally had profoundly contrasting views of the role of the people.

"The quarrel," the historian Gordon Wood rightly concludes, "was fundamentally one between aristocracy and democracy."[83] Disdainful of those they saw as inferiors, Federalists sought to systematize or institutionalize virtue, believing that their Constitution "put to an end the need for [civic] activism."[84] The neutralized factions of Madison's tenth *Federalist* would allow public-spirited gentlemen to prevail.[85] At the risk of oversimplifying, we can say that what the Federalists wanted were voters. Indeed, some Federalists were apprehensive of opening that role to the common people. Roger Sherman, in opposing the direct election of the lower house by the people, maintained that "the people should have as little to do as may be about the government. They want [i.e., lack] information and are constantly liable to be deceived." For Thomas Jefferson and most Anti-Federalists, this was reason to see that the people were better informed.[86] To nearly all Federalists, the virtue of these voters would be embodied not in traditional republican vigilance but rather in a traditional respect for their public officers once chosen.

The Federalists, and the Pennsylvania lawyer James Wilson especially, had first and most doggedly argued that the people, and not the states, were the ultimate sovereigns in America. As nationalists, they were concerned with combatting the localist claims of the Anti-Federalists. And, though there is something "decidedly disingenuous" in the Federalists' appeal to the people,[87] we should once again be careful to look beyond the political motives to assess the theoretical significance of this conceptual shift. Wilson provides an important and interesting case in point: important, because he was among the most influential Federalist statesmen, and interesting, because he was the one who spoke most fervently of popular sovereignty. In fact, Wilson did see the people as the *ultimate* sovereigns, but, in his view, they are sovereign only at that extreme. His Blackstonian view of the press, with its support of punishment for printed criticism of public men and measures, suggests as much.[88] Anti-Federalists, as we will soon observe, generally saw public officials as servants who could be directly controlled by their masters, the people. Wilson, to the contrary, saw political participation as chiefly symbolic and employed a "pyramid" metaphor, leaving the people at the base and exalting the likes of Wilson.[89] And, as Edmund Morgan shrewdly reminds us, "popular sovereignty" is always in part a fiction; it is the distance between fact and fiction that matters.[90] Nevertheless, the increasing power and stature of the language of the people's sovereignty is evident in the fact that it is this language that ardent Federalists were bound to incorporate.

Though they had little faith in the Federalists' national representative government, the Anti-Federalists saw the need for a citizenry that was not only ultimately sovereign but also actively involved, informed, and vigilant. "To many Anti-Federalists . . . genuine democracy was more than just a matter of popular elections."[91] Virginia Anti-Federalists, for example, included in a list of proposed amendments a clause that would protect the people's right to instruct their representatives.[92] When a similar amendment was proposed in the First Congress, many Federalists feared that legislators would be bound by such instructions.[93] Most Anti-Federalists, on the contrary, were fearful of the end of meaningful political citizenship, especially for members of the "middling" orders such as themselves. Rejecting "the deferential political message implicit in Federalist ideology," the vast majority of Anti-Federalists defended an ideal "in which republican liberty and popular participation were the defining characteristics of political life."[94]

These contrasting views of the people's proper role in the new republic led, in turn, to differing views of a declaration of rights. Federalists wanted to avoid the issue altogether, viewing it as mere obstructionism, and they frequently—and sincerely—dismissed such "parchment barriers" as useless.[95] Yet, in those rare moments when one of them discussed what impediments there were, the reasoning is revealing. "The only barrier against tyranny, that is necessary in any State," Noah Webster explained, "is *the election of Legislators* by the yeomanry of that State. Preserve *that*, and every privilege is safe."[96]

For the Anti-Federalists, a charter of rights was not useless, for it would serve both a practical, legal function and a symbolic, educational function. It would at once be a "test" of all national laws and a "plain, and pithy" reminder of the country's fundamental principles.[97] It was the "legal check" on majority tyranny that Thomas Jefferson had advocated to James Madison in March 1789; by June, Madison would be lecturing the House on it.[98] The widely reprinted *Address* of the minority of the Maryland Convention explained this use of a press clause: "In prosecutions in the federal courts for libels, the constitutional preservation of this great and fundamental right, may prove invaluable."[99]

In its symbolic and educative role, a declaration of rights could sanctify and confirm pre-existing natural rights. "We do not by declarations change the nature of things, or create new truths, but we do give existence, or at least establish in the minds of people truths and principles which they might never otherwise have thought of, or soon forgot."[100] With the Constitution ratified, even Madison had begun to see things differently. More than merely reminding the people, he argued, "the political truths declared in that solemn manner acquire by degrees the character of fundamental maxims of free Government, and as they become incorporated with the national sentiment, counteract the impulses of interest and passion."[101] While most Federalists were concerned with giving and reserving powers, the Anti-Federalists were keen to protect and substantiate pre-existing rights.

The Role of the Press

Chief among the fundamental rights the Anti-Federalists wanted to safeguard and confirm was press liberty. Indeed, because they "championed an expanded sphere of public discourse," "no form of liberty was more important" to influential Anti-Federalists like Centinel "than freedom of the press."[102] And, though it is largely true that "so far as we can tell, Congress never debated the merits or meaning of freedom of the press," we do have some evidence of a conservative reaction to Anti-Federalist views of the press.[103] The Senate, meeting behind closed doors, saw the introduction of a motion to amend the press clause to protect press liberty "in as ample a manner as hath at any time been secured by the common law." As the common law originated in England, this language would have invited restrictive, Blackstonian interpretations. The Senate rejected this motion the same day it accepted one to include common law rules in the Seventh Amendment.[104] Still, some clearly wanted to narrow the definition of press liberty. James Wilson, for one, maintained that "what is meant by the liberty of the press is, that there should be no antecedent restraint upon it." Others clearly held similar views.[105] Finally, the conservative Pennsylvania Constitution of 1790 allowed for subsequent punishment of public libel, though it—in Zengerian fashion—made truth a defense and established the jury as the finders of law, as well as of fact. John Adams interpreted the Massachusetts Constitution to warrant similar provisions.[106]

The resurgence, or at least the resurfacing, of qualified Blackstonian views of press liberty corroborated escalating Anti-Federalist fears of a

Federalist attack on the press. That freedom of the press was a central concern for the opponents of the constitution is clear from one sarcastic Federalist's "Receipt [i.e., recipe]" for an Anti-Federalist essay, which included, among other ingredients, "WELL-BORN, nine times—*Aristocracy*, eighteen times—*Liberty of the Press*, thirteen times repeated."[107] It is no less clear that Anti-Federalists had reason to be concerned. In addition to the fact that Federalists dominated most of the presses and were pressuring printers to require pseudonymous Anti-Federalists to surrender their names, the new Postmaster General effectively cut off newspaper circulation between the North and the South of the Confederation.[108] "Although modern accounts have tended to dismiss Anti-Federalist complaints as paranoia or propaganda," Saul Cornell concludes that "the surviving evidence about publication tends to support the indictment. Anti-Federalists did have trouble getting their message into print."[109] Against this background, it is perhaps not surprising that the Anti-Federalists took to enlarging upon the advantages of a sovereign press.

The Anti-Federalist Press of Sovereignty

The framing of a new government is the most important step a sovereign people can take; thus, it was only natural for those critical of the Constitution to stress the role of the press as a critical medium for public discourse. In explaining his editorial policy, Matthias Bartgis, of the *Virginia Gazette and Winchester Advertiser,* observed "that it must be evident to the least thoughtful, that the *body of the people* should be well-informed of the nature of any [proposed] Government." Adhering to the public/private distinction, Bartgis assured his readers that "*private characters* shall be secure from the poisoned shafts of envy and malice, cast through the medium of his Press."[110] Jefferson, an advocate of the Constitution provided it contained a declaration of rights, would have altered Madison's proposed federal press clause to protect against "false facts affecting injuriously the life, liberty, property, or reputation of others."[111]

Anti-Federalist voices took to emphasizing and extending the conception of press liberty that I have been calling the "press of sovereignty." One of the most often reprinted Anti-Federalist documents—one now generally ignored—began by declaring that governmental personnel were "Servants of the Public, and as such accountable for their conduct." Accordingly, the ubiquitous piece went on to propose an amendment stating "that the Freedom of the Press ought not to be restrained, and the Printing Presses ought to be free to examine the Proceedings of Government, and the Conduct of its Officers."[112] Some of the more radical Anti-Federalists explained the common people's role as masters in even more explicit terms. Quoting his own state constitution to make his point, one anonymous newspaper correspondent wrote, "the magistrates can, & must be *accountable to the people*— they are our '*substitutes and agents,*' that is, *acting under & for us. . . .* We chose them to deliberate for us, not that they were wiser or knew more than we; but because we cannot spare time."[113] Others defended Anti-Federalist newspaper correspondents from often offensive and threatening responses by stressing the duty of citizens to contribute to the public discourse. "For my part," wrote "A Citizen of Georgia," "I always thought it not only the indubitable right, but the bounden duty, of every citizen freely to declare his sentiments when anything of consequence to this country was in agitation."[114]

The Anti-Federalists also wanted to establish that the press was not solely a medium for the elite. "[The press in a free state] gives all the people an opportunity to learn and be wise, to choose or refuse, in all important matters." The channel of the press, another Anti-Federalist asserted, enabled "fellow-citizens . . . to inform the minds and enlarge the understandings of the bulk of the people, as to those leading and essential points which contain every thing dear to them as men and members of society."[115] Finally, Thomas Jefferson maintained—even before the Constitutional Convention—that "the people are the only censors of their governors." To keep the people from even momentary errors, though, it was critical to "give them full information of their affairs thro' the channel of the public papers, and to contrive that those papers should penetrate the whole mass of the people."[116] Ultimately, Saul Cornell concludes, "the egalitarian vision of the 'republic of letters' that Anti-Federalists like [the Pennsylvania radical William] Petrikin rallied around encouraged an active role for common folk who would exercise their own capacity for civic virtue by reading popular political literature, writing for the popular press, and even seeking public office."[117]

In addition to placing increased emphasis on certain aspects of a press of sovereignty, the Anti-Federalists expanded the argument by explaining the heightened significance of a vigorous press in an extensive territory such as the United States. "By means of [a free press]," the "Federal Farmer" insisted, "the people in large countries ascertain each others sentiments; are enabled to unite, and become formidable to those rulers who adopt improper measures." Liberty of the press was, for "Philadelphiensis," the "great aorta, the prime artery" that conveyed freedom, America's lifeblood "to the remotest parts of the extremities." "Centinel," one of the most widely reprinted Anti-Federalists, concurred. "In a confederated government of such extent as the United States, the freest communication of sentiment and information should be maintained, as the liberties, happiness, and welfare of the union depend upon a concert of counsels."[118] Ultimately, "the public sphere solved the central problem of Anti-Federalist political thought: how to ensure the survival of federalism without creating a powerful central government."[119] Commending the newly ratified Bill of Rights, James Madison concluded in a similar vein: "whatever facilitates a general intercourse of sentiments, as . . . a free press, and particularly a *circulation of newspapers through the entire body of the people* . . . is equivalent to a contraction of territorial limits, and is favorable to liberty, where these may be too extensive."[120]

Most Federalists were loath to give more ink to the issue of press liberty, one of their opponents' most popular issues. What hints we do have suggest that they had little faith in the common people's ability to be anything more that obedient voters. Conservatives had in fact long been skeptical about having nonelites take part in political activity. The conservative *Essex Result* (1778) posited that "the bulk of the people . . . are so situated in life . . . that they cannot have time for, nor the means of furnishing themselves with proper information, but must be indebted to some of their fellow subjects for the communication," with the result that they were prey to the "artful demagogue."[121] Noah Webster, the reader will recall, thought the election of their legislators a sufficient role for the people. Chief Justice McKean argued, at Pennsylvania's ratifying convention, that the dissent of a majority need not be included in the published proceedings of a legislature, since "the members . . . are from time to time responsible to their constituents."[122] "Cæsar," however, was the most explicit, belittling the doctrine that

> *all power is seated in the People.* For my part, I am not much attached to the *Majesty of the multitude.* . . . I consider them in general as very ill qualified to *judge* for themselves what government will best suit their pe-

culiar situations. . . . [Anti-Federalists] will admit, I presume, that men of good education and deep reflection, only, are judges of the *form* of a Government.

The people would do best to maintain "a tractable and docile disposition."[123] The Federalists, then, saw little need for conceiving of press liberty as a vigorous medium for a sovereign people.

The Anti-Federalists and the Advantages of the Press

Critics of the Constitution were more likely than its supporters to stress the advantages of an active press. Thomas Jefferson, both an advocate of the Constitution and a critic of its lack of a bill of rights, wrote to James Madison championing amendments that would secure, among other things, freedom of the press. "The few cases wherein these things may do evil, cannot be weighed against the multitude wherein the want of them will do evil."[124] More important, the Anti-Federalists, were not merely being naïve about the benefits of an unrestricted press. "Newspapers may sometimes be the vehicles of abuse, and of many things not true," the "Federal Farmer" conceded, "but these are but small inconveniences, in my mind, among many advantages."[125]

For Anti-Federalists, the disadvantages of an unlimited political press simply had to be borne, since they were interwoven with the advantages: "Restrain the *licentiousness,* and you in effect demolish the *liberty* of the press." The burden could be weighty. "A Friend to Harmony" was perhaps the most forthright about the failings of an open press, acknowledging that a vindication rarely travels as quickly or as far (or with as much entertainment value) as calumny. To make matters worse, many readers merely "conform to the publick opinion" without sufficient reflection. But, rather than deriding the people and doubting the value of the press, "A Friend" recommended an open press and exhorted the public to be more skeptical.[126]

Nor was it merely elite Anti-Federalists, mindful of their prized reputations, who bore the burdens of an open but imperfect press. Plebeian Anti-Federalists in Carlisle, Pennsylvania, took to the streets to oppose incendiary Federalist celebrations of their state's ratification of the Constitution, but they never sought to put an end to the local newspaper. "Although they resented the pro-Federalist bias of the *Carlisle Gazette,* they did not seek to silence it," the historian Saul Cornell notes. "Federalist crowds in New York did not exercise a similar restraint when they ransacked the printing shop of Thomas Greenleaf, publisher of the Anti-Federalist *New-York Journal*."[127]

Federalists were more likely than their critics to stress the disadvantages of an unrestricted press. Indicted for a libel of a private person, Eleazor Oswald published a defense of himself and press liberty, thus arguably attempting to sway potential jurors. Chief Justice McKean seized the opportunity to both lecture Oswald on press liberty and jail him for contempt of court (without grand or petit jury), thus concocting "the first successful legal assault on a partisan press since the Revolution."[128] In and out of court, McKean and Oswald merely rehearsed their divergent views of press liberty from the 1782 trial; the controversy's focus was on the "procedural irregularities."[129] This second Oswald-McKean case, then, fails to serve our purposes here (though we may be sure that it served McKean's purposes well enough).[130] Nevertheless, the chief justice's language is revealing for conservatives' thinking. An ardent Federalist, McKean claimed that an arsonist's damages to one's house "are easily repaired," but "the injuries which are done to character and reputation seldom can be cured" because "the wide circulation of public prints must render it impracticable to apply the antidote as far as the poison has been extended." Ultimately, McKean sanctioned a generally Blackstonian interpretation of press liberty, both public and private.[131]

Federalists' suspicion of an open press was in part a function of their suspicion of an actively sovereign common people. The Federalist printer Benjamin Russell excluded from his *Massachusetts Centinel* any Anti-Federalists who refused to provide their names. Defending this policy, Russell insisted it furnished

> a timely caution against those, who secure, in not being known, even to the printer, would foist into our papers their assertions and falsehoods, to excite jealousy and mistrust—Which though the *wise* would consider as too glaring to be hurtful, and too weak to merit an answer, yet the less informed would believe, and adopt as truth.[132]

In the 1780s, Americans all across the political spectrum had grown less likely to celebrate the unmitigated blessing of an open press. Still, whereas the Anti-Federalists took the disadvantages of an open press to be a call for a more informed, more active citizenry, the Federalists saw the need to restrict and narrow press liberty.

Individual Liberty, Majority Tyranny

The Anti-Federalists' vision of a sovereign people censuring their public servants through an unrestricted press amounted to an assault on the Federalists' professed hope that the new Constitution would provide an opportunity for a natural elite to legislate, unmolested, for the nation. Reflecting on the Anti-Federalists' rebuke of these aristocratic pretensions, Gordon Wood reveals a startling dimension to their arguments. By attacking the ability of any aristocracy, natural or otherwise, to speak for the public good, and by insisting that the common people speak for themselves—or, better yet, represent themselves—the Anti-Federalists were undermining the "basic similarity of interest for which an empathic elite could speak."[133] "Consequently, there was no one in the society equipped to promote an exclusive public interest that was distinguishable from the private interests of people."[134]

"Without fully comprehending the consequences of their arguments," Wood rightly concludes, "the Antifederalists were . . . undermining the social basis of republicanism."[135] Yet, what we should not lose sight of here is that the Federalists were also positing an increasingly "liberal," interest-based politics, their recourse to traditional notions of social homogeneity notwithstanding. This nascent liberal view is perhaps evident, theoretically at least, in Madison's *Federalist* 10 and 51; these texts are the well-worn scholarly sources for Federalist liberalism. But what has been ignored is that it is also unmistakable in the much more practical and widespread Federalist efforts to unmask Anti-Federalist essayists. To be sure, these efforts were part of a broader and largely transparent tactic of intimidation and pressure. This, for example, explains the frequent suggestions that those critical of the Constitution must be foreign or domestic enemies.[136] But a more compelling argument was required, since the Federalists were breaking with the longstanding tradition of pseudonymous authorship, which allowed the "better sort" and plain folks to enter the public sphere as seeming equals. What mattered was not the name or attributes of the author, Anti-Federalists maintained, but "his argument, which if it were just ought not to be suppressed, and if it were fallacious should be refuted."[137] Yet, rather than simply provide a more convincing argument and allow truth to best falsehood in an open encounter, Federalists sought to rebut critical essays by revealing and centering on the individual interests of the author.

The Privatization of Liberty

Pre-Revolutionary Tories had been accused of being the "tools" of ministerial power's assault on public liberty, but the Federalists were taking these sorts of claims to another, more individualized level. The authors and popularizers of Anti-Federalist sentiments, went the claim, were averse to the proposed constitution because of their particular economic and political interests in the continued prestige and power of state governments. Their pensions and salaries were at risk.[138] At its most explicit, this view insisted on discovering the "REAL designs" of each "hidden enemy," for fear that—"notwithstanding the absurdity and falshood" of his remarks—"some, who supposing them to be the result of honest enquiry of some friend to our country, may give them attention."[139] An author's individual interests, not his public argument, were for the first time emerging as the central concern.[140]

The decline of a republican common good in the face of the developing contest between individuals and their interests can also be seen in the first instances of people subscribing to two newspapers for the avowed purposes of hearing both sides. In the heated controversy between critics and supporters of the Constitution, a single newspaper, some suggested, could no longer be expected to be open and impartial enough to present opposing arguments fairly. "TWENTY-SEVEN SUBSCRIBERS" wrote to the Anti-Federalist editor Thomas Greenleaf, observing that "a number of gentlemen" subscribed to his *New York Journal* in addition to their customary, Federalist newspapers, "merely for the variety and to have an opportunity of seeing the arguments as fully as possible on both sides."[141] And, in a portentous item reprinted from an English paper the day before the Bill of Rights became part of the Constitution, the *Gazette of the United States* published a novel, even modern, understanding of the open press. "The great variety of the papers having separate interests and separate employers, often, by contradicting each other, set mutual errors to rights."[142]

Pace Wood, Federalists *as well as* Anti-Federalists were appealing to certain "liberal" ideas of interested individuals at the expense of more traditional, republican notions of a single, objectively identifiable public good. This observation serves to underscore the fact that, although the coexistence of liberal and republican concepts in the same political discourse remains "a puzzle yet to be solved," the solution—to the extent that one exists—lies in appreciating the fluidity, and not the distance, between them.[143] Given this fluidity, it is perhaps not surprising that the most prescient thinker, the one who most clearly saw the nascent threats to individual liberty, was a Federalist-turned-Republican, James Madison.

The Concept of Majority Tyranny

In pre-Revolutionary American thought, public liberty had been the common concern of the people in their struggle with governmental power. In post-Revolutionary America, public liberty per se was no longer the issue: The people were the government. Whereas the communal liberty had been the concern of every individual, individual liberty was now the concern of every member of the community. "THE Liberty of every man is not only dear to *himself,* but dear *to his fellow citizens,*" Eleazer Oswald proclaimed in his second controversy with Chief Justice McKean. "Oppressions and injuries to *one* individual in the great line of equal and fundamental privileges, are affecting to the *whole* community."[144] In the traditional politics of England, the people would unite to defend printers and authors who opposed the government; in the new politics of America, controversial printers and authors ran the risk of being "severely handled, not by the government, but by the populace."[145]

No one saw the threats to liberty more clearly than James Madison. His shift from Federalist to Republican reflected not a change of political theory so much as a change in the circumstances about which he theorized.[146] Madison recognized that the threats to liberty are many and do not emanate from a single source. To be sure, even in the new federal republic, there still "may be occasions on which the evil [of oppression] may spring from [the Government]." But the majority was the real threat. As he explained to Jefferson,

> wherever the real power in a Government lies, there is the danger of oppression. In our Governments the real power lies in the majority of the Community, and the invasion of private rights is *chiefly* to be apprehended, not from acts of Government contrary to the sense of its constituents, but from acts in which the Government is the mere instrument of the major number of the constituents.[147]

Madison reiterated this same theme the next summer, when he was presenting his draft amendments to the House.[148] Those amendments included a clause to be added to the limitations on the states found in Art. I, Sec. 10: "No State shall infringe the equal rights of conscience, nor the freedom of speech, or of the press, nor of the right of trial by jury in criminal cases." When the Anti-Federalist Thomas Tudor Tucker sought to strike this clause on the grounds that the Constitution "interfered too much already" with the states, Madison called the clause "the most valuable amendment on the whole list."[149] "These abuses," he said, "are most likely to take place under the State governments." Some state constitutions permitted the "rights of the community" to override press liberty and other "particular rights." Indeed, Madison had observed the actions of "overbearing majorities" in his own and other states.[150] The House passed both of Madison's press clauses with nothing more than a slight change in wording. The Senate changed the first press clause to the now-familiar "Congress shall make no law . . ." language and "passed in the negative" Madison's prized state-limiting clause.[151]

Though the First Amendment that the country ratified in 1791 was a far cry from the clause, or, rather, clauses, Madison would have wanted, it lives on in American press liberty discourse. It was his fear of majority tyranny, however, that most clearly expressed the evolving conceptions of press liberty espoused by the Anti-Federalists, while at the same time illustrating the nascent privatization of liberty. Majority tyranny presented a dangerous unification and distortion of both the "press of sovereignty" and the "advantage" arguments I have sought to elucidate. An "overbearing majority" was nothing more than the bulk of the sovereign people actively participating, though in an imperious manner. And, rather than suffer the disadvantages of an open press, such a majority will seek to restrict untrue, or at least unpopular, ideas. The net result, Madison foresaw, puts individual liberty at risk.

Conclusion

The momentous political, economic, and social transformations of the Revolutionary era occasioned pivotal reformulations of the inherited press liberty tradition. As the "press of freedom" was theoretically challenged, open press arguments returned to Patriot America, along with an increased recognition that press liberty must permit even the most unpopular sentiments. The radical remaking of American society brought increased popular participation in government and in the economy. The accelerated separation of public and private spheres prompted a bifurcation between public and private liberties.

The free and open press tradition was transformed. The distinct, rhetorical power of the terms "free" and "open" was lost as they became blurred and largely synonymous, but more consequential reformations were under way in the doctrines they had signified. Radical Americans of the Confederation period took up the task of making sense of profound changes in the very nature of government and the implications they had for the role of the press. A sovereign people required a steady flow of political information, constructive as well as critical, in order to be competent masters of their public servants; they required not a free press but a "press of sovereignty." To make this practicable, an effective if rough distinction had to be drawn between a government official's public character and his private life. Finally, as factionalism turned to calumny of the people's chosen servants, a more considered appreciation of the advantages of the press was fashioned.

In response to the Federalists' proposed constitution and their narrower understanding of press liberty, Anti-Federalists stressed and extended these evolving conceptions of press liberty. In an extensive country, a vigorous, pervasive press was all the more essential. For conservative Federalists, an abused political press was an argument for legal sanctions; Anti-Federalists instead sought a better informed populace in an effort to improve an already advantageous press. In response to Federalists' attempts to systemize virtue and to rely on the "better sort," their critics generally emphasized the continued need for broad-based citizen vigilance, participation, and dialogue. These competing views, when combined with the emergence—on *all* sides—of a more individualized, interest-based politics, laid the groundwork for the more divisive politics of the 1790s.

Within this highly fluid context, some Anti-Federalists had sufficient prescience to anticipate the threat of majority tyranny, especially in light of the Federalists' aristocratic politics. A sarcastic "Philadelphiensis" envisioned the Federalist future—and the Sedition Act (1798)—all too clearly.

> I wonder that our *well born* should allow such mean fellows to write against this their government; such base wretches ought not to live in the same country with *gentlemen*; and as soon as our new government is confirmed, these vile enemies to its *splendor and dignity*, shall quit their

carping, I'll warrant them; a federal solider with a fixed bayonet will soon give such daring dogs their quietis. Ah! what glorious days are coming; how I anticipate the brilliancy of the American court! . . . here is the president going in state to the senate house to confirm the law for the abolition of the liberty of the press. Men and brethren will not these things be so?[152]

They would be so, as Madison, former Anti-Federalists, and other Jeffersonian Republicans would soon discover.

5

The Emergence of Modern Democratic Press Liberty

The debate over the Constitution brought different definitions of republican government to light in the 1780s, but the terms of discourse were largely abstract and institutional. Federalists usually left the issue of press liberty alone, praising it broadly and insisting that the Constitution did not touch it. Even the contest over the Bill of Rights failed to furnish congressional debate over the meaning of the "freedom of the press." The controversy over the Sedition Act, to the contrary, cut right through the ostensible consensus. Yet this dispute was part of the emerging practical political context of the 1790s, which saw increased newspaper partisanship, and led to bitter divisions, trenchant criticism, and, ultimately, conceptual evolution. It was this broader context that forced even those who had once agreed on many general principles, such as Madison and Hamilton, to differ profoundly when those same principles had to be made real during the course of governing the new republic.

The practical political context tells only part of the story of the divisive politics and conceptual innovations of the 1790s. In the early years of the new republic, ideology was also vital. Here, though, it is actually the shared beliefs and not the divergent policies that are most illuminating. The common republican presuppositions of the period underwrote a political life that was plagued by conspiracy theories, as discourse became violently hyperbolic and visions of the republic's survival turned apocalyptic.[1] Americans of the 1790s were very much aware that they lived in a critical moment and saw all around them reason for despair. Every good republican knew that history had proven republics to be the most vulnerable of all political systems. And now the virtue and the broad equality that had sustained American republicanism seemed to be waning, while factionalism, the death knell of a republic, was unmistakably waxing. It seemed the American republic was on the road to a premature demise.[2]

But if the first decade after the Bill of Rights was given to divisive and distrustful politics, it was the Sedition Act (1798) that "precipitated the most serious constitutional crisis in the period after ratification."[3] In fact, the Sedition Act crisis motivated more debate and greater philosophical advances than even the pre-Revolutionary crisis. It was in response to defenses of the sedition law that the recognizably modern concept of democratic press liberty emerged. The founding of this concept involved more than a repudiation of the idea that government could be criminally assaulted by words. It required also an understanding of the need for both an ongoing discourse that represented the diversity of sentiments and a public opinion that acted as the authoritative political standard.

Yet the period did more than provide the foundation of modern American democratic press liberty. Simply put, the Sedition Act crisis was the pivotal moment in the "democratization of the American mind."[4] The effort to realize the constitutional principles of 1787 and 1791 revealed divergent ideas about the equality of all men and the role of "the people" in republican politics. These differences contributed to differing concepts of political representation. In turn, all of these divisions contributed to competing views of republican press liberty. In recognition of these interconnected ideological disputes, this chapter examines Federalist and Republican ideas about the people, representation, and the nature of republican press liberty. An additional section further analyzes rival understandings of the advantages and the dangers of absolute political press liberty in a republic. Ultimately, we arrive at an examination of the novel, indeed radical, ideas of public truth and public opinion that underwrote a recognizably modern discourse of democratic press liberty. But, before we address these issues, we turn first to important theoretical and practical events leading up to the Sedition Act, and then to some significant issues surrounding the Act itself.

Early Issues and Episodes

The earliest and perhaps most suggestive issue of the pre-Sedition Act period is actually a nonevent. A proposed newspaper tax in 1790 and the Post Office Act (1792) seemed to threaten newspaper circulation by increasing the cost of a newspaper sent through the post to subscribers, as many were.[5] This was especially important to opposition leaders, who could turn to only a handful of sympathetic newspapers in the early 1790s. Thus, the Republican *National Gazette* bemoaned the attack on necessary information, especially troubling in such an extensive territory.[6] Yet what is most remarkable about such comments is their paucity. Compared to the reactions to the Massachusetts stamp and advertisement taxes of 1785–87, or to the changes in postal policies in 1787–88, these tandem proposals elicited little response.

Perhaps the explanation lies in the rapidly expanding newspaper market and the burgeoning postal system. The "trifling" increase of a penny and a half contained in the new postal regulations would not, and in fact did not, prove enough to undermine newspaper circulation.[7] In fact, as James Madison and others noted, since a commission went to the postmasters, they would have now have a personal interest in seeing that each newspaper reached its subscriber, thus actually improving an imperfect delivery system.[8] Furthermore, the increase in partisanship and the broadening class of politically active citizens meant that even ordinary people were quite unlikely to go without political information. The restrained response, then, points to deepening partisanship and a broader, more institutionalized public sphere; accordingly, each of these interrelated transformations receives further discussion later in this chapter. In the meantime, suffice it to say that important shifts in the economic and political contexts meant that these were the first newspaper duties that threatened not popular sovereignty but merely profit margins.

The case of William Keteltas was also prophetic, and it was anything but a nonevent.[9] Keteltas, a young Republican lawyer in New York, had taken up the case of two Irish ferrymen summarily convicted of insulting a Federalist alderman. Keteltas, among others, argued that there was no law banning insulting language and further claimed that the magistrates had been partial. When he petitioned the Assembly and criticized the resulting special committee report, Keteltas was unanimously censured. Press liberty became a central issue when his next newspaper article was held a breach of privilege. With Keteltas in jail for the remainder of the session, the pseudonymous "Camillus Junius" argued that the legislature had no right to punish writers for offensive publications, even if they included "*falshoods* which have an evident tendency to destroy" public confidence.[10] Such summary proceedings were well out of the Assembly's proper powers. "I am no friend to the doctrine of libels," Camillus Junius declared, "but it is a perfect *guardian of the press*, compared to your late decision."[11] This offhand sarcasm regarding libel law would soon prove all too portentous for those who were not friends to the doctrine, but it is Camillus's hypothetical extension of such legislative privileges to the U.S. Senate that is most prophetic. Camillus's intent was no doubt to expose "so monstrous" a policy by applying it to the extreme case of the infrequently, indirectly elected Senate.[12] Nevertheless, in retrospect, the comments aptly foreshadow the Senate proceedings against William Duane, discussed later. Moreover, the Keteltas case presents the first explicit and sustained arguments that reject altogether the use of legislative privilege as a restraint on press liberty.

Notwithstanding this early assault on legislative privilege, by far the most significant press liberty issue prior to the Sedition Act was the controversy over the so-called Democratic Societies. The Democratic Societies popped up in 1793–94, in part the result of Republican enthusiasm over the new French Republic and the Jacobin Society of Paris. Yet, as much as anything, the Democratic Societies provided an avenue to public prominence and influence for political and economic parvenus who had been heretofore unable to get into power. But if the political establishment of the early 1790s—Republican as well as Federalist—had as yet no place for these new men, the late eighteenth century also had no obvious place for unofficial associations. Such Societies might very well be factions and thus "might actually inhibit the free expression of public opinion." The "self-created" nature of the Societies put their legitimacy very much in doubt, for their relationship to popular sovereignty was an open question.[13]

The discourse concerning the Societies foreshadows the coming dispute over the Sedition Act in that we see a clearly defined Republican understanding of the role of the people and the press in a republic. In many respects, the arguments about the Democratic Societies start to extend Anti-Federalist contentions about a "press of sovereignty" to include the people's elective responsibilities. The Federalists once again largely avoided the issue of press liberty, preferring instead to emphasize the questionable legitimacy of any "self-created" body.

The Democratic Societies, for their part, naturally wanted to avoid the issues of party and faction. Accordingly, "a principal theme in their statements of purpose was simply the importance of discussion, the exchange of views, the spread of information."[14] Given the dubious legitimacy of such "self-created societies," the Democratic Societies were generally eager to stress that their membership was open to all. The Political Society of Mount Prospect (New Jersey) went so far as to "invite all, within the limits of this parish" to join its deliberations, provided they not be felons or others of "immoral character."

> Are several of you disposed to advocate an aristocratical or monarchical government? Where there is real opposition of sentiment, in a well regulated discussion, the righteous cause will probably shine with an additional lustre: Come forward then, with your arguments; we are more general than cowardly; liberty is yours, as well as ours; come on, and vindicate your cause, in the open field of reason.[15]

But if the Societies maintained that the truth would probably prevail in their open discussions, their emphasis was on the "the duty of every good Citizen . . . to *detect* and *publish* to the world, every violation of our Constitution, or instance of Mal-Administration."[16] Moreover, in keeping with the "press of sovereignty" argument, the Societies insisted on continuous scrutiny of public men and measures, for, "after having set up a government, citizens ought not to resign it into the hands of agents." Employers do not cease being watchful once an employee is hired, and "the different members of the government, are nothing more than the agents of the people, and as such, have no right to prevent their employers from inspecting into their conduct."[17]

We begin to see signs that Society members were expanding on previous understandings of republican press liberty in their emphasis on the need for citizen vigilance. Vigilance, of course, had long been a republican—and, more specifically, a free press—mantra, but, with the establishment of popularly elected governments in the 1770s and 1780s, the concept receded from view as the need for such watchfulness seemed relatively less pressing. In the discourse of the societies, however, one espies an emerging belief that governmental officials, even in a republic, "ought to be watched with a *scrupulously* jealous eye." For "it is the right and duty of every Freeman, to watch with the vigilance of a faithful centinel the conduct of those to whom is intrusted the administration of Government."[18]

A second critical issue suggested by the dispute over the Democratic Societies is that of the competence of the people for active participation in politics. A New Jersey "Cato" made the necessary argument with Republican gusto:

> To declare that the affairs of government are too enveloped in mysterious intricacy as to be placed beyond the reach of common capacities, is as slavish a doctrine as ever disgraced the creed of the vilest minion of the most despotic tyrant, and is the source from which much oppression springs.[19]

Perhaps the most important arguments, however, were those that began to explore the meaning of press liberty in an elective republic. The suffrage of the people (or at least the white men among them) required an informed public. The Democratic Society of the City of New York put the matter most emphatically: "*The* RESPONSIBILITY *of* PUBLIC FUNCTIONARIES *presupposes a* RIGHT OF INVESTIGATING INTO THEIR PROCEEDINGS." The Democratic Society also thought it especially important that political discourse be encouraged in a republic so that all citizens would be prepared for public service. "It is in Republican governments . . . that it becomes a duty more particularly incumbent upon individuals, to require a perfect knowledge of the government and political institutions of their country, the administration of which they may one day be called upon to take an active share."[20]

The Democratic Societies would not last long enough to do more for the discourse of press liberty than to posit briefly a few promising extensions of earlier arguments. For example, the overall advantages of unrestrained political press liberty receive little attention in the Societies' discourse.[21] This, however, is understandable, since the Federalists were criticizing them not for libel but for being dangerous factions. Indeed, the Societies died out in large part because of Washington's accusation, in a presidential address, that they were partly responsible for the Whiskey Rebellion. Still, even in their passing, the Societies provided the opportunity for some prophetic words, this time from James Madison.

No member of the Societies, Madison rose to speak against a motion to censure the Societies as part of concurring with Washington's Address. "If we advert to the nature of Republican government," he famously lectured the House, "we shall find that the censorial power is in the people over the Government, and not in the Government over the people." Moreover, "in a Republic, light will prevail over darkness, truth over error." Having reminded his audience of traditional republican principles, Madison went further to broach a view of public opinion and press liberty that would find strong echoes in the coming controversy. As he had "confidence in the good sense and patriotism of the people," Madison "did not anticipate any lasting evil to result" from the Societies' publications. "They would stand or fall by the public opinion."[22] These are broad, unsubstantiated claims, to be sure, mere philosophical promissory notes. But, in the Sedition Act debates, it would be Madison, perhaps more than any other man, who would prove their full value.

The Sedition Act

"An Act in addition to the act, entitled 'An act for the punishment of certain crimes against the United States'" (14 July 1798) criminalized— along with actual sedition and insurrection—"any false, scandalous and malicious writing or writings against the government of the United States . . . or Congress . . . or the President, with the intent to defame . . . or to bring them . . . into contempt or disrepute." More commonly referred to as the Sedition Act, it has long been taken to be the epitome of Federalist highhandedness. Though by no means unfounded, this view is still overstated. The Federalists, of course, were drawing on a wealth of British and, in some cases, American arguments and precedents. These sources and arguments are evident if we reflect on the various conservative claims analyzed in the preceding chapters. Indeed, in some respects, the "Sedition Act controversy" began with the institution of common law proceedings against two Republican printers shortly before the law was enacted. For various reasons, however, neither of these common law cases went to trial.[23] Nevertheless, these two cases remind us of the Federalists' faith in the common law of seditious libel. More important, this turn of events proved critical because, in the absence of actual trials, the Federalists had little idea of the popular opprobrium that seditious libel convictions might bring.

Had these two cases brought lengthy, heated trials, it is at least possible that the sedition law would have been seriously reconsidered. The Alien and Sedition Acts had only halfhearted support, as the most recent authorities on the 1790s make clear.[24] If any law was the epitome of Federalist highhandedness, it was the so-called Alien Friends Act of 25 June 1798, which gave the president authority to expel any "dangerous," nonnaturalized person without trial or even explanation. The

Sedition Act that was finally approved on 14 July was "sweet reason" compared to the Alien law and to earlier versions of the sedition law.[25] The House had watered down earlier Senate bills and ended up approving the modified common law of the Zenger trial: Evidence of the truth of the alleged libel could be presented by the defense, and the jury could rule on the law, as well as the facts.

Notwithstanding these meliorations, the sedition law seemed despotic to many people. "Hostility . . . was widespread," and "mass meetings were organized, drawing crowds numbering as high as five thousand."[26] The Federalists, in fact, were not only "blindly striking back" at the vilification of the "right sort" of men but also trying to stem the growth of the emerging Republican party.[27] The Federalists did not see themselves as partisan, of course, but rather as loyal to the elected government. Still, the political nature of the sedition law was evident from its specified expiration date. The Act was to expire not at the end of the nascent international crisis with France but at the end of Adams's current term. Moreover, as the Federalist representative John Allen declared, "it is our business to wrest" the press from Republican hands.[28] But if the intent of the Sedition Act was political, its execution was all the more so. Republican editors—and only Republicans—were indicted, and most of the major opposition papers and several minor ones were targets. The timing was such that the trials would take place, and thus silence the editors, before the election of 1800.[29] "Enforced by a partisan judiciary, the Alien and Sedition Acts unleashed a bloodless reign of terror."[30]

Yet, if the political cast and draconian nature of the prosecutions are obvious, so is the "almost comic clumsiness, the sheer political ineptitude" of the Federalists' efforts.[31] The ineptitude is perhaps best seen in the attempts to muzzle William Duane, Bache's successor at the *Aurora*.[32] Duane won first an acquittal on trumped-up seditious riot charges and then an embarrassing dismissal from Federalist authorities in a seditious libel proceeding. Taking a seemingly safer path, the Senate found Duane in breach of its privileges for printing and commenting on a compromising bill. But Duane eluded arrest for the remainder of the session and then mocked the Senate in his paper. When Federalists went after him again for seditious libel, Duane argued successfully for a postponement, and by the time the trial came, Jefferson was President and all seditious libel charges had been dropped.

The draconian character of the sedition law is even more apparent in

the Federalists' desperation than in their incompetence. Federal authorities even fined a man who drunkenly and crudely remarked, as Adams
paraded through Newark, that he did not care if the celebratory can-
non fire struck the presidential posterior.[33] As pitiful as this episode is,
it suggests the importance—for Federalists—of defending the honor
and dignity of governmental officials. Seeking to defend themselves, the
only device they could think of was "the rusty principle of seditious
libel—one which, even as a theoretical premise, had come to have little
or no pertinence to the emerging state of political practice in America."[34] As we have seen, the preceding decades had brought increasingly wide practical leeway to the press, despite the fact that libel laws
were anything but settled.

The unsettled nature of the law and theory of the Sedition Act left
fertile ground for a wide variety of arguments, both for and against.
Many of these can be dispensed with quickly here, as they add little to
the evolving concept of press liberty. For example, one of the most
common critiques of the sedition law was a simple appeal to the First
Amendment. Several papers reprinted the Amendment as "Text" and
then sarcastically printed the Sedition Act's libel clause as "Commentary."[35] Federalists merely responded that they had not abridged press
freedom because that term required nothing more than a press free
from prior restraint. As we shall see, some dialogues led to illuminating discussions of the role of such a press in a republic. More often
than not, however, these exchanges remained superficial. Similarly te-
dious arguments centered on the Constitution's "necessary and proper"
clause and on the Tenth Amendment.

At least one seemingly inconsequential dispute gave rise to a deeper
issue that would come to have a pivotal role in the emergence of the
modern concept of democratic press liberty. Exchanges over the regulations that governed the use of truth as a defense often began as legal
disputes but resulted in broader debates about the nature of truth and
opinion. In the legal case, the Federalists were decidedly the victors.
Federalist courts held that the accused must prove the truth of the
opinions, as well as the facts, in their alleged libels. Moreover, the defendant's intent was inferred from the "bad tendency" of his words. All
of this left the truth defense virtually useless and the jury trial little
more than a rubber stamp, especially once the Federalist-appointed
marshal impaneled the jurymen of his choice.[36] Republicans responded
that certain types of truth did not admit of legal proof because they

were matters of argument and opinion. This forced them "to do what had never been done perhaps before, to draw a line of discrimination between fact and opinion."[37]

Given the apparently unprecedented nature of the theoretical and conceptual innovations that were required, it is not surprising that conservative Federalist judges refused to admit the distinction. Nor is it surprising that it is here that Republicans were forced to theorize their most original and advanced arguments. For now, these arguments too will have to wait until we address the genuinely philosophical differences that contributed to the Sedition Act controversy.

Another dispute frequently if not always proved illuminating: the debate over federalism and states' rights. Denials of Federal jurisdiction in the states' rights arguments were tricky, of course, because they suggested that Republicans were accepting the concept of seditious libel. Surely, some Republicans were.[38] At other times, such arguments were clearly tactical moves, as when an *Aurora* correspondent wanted state jurisdiction, despite the fact that the Pennsylvania law was effectively identical to the new federal statute. On other occasions, Republicans insisted that press liberty was an individual, not a state, right.[39]

More importantly, as heirs to the Anti-Federalists, Republicans elaborated a defense of states' rights that was interconnected with press liberty as part of a broader vision of a democratic republic of vigilant citizens and strictly limited government. As the current authority on James Madison concludes, Republican opposition "was not developed for the sake of states as states, but for the sake of the republican and liberal ideas" of the Revolution.[40] To be sure, the debate over federalism was critical to the politics of the 1790s. But Republicans could well have chosen—and might have been better off—to attack the Sedition Act on purely states' rights grounds. Nevertheless, as we shall soon see, many Jeffersonians insisted on defending freedom of expression in radically democratic, as well as state-centered, terms.

Impartiality

Before we hasten to confront the critical theoretical arguments that emerged from the debates over the sedition law, we must take one last pause to address an issue that is, in a sense, remarkably tangential: impartiality. Impartiality, as we have seen, had long been the watchword for printers. The open press doctrine that was a central feature of the American press tradition for the last three-quarters of the eighteenth century required that printers maintain their impartiality so that individuals could openly present their sentiments. Even into the 1790s, open press phrases (as well as free press notions) periodically reappeared, with *Cato's Letters* still quoted on rare occasions. Yet, for the most part, the terms "free" and "open" had evolved into vaguely synonymous terms, and, as we have seen, the related doctrines had been transformed. Impartiality, however, was still a commonplace affirmation of newspaper editors, both Federalist and Republican.[41]

These frequent claims were belied by the decline of newspaper impartiality, both in theory and in practice, that developed alongside the marked increase in partisanship that characterized the 1790s.[42] By the end of the decade, some papers were clearly partisan in tone, despite their declarations of impartiality. The editors of the *Ploughman*, for example, appealed to potential subscribers by assuring them that they would "impartially embrace the primary Objects of NATIONAL CONCERN" and remain "free from Party Rancour"; yet they also admitted they printed "under the Auspices of Federal Patronage."[43] Delving deeper into now rare sources reveals that other editors were less equivocal and more brazen. "The *times* admit of no *duplicity*," Charles Pierce proclaimed in proposing "The Oracle of the Day as A FEDERAL PAPER." "Every native *American* has but *two choices* to make. He must *rank* with the *friends* or the *foes* of America. *Neutrality* is *criminal*."[44]

Though the impartiality of early American newspapers had only very rarely maintained pristine purity, bald statements like these suggest a profoundly changed approach to the press. This remarkable decline in impartiality was in part a reflection of the nascent party system and the broader partisanship it engendered. But there were also significant shifts at a more practical level that were revolutionizing American press discourse. The new citizens of the American republic were conversing far more broadly than ever before, and they were transforming their institutions and practices to enable that expanding conversation. The number of post offices, for example, grew from only seventy-five in 1790 to more than nine hundred in 1800. The number of newspapers more than doubled in the same decade, from ninety-two to 235. Meanwhile, the time required for news to travel between Philadelphia and New York dropped from four days to about one and a half days by only the middle of that decade.[45] The increased speed and ease of news exchange from Philadelphia is especially important to the decline in impartiality, because some of the most avidly partisan papers were printed there and because the capital city's papers "acted as a kind of news service for papers throughout the country."[46] The decline of impartiality, even as a standard, can thus be followed in Philadelphia.

When John Fenno's *Gazette of the United States* became antirepublican, at least in Thomas Jefferson's view, he and Madison cajoled Philip Freneau to start the *National Gazette*, to be written "on whig principles" and "in a contrary spirit" to Fenno's paper. The result was that citizens increasingly required two newspapers to see "both sides of our politics."[47] Not only were there now unabashedly two sides to the supposedly unified politics of a republic; the sides were growing further apart. The opposition between Freneau and Fenno gave way to that between Benjamin Franklin Bache's *Aurora* and the Englishman William Cobbett's aptly named *Porcupine's Gazette*. Bache had at least claimed impartiality back in 1790 and had printed both sides as late as 1792, but after 1795 Federalists were almost never defended, Republicans almost never criticized;[48] by middecade, even his claims to truth and impartiality were gone.[49] Cobbett is perhaps the only newspaper editor who surpassed Bache in newspaper poison; as we shall see, he had only contempt for the notion of impartiality.

The decline in the norm of impartiality was not restricted to Philadelphia. Boston's Federalist *Columbian Centinel,* rival to the Republican *Independent Chronicle,* had by 1795 dropped its motto ("Uninfluenced by party, we aim only to be just") as a travesty.[50] Indeed, during the 1790s, the use of reason and the standard of impartiality gave way to the use of invective and the norm of brazen partiality. The dialogue that had once taken place within one newspaper was now expected to take place, if anywhere, *between* two or more newspapers.[51] Thus, Charles Holt, editor of the New London, Connecticut, *Bee*, defended his exclusively Republican printing in late 1798 by insisting that, since "nine tenths of the newspapers in Connecticut are decidedly partial to *one side*, and keep the *other* totally out of sight," he would print the missing Republican side.[52] The marked increase in unadorned partisanship prior to the Sedition Act was such that one could matter-of-factly state on the floor of the House, "It is well known that there are papers on both sides [of] the question and if you say you have read one; you are generally asked if you have seen the other."[53]

With the remarkable decline in impartiality in practice came unprecedented attacks on impartiality as a theoretical standard, much less an ideal. Papers on both sides of the political divide ridiculed impartiality as impossible or even undesirable.[54] Why should the theoretical assault have emerged in the 1790s? Part of the explanation probably lies in the unmistakably partisan nature of the new political context; the ongoing contradiction between certain newspapers' policies and practices was simply too glaring—and too widely criticized—to be sustained. Thus, once William Cobbett had advertised that his *Gazette* would return the Republicans "two blows for one," he could scarcely make any claims to impartiality. Instead, his first issue addressed the public with a candor impossible only a few years earlier:

> Professions of *impartiality* I shall make none. They are always useless, and are besides perfect nonsense. . . . For my part, I feel the strongest partiality for the cause of order and good government, such as we live under, and against every thing that is opposed to it. To profess impartiality here, would be as absurd as to profess it in a war between Virtue and Vice, Good and Evil, Happiness and Misery.[55]

Given the power of republican norms, even the partiality of an arch-Federalist had a public-spirited, not merely a partisan, cast. Nevertheless, the attack on the notion of press impartiality was well under way.

The prospectus of Joseph Dennie's *Port Folio* was at least as candid as Cobbett's *Gazette*, and even more hostile to the ideal of impartiality. Dennie's first promise to subscribers was a negative one: "He *will not* publish an *impartial* paper in that style of cold, callous, supine, and criminal indifference, which views, with [an] equal eye . . . a stable government, and the uproar of anarchy." "For the silly scheme of impartiality," Dennie "cherishe[d] the most ineffable contempt."[56]

But the theory and practice of impartiality was not only thoroughly implausible almost everywhere in the late 1790s; it was also unnecessary. As the expanded public sphere was institutionalized, the growth of multinewspaper towns—and, more important, the circulation of papers and news between towns—made an impartial, open newspaper much less crucial: One could just publish in an opposing paper. Indeed, in some cases editors were telling critical correspondents to take their responses to another paper.[57] The issue of an open press as such thus became less central to the modern, democratic free press discourse that would emerge from the Sedition Act crisis.

A Republican Press for a Republican People

In his classic work *Freedom's Fetters: The Alien and Sedition Laws and American Civil Liberties*, James Morton Smith aptly observed that the controversy over liberty of the press "pivoted on the concept of the relation of the people to the government."[58] As we shall now see, there was a good deal more to it than this, involving differing conceptions of representation, of the power of public opinion, and of the nature of truth. Yet the practical role of the people in the new republic was precisely the crux of the matter. The question was what concept of press liberty was most appropriate for a genuine republic. This was a question radical Englishmen and even French Jacobins simply did not face, and one that Americans of the early Republic simply could not avoid.

All men are created equal. But how so, exactly? This is the very question that ultimately divided Federalists and Republicans and served as the basis of their competing views of press liberty. As the historians Stanley Elkins and Eric McKitrick conclude, the Republicans devised a "politics of inclusion," while "Federalism ended up as little more than a kind of strident exclusivism."[59] The differing visions of the people and of popular sovereignty are most clearly summarized in Madison's essay, "WHO ARE THE BEST KEEPERS OF THE PEOPLE'S LIBERTIES?," the last in an increasingly partisan series written for Freneau's *National Gazette*. Predictably, Madison's "Republican" answers, "The people themselves. The sacred trust can be no where so safe as in the hands most interested in preserving it."

> *Anti-Republican.*—The people are stupid, suspicious, licentious. They cannot safely trust themselves. When they have established a government they should think of nothing but obedience, leaving the care of their liberties to their wiser rulers.
>
> *Republican.*— . . . because the people *may* betray themselves, they ought to give themselves up, blindfold, to those who have an interest in betraying them? Rather conclude that the people ought to be enlightened, to be awakened, to be united, that after establishing a government they should watch over it, as well as obey it.[60]

This is highly polemical, of course. Alexander Hamilton, probably the "Anti-Republican" caricatured here, was never this extreme. Still, John Rutledge would write Hamilton privately, acknowledging the Federalist fear that a Jeffersonian presidency "would begin by democratizing the people & end with throwing everything into their hands." And, indeed, Federalists would soon publicly lament that, "in this country, almost every man considers himself a politician, and a judge of the affairs of state."[61]

Private fears and public railings aside, the conceptual distinction that best captures the contrasting views of the people and popular sovereignty is that which arose over whether vigilance or confidence is the proper attribute of a republican people.[62] For Republicans, it "remained axiomatic" that government, even republican government, "had a tendency to trespass on popular liberties."[63] "Implicit confidence is the parent of tyranny," insisted John Thomson. "Vigilance" is "the first duty of every republican." Defending himself against seditious libel charges, Thomas Cooper cautioned that any confidence placed in government "ought not to be unlimited, and need not be paid up in advance; let it be earned before it be reposed." Madison instead placed "confidence in the good sense and patriotism of the people."[64]

Federalists, however, insisted that confidence was properly placed in the government. The problem with the publication of falsehoods, Hamilton explained, was that they "destroy the confidence of the people" in government officials and supporters. To the Republican insistence on vigilance and jealousy of governmental power, one Federalist replied that

> nothing can be more mischievous . . . than the raising and harboring of idle fears and jealousies. The government stands on higher ground than we do, and of course sees to a greater distance, and are enabled to form a better judgment of what is necessary for the public welfare; and they are entitled to a generous and manly, not a blind confidence.

Other Federalists agreed and were much less equivocal. Verbal abuse of government officials elected by the people "was in direct opposition to the duties of a good citizen."[65] By late 1799, Hamiltonian Federalists were privately discussing a proposed law, in addition to the Sedition Act, to punish "seditious practices" and thereby "preserve confidence in the officers of the general government."[66]

Federalist Representation, Federalist Press Liberty

The Federalists' views of the people and of popular sovereignty naturally played a role in their understanding of representation and, in turn, their conception of press liberty. Madison's *National Gazette* parody of the "Anti-Republican" contained a grain of truth in that it captured the Federalist stress on the obedience of the people. The Federalists of the 1790s were still clinging to the version of republicanism that had held sway for much of the eighteenth century and included the elitist assumption that "men of the right sort" would govern and the people would obey. But, by the 1790s, traditional notions of status and authority had lost much of their significance. Nevertheless, "this principle—men of the right sort—comes close to holding the key to the entire Federalist idea."[67]

If men of the right sort were to govern a representative republic, what of the sovereign people? As we saw in chapter 4, Federalists held that the people's primary virtue was to choose wisely. Elections, not a free press, were seen as "a security paramount to all others." Opposition discourse would be confined to the period prior to balloting, after which confidence in, and obedience to, the chosen rulers would be the norm. For Hamilton, the act of election "committed the administration of our public affairs" to government officials. To the Federalist mind, opposition to public men and measures between elections was antirepublican precisely because voting was the act of relegating the public business to the elected officials. "Those, who choose their civil magistrates, do voluntarily pledge their obedience," the Reverend Nathanael Emmons preached in a fast day sermon. "By putting power into the hands of their rulers, they put it out of their own; by choosing and authorizing them to govern, they practically declare their . . . intention and willingness to obey."[68]

Some Federalists would go further yet, wondering whether popular discussion even immediately prior to elections was in the best interests of the people. Many feared that some publications had "been too unrestrained for the benefit of our citizens. Can it be beneficial to the community to have our gazettes crowded, as they sometimes have been, on the subject of elections, of public men?" Ultimately, regulating the press was especially necessary in a republic because, as James Bayard explained on the House floor, "that falsehood which deprives men of the means of forming a true judgement of public affairs, in this country, where the Government is elective, is a crime of the first magnitude."[69]

The Federalists' notion of representation and view of the people, then, helps us understand their conception of press liberty. Punishing untrue criticism of public men and measures was further required by their view of the "government." Most Federalists used the words "administration" and "government" interchangeably.[70] And, "from the beginning, the Federalists had equated support for the government with support for the Constitution."[71] Thus, for them, opposition to the current Federalist administration was tantamount to treason. Republicans again and again argued that the Federalists were—perhaps intentionally—failing to distinguish between the administration, the government and the Constitution, and thereby confusing dissent with sedition.[72] While the Federalist position may seem a bit overdrawn to us in retrospect, we must recall that the relationships between a sovereign people, a republican government, and a written constitution were only now being fleshed out for the first time in history. Republicans hoping to elect one of their own to the presidency in 1800 had every political reason to conceptualize this new distinction between a temporary administration and a permanent constitution. Federalists like Washington and Hamilton, who spent little time addressing this relationship, remained "quite unable to imagine that opposition could be loyal opposition."[73]

By elevating their administration to the level of the Constitution itself, and by relegating the people to mere choosers of wise rulers, the Federalists had "corrupted that very principle—the sovereignty of the people—that had enabled them a dozen years before to ride down the opposition to their new Constitution."[74] This did not mean that the Federalists were abandoning popular sovereignty as such. Rather, they were realizing it as they genuinely understood it. The people, as they saw it, were being molested by Republican critics *through* their elected officials. Vilifying President Adams as a "mock Monarch" was therefore an "indignity offered to their majesty of the American people, thro the Chief Magistrate," according to Noah Webster's *Commercial Advertiser.* "How long ye slumbering Americans, will you be thus insulted?" In defaming Congress and the president, Republican papers were "of course openly vilifying that very PEOPLE for whom they profess so deep a respect."[75] Officials had a right to the people's good opinion for the people's own interests. Even finding William Duane in breach of Senate privilege was a matter of defending the public: "It is for the interest of the people, and not for our own peculiar advantage, that we enjoy these privileges."[76] This, the reader will recall, had been sound logic through midcentury. Now, however, the Federalists' notion of exalting the people by exalting themselves was the object of Republican sarcasm.[77] Republicans, for their part, were busy shaping a concept of press liberty that exalted the people as active members of the republic's politics.

Republican Representation, Republican Press Liberty

Just as the Federalists' conception of press liberty is best understood in relation to their views of representation, so too the Republican's efforts to formulate a conception that legitimated unrestrained political expression can be comprehended only in correlation with their understanding of representation. As the philosophical descendants of the Anti-Federalists, the Republicans of the 1790s held that the people were the continual masters of their political servants. Such servants, of course, were still men whose reputations deserved protection, and so the public/private distinction that had emerged during the previous decade was maintained and advanced. Recounting his own use of this argument in a seditious libel trial, the lawyer George Blake simply asserted that "the distinction we presume is neither novel nor unfounded." That the public expected the distinction to be drawn (and public conduct to be scrutinized) is equally apparent from private correspondence and public declaration.[78] Indeed, Hamilton, Washington, and other Federalists understood that the people anticipated news of public men and measures.[79] And Republicans were sure to stress the government official's continuing recourse to civil suits for private damages. Nevertheless, most Federalists, Hamilton among them, persisted in maintaining that criticism of public men could be criminal.[80]

For Republicans, of course, these public men were public servants and thus were just as subject to criticism as any servant. In the 1790s, radicals took to extending this notion. The people were the masters, and "the *President*—even the great Washington—the first *servant*." "The independent citizens of the United States," the *Independent Chronicle* asserted, "will never be deterred, from a manly censure on their servants." But an official is not only a servant; he is an employee, and "in case of mal-performance on his part, the people who *employ and pay him*, have a right not only to complain, but to punish; whereas, when he has done his best, he has done but that which is his duty."[81] Alternatively, the government official was characterized as a mere "substitute," a "tenant," and a "creature of the people."[82] Republicans, however, did more than merely expand their list of appropriate metaphors. They began to argue that scrutinizing the conduct of annually elected assemblymen, no less than executive officers and indirectly elected senators, was central to the nature of a *republican* press liberty.[83]

What, then, did a genuinely republican government require of the press? Most clearly, it demanded a concept of press liberty that was sufficiently broad as to make room for unrestrained exchange of political information and opinion; otherwise, the power of elections would be chimerical. In one of the relatively few critiques of the proposed stamp tax in 1792, a contributor to the *National Gazette* fleetingly made this connection, arguing that if the stamp tax left the people uninformed about their public servants' conduct, it would "make the ensuing general election not so satisfactory a touchstone of the public mind as it ought to have been." For one thing, elections would not be fair if, as under the Sedition Act, incumbents were protected from public criticism while candidates had no such protection. With a sedition law, "you in fact render [the people's] right of electing nugatory," Albert Gallatin admonished Congress. Thomas Cooper defended himself from seditious libel charges by asking "how the people can exercise on rational grounds their elective franchise, if perfect freedom of discussion of public characters be not allowed." For the Virginia jurist St. George Tucker, it was really quite simple: "Where *discussion* is *prohibited* or *restrained, responsibility vanishes.*"[84]

For Republicans, then, the "perfect freedom" of political discussion was a matter of actualizing a truly republican form of government. Yet their vision of republican press liberty went further still. Having established the need for continual citizen vigilance, even in a republic, nascent Jeffersonians built on the Anti-Federalist notion of ongoing, active participation. Not surprisingly, it was Madison who most eloquently combined the negative and positive features of a republican press freedom. In his "Virginia Report" of 1799, he defended the Virginia Assembly against criticism of its Resolutions opposing the Alien and Sedition Acts. Concerning any faulty governmental proceedings,

it is the duty was well as right of intelligent and faithful citizens, to discuss and promulge them freely, as well to control them by the censorship of the public opinion, as to promote a remedy according to the rules of the Constitution.[85]

Other Republicans saw a need to be very explicit that the people's positive contribution was more than a matter of electing public men. "In

Popular governments," wrote John Park, "*the People* have a direct influence on the measures of the administration, possessing the right to approve or condemn." "A TRUE AMERICAN" conceptualized the interconnection of absolute political press liberty, active citizenship, and republican government.

> The most unlimited disquisition, as to the conduct of public men in their official character is the only channel, thro which *real* knowledge can be diffused among the People. The theory of every Government really free, presupposes a continued appeal to the public understanding; and, in what manner, can this be made, except thro the *medium* of the Press?[86]

St. George Tucker and other partisans of the Jeffersonian cause took the further, final step of making absolute freedom of public, political expression—not mere elections—the sine qua non of popular government.

> True it is, that where that freedom [of political expression] be *abridged* or in any wise impaired the nature of government will instantly be changed from a representative democracy, in which the *people* are the *sovereign*, and those who administer the government their agents, to complete oligarchy, aristocracy, or monarchy.[87]

With this recognition of the essential character of continuous and unlimited popular scrutiny and sanction, one can see a recognizably modern discourse of democratic press liberty emerging.

The Other *Half of Democratic Press Liberty*

The notion of a continuous and active popular sovereignty gave the people the practical right, even the duty, of vigilant, democratic press liberty. This argument, however, only begged the question whether such a practice was pragmatically warranted. What if a good, popularly elected government could be undermined by a few vicious men and their libels, despite the otherwise continuing approbation of the people? Would not the public interest require investing government with some power to control these abuses of the press?

Conservatives of varying stripes, of course, had long made similar arguments, insisting that a licentious press was not only a disadvantage to government but a threat to liberty of the press, properly understood. But, as active popular sovereignty was realized on a relatively widespread scale, and as newspaper discourse proliferated, the argument seemed especially persuasive. An unrestrained press was particularly dangerous in an elective government, because artful demagogues could gain power by "falsely and deceitfully stealing the public opinion."[88]

The Truth Shall Probably Prevail

The traditional response to this argument, as we have seen, was the open press contention that the "truth will prevail." And, despite the changed context of an increasingly practical popular sovereignty, this well-worn notion was the Republicans' single most common retort, more prevalent even than the claim that an elective government required an unlimited political press. Republicans also appealed to the familiar corollary, insisting that good governments have nothing to fear from open debate; only tyranny needs protection.[89] The nascent Jeffersonians even extended these arguments, claiming that political virtue would prevail, even shine, from unrestricted examination. Writing as "Hortenius," the Virginia lawyer George Hay was confident that "truth, liberty, and virtue, must prevail in America." "Truth and merit are so far from tarnishing by examination, that they receive additional strength and lustre from the trial," "FRANKLIN" declared. "A sound character, therefore, will not be hurt by the strictest investigation."[90]

This elaboration of conventional notions had a significant amount of traditional appeal. But to men of both parties who had experienced the hurly-burly of political discourse in the 1770s, 1780s, and 1790s, these assertions began to sound hopeful at best and deliberately naïve at worst. Just as the Anti-Federalists conceded that the conquest of truth was too often late and even uncertain, the Republicans of the 1790s were circumspect about the progress of truth. "The sentiments of reason and truth will always ultimately prevail," John Thomson maintained, but he admitted adverse proceedings "may for a time be carried on."[91]

The Federalists were even less sanguine. Richard Buel, Jr., in his study of late-eighteenth-century free press discourse, concludes that "in effect, [the Republicans] assumed what the Federalists denied, that when ideas could compete freely true opinions would always triumph." This perhaps oversimplifies the Federalist position no less than the Republican.[92] Still, many Federalists looked at the "Jacobin" newspapers and despaired that truth would ever prevail. Senator Uriah Tracy certainly did, convinced that "the defamation and calumny of yesterday, circulated in the newspapers, out-travel the slow and tardy steps of truth."[93]

James Bayard, Tracy's Senate colleague, put the Federalist argument candidly. The belief that truth would prevail "was a fine moral sentiment, but our limited knowledge of events did not verify it." "Truth had power to prevail in the end," Bayard conceded. Yet, "before the victory was obtained by truth it often happened that much mischief was done by falsehood."[94] Perhaps no one felt as wounded by that mischief as Alexander Hamilton. Hamilton saw as central to the "Jacobin Scandal-Club" the maxim "that no character, however upright, is a match for constantly reiterated attacks, however false. It is well understood by its disciples that every calumny makes some proselytes, and even retains some; since justification seldom circulates as rapidly and as widely as slander."[95]

Faced with bald assertions that truth would *not* prevail, claims they themselves half-believed anyway, Republicans looked elsewhere to combat the claim that an unrestricted political press liberty would be dangerous even to a genuinely republican government. So they simply turned the argument on its head: Even if truth did not prevail, falsehood and error were not dangerous, at least not to government. "Where discussion is free, error ceases to be dangerous." Or, as Republican Congressman John Nicholas argued, it was the issuing press, not government, that suffered, "because falsehoods issued from a press, are not calculated to do any lasting mischief. Falsehoods will always depreciate the press from whence they proceed." With the expiration of the Sedition Act, John Thomson went so far as to say that errors let the truth "appear with increased lustre." Of course, it is Jefferson's phrasing that has proven most enduring:

> If there be any among us who would wish to dissolve this Union or to change its republican form, let them stand undisturbed, as monuments of the safety with which error of opinion may be tolerated where reason is left free to combat it.[96]

The Advantage of an Unrestrained Press

The Jeffersonians' arguments were not only a new twist on the "truth shall prevail" logic of traditional open press doctrine; they were further a modification of the Anti-Federalists' "advantage" argument. For, if falsehood and error truly were harmless, then even an ardent Federalist would have to concede the advantages of an unlimited, republican political press liberty. Federalists, not surprisingly, had no intention of conceding the argument regarding the advantages of press liberty. Or, more precisely, they praised the advantages of press *liberty* but were more concerned to explicate the egregious disadvantages of press *licentiousness*. Seizing on this longstanding distinction, Federalists time and again insisted that they were only trying to restrain a perilously licentious press. Rejecting the Virginia Resolutions, the Massachusetts Legislature maintained that "the constitutional right of the citizen to utter and publish the truth, is not to be confounded with the licentiousness in speaking and writing, that is only employed in propagating falsehood and slander."[97]

The response to this traditional argument was almost as longstanding: The distinction was practically untenable.[98] Even Federalist officials employed this argument shortly before the Sedition Act crisis. When the French foreign minister, Charles-Maurice de Talleyrand-Périgord, complained of the treatment the French were getting in the Federalist press, the American envoys said that, though press "licentiousness is seen and lamented," "the remedy has not yet been discovered[;] perhaps it is an evil inseparable from the good with which it is allied: perhaps it is a shoot which cannot be stripped from the stalk, without wounding vitally the plant from which it is torn."[99] Republicans doggedly maintained that the distinction was "impossible," or, at the very least, "difficult." Liberty and licentiousness "cannot be separated." "Some degree of abuse is inseparable from the proper use of everything," Madison explained. Then, deftly echoing the envoy's response, he claimed that it "has accordingly been decided by the practice of the states, that it is better to leave a few of its noxious branches to their luxuriant growth, than by pruning them away, to injure the vigour of those yielding the proper fruits."[100]

Having established—at least to their own satisfaction—that a genuinely republican political press liberty had to be assessed in its totality, warts and all, the Republicans took recourse to the Anti-Federalists' contention that an unrestricted political press was ultimately an advantage, if not an unmitigated blessing. Though this argument had been elaborated only a decade earlier, it had roots deep in the radical Whig tradition. Indeed, the *Bee* made this claim by paraphrasing *Cato's Letters* (with adaptations but without attribution). The *Bee* need not have looked so far afield for eloquent adherents of this view; there were contemporary champions, Madison again chief among them: "To the press alone, chequered as it is with abuses, the world is indebted for all the triumphs which have been gained by reason and humanity, over error and oppression."[101] Eloquence aside, it was by arguing that error did little or no harm that one could assert the aggregate benefits of unrestricted press liberty. As one Republican polemicist put it in the New York *Timepiece*, "suppose even that the supercilious pride of men in place, should sometimes be slightly wounded; is that a reason for depriving the human race of the mine of knowledge[?]"[102]

Overt Acts Only

Nascent Jeffersonians had laid the conceptual groundwork for the claim that only overt acts of violence or sedition should be criminal in a republic. They did this by arguing, first, for the essential nature of unrestricted political press liberty to a genuinely republican popular sovereignty and, second, for the relatively trivial and easily mitigated harm of an intemperate press. To be sure, actual breaches of the peace would still be punished in America, but anything less could and must be tolerated.

To Federalists, this was outright heresy. The false, scandalous, and malicious sentiments of a seditious libel had a "direct tendency" to breach the peace. And, in any event, such libels undermined the "confidence" the people should have in elected officials. Even the rare conservative Republican, like the haughty Federalist-turned-Republican Thomas McKean, held to this view. McKean, of course, had been a stalwart advocate of seditious libel law since at least the first Oswald trial in the early 1780s, and he had been hanged and burned in effigy by Anti-Federalists, and later by Democratic-Republicans, as a dangerous elitist.[103] In a case prior to the Sedition Act crisis, McKean candidly explained traditional common law doctrine to a Pennsylvania grand jury in a vain attempt to indict the avid Federalist William Cobbett. "The direct tendency of these libels is the breach of public peace which it would be impossible to restrain by the severest laws, were there no redress from public justice for injuries of this kind." For congressional Federalists, this logic was self-evident. "If gentlemen would agree" that acts such as sedition were criminal, Harrison Otis asserted, "it follows that all means calculated to produce these effects, whether by speaking, writing, or printing, were also criminal." This was true, as Judge Alexander Addison explained in his oft-reprinted grand jury charge, because seditious libels "have a direct tendency, differing only in degree from force."

Once the Federalists had candidly maintained that the difference between physical and verbal violence was a difference not of kind but only of degree, it was but a small step to equating the two. The Federalists took this philosophical step in the most public and authoritative manner possible. The Select Committee charged with reviewing the myriad public petitions for repeal of the Alien and Sedition Acts reported back to the House: "As the liberty of speech does not authorize a man to speak malicious slanders against his neighbor, nor [does] the liberty of action justify him . . . in assaulting any person whom he may meet in the streets."[104] As soon as the Federalists had equated liberty of expression with liberty of action, character assassination was tantamount to corporeal assassination. Radical Republicans like Matthew Lyon, however, could scarcely begin to comprehend the equation.[105]

Drawing from their "advantage" argument, their contention that error was virtually harmless given free discussion, and their conviction that the press's abuses could not be safely trimmed away, the Republicans advanced press liberty discourse by arguing that only overt acts could be punishable in a republic. To the argument that the press would then be abused, they replied, "Wretched subterfuge. Is not every thing abused? . . . As long as Government performs its functions entire, and undisturbed by actual opposition, this is all that in the nature of things it has a right to expect. Opinion is nothing, if it be not accompanied by an overt act." As early as 1796, Republicans were professing that "it is sufficient for the laws of a Republic, to restrain from violence the conduct and actions of its citizens." To the Republican mind, of course, "there can be no doubt" that the government would always have plenty of defenders, and, as they often repeated, actual insurrections remained punishable.[106]

To the Federalists' "direct tendency" argument, the very backbone of traditional seditious libel law, the Republicans responded with derision. Sarcastically extending Otis's argument, George Hay asserted that, "under this system of reasoning," since the government criminalizes murder, "it would have of course a right to punish an insult, because insults lead to quarrels, and quarrels to murder." Criticism of public men and measures exists "without the most remote design" to actual sedition. In fact, it was not any alleged seditious libel that had a dangerous tendency, one Republican lawyer argued; it was rather "the tendency of measures, which are adopted to correct it" that is menacing.[107]

Perhaps John Thomson best summarizes the Republicans' innovative view of absolute political press liberty.

> Political opinions never can be destructive of social order, or public tranquility, if allowed a free operation. The law is at all times sufficiently energetic to punish disturbers of the public peace. When men are found guilty of this, let them be punished; it is well. It is not then punishing *opinion*, it is punishing actions injurious to the peace of the community.[108]

The nascent Jeffersonians had already conceptualized and defended the genuinely republican *right* to an active, critical, and unrestricted political press liberty. But if this right could be exercised, should it be? Republicans resoundingly answered in the affirmative. With their newly developed "overt acts" argument, the Republicans were not only refuting the perennial claim that such a press had a "direct tendency" to breach the peace or undermine the government, but also vindicating their democratic conception of press liberty.

A Modern Concept of Press Liberty

The partisans of Jefferson and Madison were not only formulating a decidedly democratic notion of press liberty during the 1790s; they were conceptualizing a *modern* press liberty, as well. Though largely neglected in the secondary literature on press liberty, this characteristic of the Republicans' novel conception was part of a philosophical revolution at the very core of the dispute between Federalists and their opponents. This transformation involved competing understandings of the power of popular opinion and the nature of truth. Gordon Wood has recently explained this shift by arguing that, while the Federalists adhered to the established notion that there is a constant, universal, and discoverable truth, nascent Jeffersonians, to the contrary, were beginning to develop the notion that the "truth was actually the creation of many voices and many minds, no one of which was more important than another."[109]

Though this characterization aptly captures the practical, modernizing effect of the conceptual evolution under way, it obscures the actual philosophical claims that gave rise to this change. Republicans of the 1790s were not so much repudiating universal truth as marginalizing it. In reaction to the Federalists' Sedition Law, and specifically its allowance of truth as a defense, the Republicans elaborated their novel distinction between facts and opinion. While American adherents of the Scottish Enlightenment were trying to make a science of politics, many Republicans argued that the domain of universal political truths was small, including "mere" facts that were rarely decisive to the discourse of a genuinely sovereign, republican people. It was instead political opinions that mattered, and it was ultimately the "public opinion" that was the great arbiter. Regarding those types of political discourse that Federalists would call seditious libel, Republicans argued that "very few of them will probably ever relate to mere matters of fact." "Matters of opinion admit of no other proof than the argument by which they are supported," concluded a memorial from Suffolk County, New York.[110]

For Judge Samuel Chase and other Federalists, this distinction between fact and opinion was a "departure from common sense." To the Federalist insistence that "opinions may be false," Republicans answered that such a view was "absurd." "An opinion may be incorrect." By 1800, the *Bee* claimed that it printed matters *"all neither wholly false, nor wholly true."*[111]

Republican arguments notwithstanding, Federalists insisted that opinions could be false, and, as the 1790s proceeded, it seemed to many of them that the opinion most likely to be furthest from the truth was "public opinion." More important, by the mid-1790s, popular opinion was becoming the dominant force in the politics of the new Republic. Capitalizing on the abrupt shift in popular opinion in favor of their Jay Treaty during 1796, Federalists used this public approbation to win necessary funding for the treaty in Congress. John Fenno immediately rebuked his Federalist allies for such behavior. "The recent appeal to the people by the friends of the Constitution . . . has been irregular; it is all improper; it is an extraneous influence, unknown to the regular governmental proceedings."[112]

Fenno need not have worried; this was a unique aberration. As Elkins and McKitrick point out, Federalists did not "have much taste for pandering to the multitude, and they frequently said so." The proper role for Federalists was rather Burkean: "not to mirror public opinion but to lead and correct it." Indeed, ardent Federalists mocked a moderate colleague because he tended to "quote the [people's] opinions as an evidence of truth."[113]

Republicans, as we have seen, were dubious that there were any simple political "truths." But, if there were any, public opinion was not merely evidence for it; it was the *principal* evidence for it. Public opinion could not be corrected so much as informed. The aim of republican press liberty was precisely that: to inform the whole people so that they might collectively choose the proper approach to any given political issue. Human nature, of course, was imperfect, and so even popular opinion would not be "infallibly correct." But, for John Park, this only elevated "the absolute necessity of giving to popular sentiment the highest possible degree of intelligence." Charles Holt concurred; newspapers in a republic must "contain the most useful and important information for all ranks and conditions of men." In turn, "the people *read, scan* and *spell out* all the truth," despite attempts to deceive them.[114]

Ultimately, the Republicans were arguing, they "knew of no such thing" as "slanders against the Government." The only response to political criticism was "to disprove it," "by the force of reason," and "let the public judge."[115] "Let the presses stand on the footing of equality, and the good sense and virtue of the people will decide between them." With sufficient discussion, one Republican explained, "it is never difficult for common sense to recognize Truth." By 1801, even pamphlets remarkable for their "unusual . . . temperateness" concluded that, where political issues were concerned, "there can be no standard, besides that of the public opinion."[116]

The Discourse of Modern Democratic Press Liberty

With the marginalization of political "truths" that were "mere facts," and with the conceptualization of public opinion as the final authority on political legitimacy, a recognizably modern concept of democratic press liberty had emerged. A crucial step in that process was a robustly developed, theoretical repudiation of the legal concept of seditious libel. Time and again during the eighteenth century, printers, lawyers, gentlemen, and commoners advocated increasingly broad understandings of political press liberty. Yet they rarely assaulted the very idea of seditious libel. To be sure, most were reluctant to take such a radical stance, believing that some controls on seemingly dangerous words were necessary. Others, no doubt, might have taken this stand had they been forced to do so; yet they were often able to achieve the widening of press liberty they immediately required by taking a less extreme, and therefore less threatening, position.

Substantiating political press liberty in the new republic allowed no such room for equivocation. And, once lines were drawn, as they were with the Sedition Act, the rhetorical pressure to elaborate a concept of press liberty that explicitly undermined seditious libel was intense. Some of the more radical adherents of the emerging Jeffersonian party took up the task of arguing that the government simply cannot be criminally assaulted by words. Actual insurrections and instigations to immediate violence were punishable in the Republic, but seditious libel could not be. To begin with, they conceded that government might be harmed by words but argued that such injury would be minimal, even if the words were false, scandalous, and malicious. Drawing on recent Anti-Federalist advances, the Republicans of the 1790s insisted that such harm was also far outweighed by the good to the community. In addition, criticisms that were false, scandalous, or malicious could be easily contradicted by truthful vindications, since a republican people would be able to examine and judge properly. Americans of all ranks could be trusted with the incisive weapon of unlimited political press liberty. Finally, there really was no choice in the matter, for the universally exalted features of press liberty—the exchange of ideas, the advance of knowledge, even the respectful appraisal of government—were inseparable from the vituperation of press "licentiousness." In the final analysis, only overt *acts* should be punishable in order to allow public discourse to follow its virtuous, if not pristine, path.

Yet there was more to formulating a modern concept of democratic press liberty than merely the absolute denial of seditious libel. Repudiation is a decidedly negative process. The radical thinkers in the first decade of the First Amendment were more broadly concerned with elaborating a more constructive notion of press liberty, one that made room for popular government. This concept of democratic press liberty required, first, the contention that it is the right of a sovereign people not merely to elect but to scrutinize and criticize vigorously their public servants. The nascent Jeffersonians developed the additional understanding that it is essential to democratic government that public opinion continually and ultimately act as the standard of political right. Finally, they argued that public opinion and political "truths" of any significance are the creation of many diverse and oft-colliding sentiments; it is thus necessary that citizens of all ranks contribute to that discourse. While they did not deny the existence of universal truth, Republicans were far more skeptical of such a notion than their Federalist countrymen; they accordingly argued that practical, political truths were accessible to, indeed created by, the aggregated citizenry. In contrast to the British monarchical tradition they had inherited, early Americans had now—for better or for worse—crowned public opinion king.[117]

Federalists no less than Republicans were stepping into the future while inevitably looking to the past. Federalists sought to preserve from the recent past the notion of a hierarchical order, ruled for the people by the "right sort" of men. For them, the future had arrived with the institution of a representative polity in which almost all significant governmental officials were answerable to the people directly or indirectly. For the Republicans, the future was only now in the making. Their future too would be built on a notion from the past, that of the constantly vigilant people, ever watchful of governmental power. The future lay in realizing popular government, meaning not only an expanded political class but also an adaptation of traditional vigilance to include all of the people's servants, all of the time.

Given their view of the future, the Republicans argued that seditious libel law made elections meaningless. Yet, ironically, it was the first election after the widespread use of the Sedition Act that proved most significant for their view of republican—or, as it was now increasingly called, "democratic"—government. In the "Revolution of 1800," "the political nation had spoken resoundingly for Jefferson," and Jeffersonian versions of popular government and press liberty.[118] It was this revolution that provided the founding for a broader, more participatory democratic politics, as well as the modern concept of press liberty that went with it.

Conclusion
The Foundation of American Press Liberty

The emergence of a recognizably modern concept of democratic press liberty was the culmination of more than a century and a half of conceptual and political struggle, development, and redefinition. Capitalizing on the first experience of de facto freedom of the press in the Anglophone world, the English radicals of the 1640s employed a variety of arguments to challenge and revise the customary limits on free expression. They held that Truth would prevail, claimed the parliamentarian's right to free speech, indicated that a free press would check government, and suggested that only overt acts should be punishable. Though some of these contentions would prove their staying power decades later, the radicals' ideas would all but disappear for half a century.

With the end of censorship, Diests and radicals such as Matthew Tindal defended against the return of licensing by forcing these more expansive understandings of press liberty back into political discourse, recasting and honing the arguments in the process. Trenchard and Gordon further refined the discourse of press liberty in reaction to libel laws that threatened subsequent punishment, resulting in the emergence of the free and open press tradition. Cato's discourse simultaneously defended a press open to sentiments on all sides of an issue and maintained that the people's liberty was the one concern to which all others must be sacrificed.

This ambivalent tradition of thought was exploited by colonial Americans who sought a widening of the range of acceptable comment in public discourse. At once contributing to and benefiting from the popularization of government, the discourse of the free and open press was used to argue for an end to criminal punishment for expression. The growth of general verdicts in libel cases and the developing distinction between the public lives and the private characters of government officials proved to be crucial steps in the transformation of press liberty in the pre-Revolutionary, Revolutionary, and Founding eras.

All of these changes were necessary for the development of modern democratic press liberty; they were not, however, sufficient for such a development. Behind much recent free speech theory and First Amendment jurisprudence lie three fundamental claims that, I argue, make up the modern concept of democratic press liberty; all three reveal their roots in the free and open press. Inherent in our concept of modern democratic press liberty is the claim that a comprehensive liberty of political expression—not mere elections—is essential to genuinely democratic government. Drawing on the free press ideal of an ever-vigilant people checking their public servants through the press, many figures in the decade after passage of the First Amendment argued that a representative government instantly and unavoidably became an oligarchy with any abridgement of free political expression.

The second element crucial to the modern understanding of press liberty is the claim that only overt acts—not expression—should be punishable. Central to this claim is a sophisticated view of the open press declaration that the truth shall prevail. Americans of all political stripes had, by the 1790s, come to realize that truth does not always prevail, at least not for significantly long periods. Nevertheless, Jeffersonians maintained that the disservice done by faulty information was minimal when compared to the damage done to valid dialogue by legal efforts to excise falsity. The modern democratic impulse rests on the belief that democracy is, in many respects, the worst kind of political system *except for all the others*. Similarly, modern democratic free press discourse concedes that criminalizing only overt acts permits falsity to do its harm but contends that any attempt to outlaw falsity risks doing even more serious injury to the accuracy and robustness of public discourse.

The third and final underlying tenet of our modern concept of democratic press liberty is the belief that public opinion is the authoritative measure of political legitimacy. Conceding that they printed things *"neither wholly false, nor wholly true,"*[1] many Jeffersonian printers and theorists argued that political "truths"—if any existed—were few and rudimentary and therefore rarely pivotal in deciding public debate. In keeping with their unprecedented faith in the *demos*, these radical theorists maintained that there could be no other ultimate standard in public life but public opinion. It is this faith that made the new concept of press liberty at once modern, democratic, and distinctively American.

A Theorist of Modern Democratic Press Liberty

The modern concept of democratic press liberty was the work of no one person. By fits and starts, as circumstances shifted and as theoretical assertions were attacked or ignored, conceptual changes both great and small were introduced, often only semiconsciously, by a vast array of patrician and plebeian thinkers. Nevertheless, one man personifies the emergence of modern democratic press liberty and thus serves as the spokesman for press freedom as Jeffersonian Republicans faced the new century.

The New York lawyer Tunis Wortman has received little attention in most recent free press history. Levy, to his credit, called Wortman's treatise on press freedom "the preeminent American classic," "the book that Jefferson did not write but should have."[2] But Levy also claimed that the libertarian theories of the Sedition Act crisis unexpectedly appeared, almost without precedent. In their welcome efforts to dispel this misinterpretation, both Jeffery Smith and David Rabban stress earlier developments and other thinkers, scarcely discussing Wortman at all.[3] As we have seen, Wortman had many conceptual and theoretical precedents on which to draw, and he was hardly alone in responding to the Federalist view of free expression. Yet Wortman took the existing arguments the furthest, thus providing the epitome of a comprehensive, explicit, and coherent discourse of modern democratic press liberty.[4]

Though Wortman was a lawyer and a devoted partisan of Jeffersonian politics, his contribution to the press controversy of the Sedition Act era was remarkably lacking in legal forensics and partisan vitriol, two commodities amply supplied in most opposition literature. Instead, he tended to be more abstract and circumspect. "There is no natural right more perfect or more absolute," Wortman maintained, "than that of investigating every subject which concerns us." To government he would have us declare, "'You have no legitimate empire over opinion.'" Thus, if there is no actual public injury, there should be no law. "If our conduct is not injurious, it is immoral to interpose the shackles of restriction. Every unnecessary law is . . . an infringement of the rights of personal liberty and judgment." Wortman further asserted that the advantages of an unlimited political press are clear: Misrepresentations are less dangerous than public prosecutions for libel, and knowledge is "a more powerful corrective than coercion." Ultimately, only overt acts should be punished. Government's authority should be constantly interposed to prevent violence and crimes and never exerted to restrain that circulation of knowledge and sentiment which is essential to general improvement.[5]

But the abstract right to unlimited press liberty was not enough. Wortman knew that exercising such a right would be deemed imprudent if the people were not able to exercise it wisely. "Little would be gained by a most decisive victory in the argument, unless it should be equally evident, that *abilities* may reside in society, adequate to the formation of a correct and pertinent opinion." Like most Republicans, Wortman had considerable confidence in the people, as is implicit in the view that even willful misrepresentations would do little harm because the people could sift out the "correct" opinion.[6] The New York lawyer, however, went further to elucidate the connection between the people's capacities and the Republicans' changing view of truth, that modernizing element too often overlooked in the secondary literature. "Whatever may be the abstract nature of truth, its evidences are capable of equal presentation to the percipient powers of all men." "Whether it relates to principles or facts, it is to be discovered and ascertained by judgment; and judgment is a faculty possessed in common by mankind." Wortman felt the whole merit of his treatise was contained in this proposition.[7]

Wortman also conceptualized the relationship between public opinion and representative government. In a chapter whose running title is "Freedom of Enquiry Essential to Representative Governments," Wortman argues that "if my suffrage is requested in favor of any individual, it is my duty to enquire" into his conduct and character.[8] But he again went further than most Republicans to elaborate on the process through which individual investigation and reflection relates to public opinion. "By Public Opinion," Wortman explained, "we are to understand that general determination of private understandings which is most extensively predominant," "an aggregation of individual sentiment." Ultimately, "the opinion of the majority is to be deemed the general opinion."[9]

Individual reflection and community deliberation combine, for Wort-

man, to create an aggregate majority sentiment that *is* the "public opinion." "In proportion as investigation continues free and unrestricted, the
mass of error will be subject to continual diminution, and the determina-
tions of distinct understandings will gradually harmonize." The result is
"public opinion," and, "with relation to government, public opinion is
omnipotent."[10] Public opinion not only directs and controls government,
Wortman maintained; it also controls its own extremes. "Public Opinion
will always possess sufficient discernment and authority to curb its tendency towards licentiousness."[11] In the end, unlimited democratic political expression takes the contributions of diverse, sometimes extreme
views and creates public opinion.

> The collision produced will be favorable to the eventual reception of
> Truth. The heresy of Sectarists will be sure of becoming vanquished in
> such a state of intellectual fervor and activity; and Society, at length, hav-
> ing heard the arguments, and examined the pretensions of both parties,
> will finally decide the controversy.[12]

During the late 1790s, Americans heard the arguments and examined
the pretensions of both parties. And, with the Jeffersonian's electoral
"Revolution of 1800," society decided the Sedition Act controversy.

The Forgotten Years

The Sedition Act controversy would not be the last press liberty struggle, of course. The Republican development of a recognizably modern
concept of democratic press liberty did not instantly establish it as the
indisputable standard. Indeed, more traditional and less libertarian understandings of press liberty would remain dominant throughout the
nineteenth century, the "forgotten years" of First Amendment scholarship.[13] What's more, Republicans would play a conspicuous role in the
maintenance of conventional elements of the law of seditious libel.

The most notorious example of Republicans not adhering to the nascent modern conception of press liberty is undoubtedly that of Thomas
Jefferson's own letter to Governor Thomas McKean (19 February
1803). Jefferson argued that the Federalists, having lost their Sedition
Act, had been seeking to undermine the press by making it so full of lies
that it no longer had any credit with the public. To restore its credibil-
ity, the president suggested "a few [state] prosecutions of the most

prominent offenders."[14] Jefferson's request that his words be kept "entirely confidential" give the letter a sinister tone. But, in fact, Jefferson publicly expressed the same spirit in his Second Inaugural, in which he said that state officials who can afford the time might well use the "salutary coercions of the law" to correct the falsehood and defamation of the press.[15]

Contrary to Wortman's writings but in keeping with Jefferson's provisos, state officials pursued a few Federalist printers in the courts. The cases against partners Barzillai Hudson and Thomas Goodwin, in Connecticut, and Joseph Dennie, in Pennsylvania, ultimately came to nothing. The seditious libel conviction of Harry Croswell, printer of the Hudson, New York, *Wasp*, however, laid the groundwork for the nineteenth-century dominance of a modified form of the Zengerian principles of truth as a defense and the jury's right to a general verdict. The case is also replete with ironic twists. The staunch Jeffersonian Chief Justice Morgan Lewis, in his role as trial judge, refused the defense opportunity to prove the truth of the *Wasp*'s attack on Jefferson; furthermore, he instructed the jury that truth was no defense and that they could find only a special verdict, leaving to the bench the determination of whether the words were libelous.

Heightening the irony, it was none other than Alexander Hamilton who defended Croswell, on appeal, against this pre-Zengerian interpretation of the common law of seditious libel. Hamilton's apt defense speech espoused modified Zengerian principles and ultimately divided the Court. Thus divided, the Court could not award Croswell a new trial, but his Republican prosecutors shrewdly dropped the case. In contrast, Hamilton's victory outside of court was unconditional. The New York legislature soon passed a libel law giving the jury uncontestable authority to find a general verdict and making truth a justification *if* "published with good motives and for justifiable ends."[16] This Hamiltonian standard was thus a *weakening* of the Zengerian principles that even the Sedition Act had not watered down. Nevertheless, this interpretation of libel became the model for laws in many states throughout the nineteenth century.[17]

As we are by now well aware, such legal precepts are seldom a sure guide to actual practice, though recent research suggests that restrictive laws were occasionally enforced.[18] Nevertheless, the Madison administration established that a modern, democratic conception of press liberty could be actualized in nineteenth-century America. Whereas the patriots in the Revolutionary War and Federalists in the "Quasi-War" with France had thought nothing of using press restrictions to silence their adversaries, Republicans in the War of 1812 tried nothing of the sort. As Drew McCoy explains,

> although few Presidents have been subjected to so much personal invective and abuse, [Madison] never hinted at measures abridging freedom of speech or press, even in the face of rampant obstruction of his government's policies and countless cases of outright treason in the "eastern states" of New England.[19]

Yet if Madison provides a heroic example of the modern democratic press liberty that Wortman's *Treatise* advanced and epitomized, the fact remains that the nineteenth century was a long period in which this newly fashioned understanding of press liberty was the minority view. Elements of the new, modern concept would reappear now and again throughout the century, at times in conspicuous places. St. George Tucker would become the "American Blackstone," and his edition of the *Commentaries*—complete with its thirty-page appendix defending the new American concept of press liberty—would become the standard legal text for a generation of lawyers.[20] Midcentury libertarians like Frederick Grimké would give rise to the conservative libertarianism of late-century thinkers such as the famed jurist Thomas Cooley.[21] Nevertheless, these ideas remained subordinate. Just as the Levellers' arguments lay fallow for decades after their emergence in the 1640s, so too would the modern concept of democratic press liberty have to await broader renewal. This fact, however, only provides evidence, if any more were needed, that conceptual change does not guarantee the dominance of the new conceptualization.

A Persistent Tradition

In retrospect, Wortman's *Treatise* surely is the most articulate exposition of the modern concept of press liberty to emerge in the aftermath of the Sedition Act. Not only does the *Treatise* embody the founding of the American tradition of democratic press liberty; it also points forward to an America of partisan politics and individual rights. Indeed, there certainly were two parties now, despite the Federalists' insistence to the contrary. This new partisanship, however, did not seem ominous to Wortman. "Associations may be rendered subservient to the particular views of sectaries or factions. Admitted. Their opponents will have the same right and the same spirit of association." Instead of fearing parties, Wortman valued "diversity of sentiment," because "it produces Collision, engenders Argument, and . . . corrects our errors."[22]

Wortman's text also serves to highlight the developing hegemony of a stress on individual rights, interests, and sentiments, an emphasis we would characterize as "liberal." As we observed in earlier chapters, these ideas took shape during the debate over the Constitution and the Bill of Rights. These issues took center stage in Wortman's book when he wrote of "personal liberty and judgment." The right of unlimited press freedom left the individual at liberty to reflect alone and to deliberate in society. In turn, "private understandings" and "individual sentiment" would be "aggregated" into public opinion.

Jefferson apparently would have concurred with Wortman's view, for Jefferson reportedly said "that the public good is best promoted by the exertion of each individual seeking his own good in his own way." Gordon Wood takes such a claim to mark the end of classical republicanism and the beginning of liberal democracy.[23] Yet Wortman, as modern as he is, provides us with reason to be skeptical about *any* end to the critical role of community norms and civic duties. A modern thinker, he believed—no less than Jefferson—that "the moral system of the universe has in reality wisely united general good with individual interest." "True virtue," Wortman explained, does not require that "men should become totally detached from themselves." For "the same conduct which ensures our own substantial good, shall also contribute to the general benefit of mankind." But, for Wortman, "our natural and social existence presents a system of continual duties." My individual rights and interests notwithstanding,

> it is not indifferent to Morality whether I conceal the perceptions of Truth within the dungeon of Solicitude, or whether I apply its evidences to remove the errors of my companion. We are not entitled to waste our hours in lethargic inexertion.

Rather, "it is incumbent upon me . . . to exercise my faculties for the production of the greatest sum of good."[24] Even as he was conceptualizing a novel, "liberal" view of democratic politics and press liberty, Wortman could not altogether abandon "republican" norms and obligations. Perhaps neither can we.

Whether the "republican" norms of early America continued to influence the concepts that inhabit early-twenty-first-century America is a question this book has not directly addressed. Certainly, our study of early American conceptions of press liberty suggests that the power of republican notions did not end with the turn of the century. Rather, we have seen that "liberal" and "republican" ideas and ideals functioned in a vague unity during much of the eighteenth century. Moreover, that ambiguous tradition belies the ends/means distinction recently posited by Michael Zuckert. In fact, the evidence presented here demonstrates a longstanding interdependence—simultaneously in theory and in practice—between the individual rights holder and the duty-bound community member. This complex interrelationship was embodied in the open press conception that emerged, became pivotal, and was transformed in the period analyzed here. Most critically, open press doctrine philosophically defended every citizen's right to air his sentiments on any side of an issue, leaving it to others to weigh their merits. But the press was open to each individual's sentiments only because another individual's private property—a printer's press and his newspaper—was thought of as a communal good, something the printer was beholden to make available to the community as the primary institution of an expanding public sphere.

The complex nature of eighteenth-century American discourse over freedom of expression demonstrates the reductionism inherent in the binary debate between "liberal" and "republican" interpretations of early American political discourse. Because the concept of press liberty provides a revealing window into this discourse, we have seen not only that the longstanding interdependence between "liberal" and "republican" notions must be analyzed; we have further seen that other strains of thought, for example, monarchical theory or Protestant theology, played notable roles in the development of early American political thought. Ultimately, these findings show how important it is that we move beyond the academic "liberal/republican" debate to analyze concrete debates in early America.

Our examination of the actual eighteenth-century debates over press liberty has provided a means for making sense of the contrary bodies of evidence provided by the free speech historian Leonard Levy and his "libertarian" critics. This was made possible by a conceptual history that revealed and elucidated the central dynamic of early American press liberty discourse: two rival doctrines evolving within one shared tradition. This history, in turn, illuminates the interdependence between the founding of democratic press liberty and the development of a public sphere of unprecedented (if still sorely limited) depth and breadth. Finally, the recourse to actual disputes taken here also provides us with a more nuanced sense of the political thought of the Founding and Early Republic. For instance, *pace* Wood, Jeffersonians at the turn of the century were not so much arguing that absolute truth was created by the people as they were contending that, because genuinely knowable truths were few and rarely decisive, the ultimate standard for significant community affairs in a democratic republic must be public opinion.

Epilogue

The conceptual history presented here has sought to advance our understanding of early American political thought in general, and specifically early American theories of press liberty and popular government. But we often turn to history not only for a richer comprehension of our past but also for a better grasp of the present and a clearer sense of the future. Conceptual history is especially important in this regard, for only if we know the limits and potentials of the concepts that shape our political language can we fulfill the promise of our politics.

Capitalizing on that promise requires that we avoid idealizing the similarities between our current predicaments and a two-centuries-old founding that we can understand only after considerable historical labor. To be sure, we continue to echo the language of a free and open press when we respond to political conflict with calls for "free and open debate." And some of the Jeffersonian Republicans' arguments are still with us in remarkably similar form. For example, the Supreme Court's adherence to the "overt-acts" doctrine is evident in the continuing dominance of variations of the "clear and present danger test": Government can punish speech only if it constitutes "incitement to imminent lawless action."[25] The Court has thus calibrated the overt-acts doctrine to recognize that on rare occasions speech can be so "brigaded with action" that a strict policy of punishing only overt acts may be imprudent.[26] Concerning other free expression claims, however, the connection with the foundation of the tradition is much more extenuated. The Freedom of Information Act may well echo the people's "RIGHT

TO KNOW" that Sam Adams's *Independent Advertiser* claimed,[27] but he would find incomprehensible the impunity with which the lurid details of public figures' private lives are circulated.

Conspicuous similarities and disjunctures notwithstanding, there are more nuanced ways in which a tradition founded at the turn of the nineteenth century defines the character of free expression discourse even as we enter the twenty-first. Two of the most powerful challenges to conventional First Amendment thinking to emerge in the past quarter century have addressed the provocative issues of pornography and racist "hate speech." The work of the law professors Catharine A. MacKinnon and Charles R. Lawrence III evince some of the most cogent theorizing to confront the absolutist notion that the only response to dangerous speech is more speech. Yet, despite their thoroughgoing critiques of a patriarchal and racist society, both legal theorists draw on the persistent tension at the core of a press liberty tradition that evolved from the free and open press: the conflict between the community and the individual. Emphasizing the "victim's story," these theorists examine the claim that offensive speech must be tolerated for the greater good of the community, an inviolable freedom of expression. But which individuals bear the burden of this toleration? In answering this question, Lawrence explicitly appeals to democratic values forged in the Stamp Act crisis:

> Whenever we decide that racist hate speech must be tolerated because of the importance of tolerating unpopular speech, we ask Blacks and other subordinated groups to bear a burden for the good of society—to pay the price for the societal benefit of creating more room for speech. And we assign this burden to them without seeking their advice or consent. . . . It is taxation without representation.[28]

These radical leaders of the Critical Race Theory and antipornography movements also "march backward into battle"[29]—that is, appeal to established justifications even as they try to legitimate iconoclastic theories—when they address the now-standard free expression argument that more, not less, speech allows for the truth-finding function of the democratic public sphere. Though this argument may have its most famous expression in John Stuart Mill's *On Liberty*, we have seen that it has deep and broad roots in eighteenth-century American political discourse. Both MacKinnon and Lawrence challenge the "laissez-faire" or "marketplace" ideal.[30] Lawrence perhaps takes this line of reasoning furthest, contending that systemic racism makes this "marketplace" "dysfunctional" in both directions: first, by muting or silencing the ideas of minority group members and, second, by distorting white people's reception of those ideas.[31] He concludes by echoing values and arguments that contributed to the founding of modern American democratic press liberty:

> I do not believe that truth will prevail in a rigged game or in a contest where the referees are on the payroll of the proponents of falsity. The argument that good speech ultimately drives out bad speech rests on a false premise unless those of us who fight racism are vigilant and unequivocal in that fight.[32]

Here, Lawrence's language most clearly echoes—I presume unintentionally—the New York printer John Holt's free press insistence that ministerial influence made a "fair hearing" impossible.[33] Lawrence, like Holt before him, fears that an open press insistence on individual freedom of expression will undermine precisely the public good that free press doctrine seeks to protect. After two centuries, the concept of democratic press liberty analyzed in these pages continues to outline the contours of our free speech tradition.

It is my contention, moreover, that the form of conceptual history pursued here does more than reveal the historical roots and current influence of our modern concepts. It also leaves us well placed to reflect critically on the ways in which other contextual factors occasion our current First Amendment controversies. For example, just as we saw how the economic and demographic contexts contributed to open press doctrine in the 1720s and 1730s, we can now better perceive how professional standards, as well as economic and technological forces, weigh into contemporary media politics.

The norm in our cities of having a single major daily newspaper that espouses "objectivity" and provides an opinion page open to all is reminiscent of its colonial precursor, but new journalistic standards have altered our conception of press liberty—to the detriment of democracy. As we have seen, the notion of impartiality, a traditional mainstay of open press doctrine, was coming under direct and indirect attack as early as the late 1790s. Two centuries later, the analogous standard is that of "objectivity." The difference is subtle but momentous. Journalists, reacting to accusations that they are "soft" or biased, have responded by asking the "tough" questions (i.e., those concerning hidden political tactics) and stressing the (seemingly) most objective news (e.g., polling data). And, as has been widely bemoaned, democratic politics has thus been depicted as a "horse-race."[34]

The message here is unmistakable, but this should not surprise us. Permitting early-eighteenth-century contributors to use Latin phrases, Roman pseudonyms, and classical references sent a subtle but effective message of the exclusivity of public discourse; just as effectively, the *Independent Advertiser*'s promise to describe "foreign parts" to "Gentlemen and others" sent the countervailing, inclusive message.[35] Similarly, by depicting politics as a horse race, "objective" journalists construct a public life in which there can only be a few "players." The rest of us must be mere spectators, and spectators, whether animated or lethargic, are powerless. Indeed, even the critical reflection on this "game" is left to "commentators" who analyze the political tactics, rather than the public good.[36]

Of course, the established press has never been the only medium of public discourse, even if it has traditionally been the most central. Happily, the emergence of communication technologies of unprecedented public accessibility—from electronic mail to desktop publishing— promises remarkably numerous and unobstructed avenues for discourse. Yet, awash as we are in this sea of expression, the problem is no longer one of having a voice; it is the likelihood of having that voice drowned out by others. Citizens searching for an opportunity to air their sentiments no longer work to combat suppression but strain to merit our attention. This dynamic clearly advantages the sensational over the thoughtful and thus all those with the economic wherewithal to dress their political messages in "entertainment value" and saturate the "market."

Significantly for American democracy, many of the entities with both a political message and the requisite economic might are the campaign organizations of the well heeled or well placed. Our analysis here in turn puts the persistent debate over campaign finance reform into sharp relief. Perhaps those who champion the individual's right to freely express himself—with countless millions of dollars, if he so chooses—will find support in these pages. To be sure, the open press discourse we have followed through much of the eighteenth century upheld the right of the individual to air his sentiments as prominently as he could manage. And, as the Democratic-Republicans of the Sedition Act Crisis made clear, one could even voice views that might very well undermine a popularly elected administration during an undeclared war.

Early Americans, however, clearly saw the tension between individual rights and the public good, between an open press and a free press. Even their open press discourse defended the right to press liberty not for individual expression in our current, increasingly self-indulgent sense but rather so that the community might hear and judge the merit of others' views. At its most individualistic, the Framing generation saw press liberty as serving the public good by contributing to the democratic public sphere. Thus, a theorist as modern as Tunis Wortman saw the right of individual free expression as subordinate to the duty of public deliberation.

Wortman's fellow Democratic-Republicans, like the Anti-Federalists before them, had also seen firsthand how political and economic power could be used to distort the public sphere, and they roundly condemned the way this manipulation undermined the democratic core of the right to press liberty. Similarly today, many observers criticize—justly, in my view—both the valuing of individual freedom of expression over a public liberty founded in democratic self-government and the way such values permit money and power to increasingly control our major media. Significantly, those media now include the Internet, a medium with radically inclusive potential but persistent exclusionary patterns of access.

These and other genuine shortcomings are highlighted by our attention to the conceptual legacy of the free and open press. But, as we reveal and address these problems, we must not neglect or casually deride the potential of universal access inherent in the current technological revolution. As we have seen, the remarkable economic and demographic growth of the 1740s and 1750s failed to bring about significant change in the existing press liberty tradition until the political and ideological transformations of the 1760s. Similarly, the "information revolution" at the turn of the twenty-first century will require considerable democratic rethinking and political restructuring if we are to realize the potential of a public discourse that is genuinely open to all. This will require a revolution in our concept of democratic press liberty on the order of that wrought by the Revolutions of 1776 and 1800. Those revolutions occasioned the founding of the modern American tradition of democratic press liberty. In many respects, we have yet to fulfill its promise.

Notes

NOTES TO THE INTRODUCTION

1. James Morton Smith, *Freedom's Fetters: The Alien and Sedition Laws and American Civil Liberties* (Ithaca, N.Y.: Cornell University Press, 1956), postscript.

2. Ira Glasser, "Introduction," in *Speaking of Race, Speaking of Sex: Hate Speech, Civil Rights, and Civil Liberties,* ed. Henry Louis Gates, Jr., et al. (New York: New York University Press, 1994), 1.

3. Robert C. Post, *Constitutional Domains: Democracy, Community, Management* (Cambridge, Mass.: Harvard University Press, 1995), 8. See also Owen M. Fiss, *The Irony of Free Speech* (Cambridge, Mass.: Harvard University Press, 1996).

4. Recent political theory is rife with such language; see, e.g., James Bohman, *Public Deliberation: Pluralism, Complexity, and Democracy* (Cambridge, Mass.: MIT Press, 1996), 16; Jürgen Habermas, *Between Facts and Norms: Contributions to a Discourse Theory of Law and Democracy,* trans. William Rehg (Cambridge, Mass.: MIT Press, 1996), 369; Iris Marion Young, "Communication and the Other: Beyond Deliberative Democracy," in *Democracy and Difference: Contesting the Boundaries of the Political,* ed. Seyla Benhabib (Princeton: Princeton University Press, 1996), 121, 123; and James Johnson, "Comment: Public Sphere, Postmodernism, and Polemic," *American Political Science Review* 88 (1994): 430. For use in recent First Amendment literature, see, e.g., Fiss, *Irony of Free Speech,* 3, 12, 21, 46, 80; in common parlance, see, e.g., David Coward, "Independent Minds," *New York Times Book Review,* 31 January 1999, 20.

5. William Waller Hening, *The Statutes at Large Being a Collection of All the Laws of Virginia, 1619–1792,* 13 vols. (Richmond, Va., 1809–1823), 2:517.

6. James Madison, *The Virginia Report of 1799–1800* (Richmond, Va.: J. W. Randolph, 1850), 223.

7. Hening, *Statutes,* 2:518. On Berkeley and the early Chesapeake more generally, see David D. Hall, *Cultures of Print: Essays in the History of the Book* (Amherst: University of Massachusetts Press, 1996), 97–150, esp. 99–101.

8. Madison, *Virginia Report,* 221.

9. Similarly, I use "free and open press" specifically to refer to this ambivalent tradition. Since I use the terms "free press" and "open press" exclusively to refer to their respective doctrines, I have chosen to employ the terms "free speech," "press liberty," and "freedom of expression" to refer broadly and generically to the freedom of expression.

10. *Pennsylvania Journal*, 17 August 1774.

11. Dwight Teeter, "From Revisionism to Orthodoxy," *Reviews in American History* 13 (1985): 518.

12. Teeter, "Revisionism to Orthodoxy," 522.

13. Zechariah Chafee, Jr. *Free Speech in the United States* (Cambridge, Mass.: Harvard University Press, 1941), 21. See also Chafee, "Freedom of Speech in War Time," *Harvard Law Review* 32 (1919): 947.

14. Teeter, "Revisionism to Orthodoxy," 518.

15. Leonard W. Levy, *Legacy of Suppression: Freedom of Speech and Press in Early American History* (Cambridge, Mass.: Harvard University Press, 1960). Though radically revisionist, Levy's book was not entirely without precedent; see Edward S. Corwin, "Freedom of Speech and Press under the First Amendment: A Resume," *Yale Law Journal* 30 (1920): 48–55; see also David A. Anderson, "Levy v. Levy," *Michigan Law Review* 84 (1986): 781n22, and accompanying text.

16. Levy, *Legacy*, vii.

17. *New York Times Co. v. Sullivan* (1964), 376 U.S. 273.

18. For a sample of the critical literature, see esp. George Anastaplo, "Book Review," *New York University Law Review*, 34 (1964): 734–74, and *The Constitutionalist* (Dallas: Southern Methodist University Press, 1971); see also, e.g., Herbert Storing, "Book Review," *American Political Science Review* 55 (1961): 385–6; Gerald J. Baldasty, "Toward an Understanding of the First Amendment: Boston Newspapers, 1782–91," *Journalism History* 3 (1976): 25–30, 32; Maryann Yodelis Smith and Gerald J. Baldasty, "Criticism of Public Officials and Government in the New Nation," *Journal of Communication Inquiry* 4 (1979): 53–74.

19. Merrill Jensen, "Book Review," *Harvard Law Review* 75 (1961): 456–8. For subsequent documentation, see, e.g., the work of Dwight Teeter: *A Legacy of Expression: Philadelphia Newspapers and Congress during the War for Independence, 1775–1783* (Ph.D. diss., University of Wisconsin at Madison, 1966); "Press Freedom and the Public Printing: Pennsylvania, 1775–83," *Journalism Quarterly* 45 (1968): 445–51; "The Printer and the Chief Justice: Seditious Libel in 1782–3," *Journalism Quarterly* 45 (1968): 235–42, 260.

20. David A. Anderson, "The Origins of the Press Clause," *U.C.L.A. Law Review* 30 (1983): 455–541; William T. Mayton, "Seditious Libel and the Lost Guarantee of a Freedom of Expression," *Columbia Law Review* 84 (1984): 91–142.

21. Levy, "On the Origins of the Free Press Clause," *U.C.L.A. Law Review* 32 (1984): 177–218; and Levy, "The *Legacy* Reexamined," *Stanford Law Review* 37 (1985): 766–93.

22. Leonard W. Levy, *Emergence of a Free Press* (New York: Oxford University Press, 1985), vii; more recently, Levy published an excerpt from *Emergence*: "Freedom of Speech in Seventeenth-Century Thought," *Antioch Review* 57 (1999): 165–77. See also Levy, *Origins of the Bill of Rights* (New Haven: Yale University Press, 1999), 103–32.

23. Levy, *Emergence*, viii–ix.

24. Levy, *Emergence*, x.

25. Levy, *Emergence*, xi, xii.

26. Anderson, "Levy v. Levy," 785; on the resulting confusion, see 785–6, and David M. Rabban, "The Ahistorical Historian: Leonard Levy on Freedom of Expression in Early American History," *Stanford Law Review* 37 (1985): 812–6.

27. Levy, *Emergence*, xii.

28. Levy, *Emergence*, xv–xvii.

29. Levy would no doubt disagree with this assessment of *Emergence*, but see his admittedly one-sided critique of Thomas Jefferson's checkered record on civil liberties: Levy, *Jefferson and Civil Liberties: The Darker Side* (Cambridge, Mass.: Harvard University Press, 1963).

30. Levy, *Emergence*, xvi, xvii.

31. Rabban, "Ahistorical Historian," 800.

32. Rabban, "Ahistorical Historian," esp. 806–11.

33. Rabban, "Ahistorical Historian," esp. 821–8.

34. Jeffery A. Smith, *Printers and Press Freedom: The Ideology of Early American Journalism* (New York: Oxford University Press, 1988).

35. For more on Franklin, see Smith, *Franklin and Bache: Envisioning the Enlightened Republic* (New York: Oxford University Press, 1990). For more on press liberty, see also Smith, *War and Press Freedom: The Problem of Prerogative Power* (New York: Oxford University Press, 1999).

36. Smith, *Printers and Press Freedom*, 6.

37. Rosenberg, "Another World," 555, 556.

38. Richard E. Ellis, "Book Review" (of Smith, *Printers and Press Freedom*), *American Historical Review* 95 (1990): 255.

39. Smith, *Printers and Press Freedom*, 11.

40. Richard Buel, Jr., "Freedom of the Press in Revolutionary America: The Evolution of Libertarianism, 1760–1820," in *The Press and the American Revolution*, ed. Bernard Bailyn and John B. Hench (Worcester, Mass.: American Antiquarian Society, 1980), 59–98.

41. See, for example, Stephen Botein, "'Meer Mechanics' and an Open Press: The Business and Political Strategies of Colonial American Printers,"

Perspectives in American History 9 (1975): 127–225, esp. 177, 180; also, Botein, "Printers and the American Revolution," in *The Press and the American Revolution*, ed. Bernard Bailyn and John B. Hench, 11–58.

42. John Nerone, *Violence against the Press: Policing the Public Sphere in United States History* (New York: Oxford University Press, 1994), 27, 29, and passim.

43. For the most recent history of this debate, see Daniel T. Rodgers, "Republicanism: The Career of a Concept," *Journal of American History* 79 (June 1992): 11–38. See also Peter S. Onuf, "Reflections on the Founding: Constitutional Historiography in Bicentennial Perspective," *William and Mary Quarterly*, 3d ser., 46 (1989): 341–75; Robert E. Shalhope, "Republicanism and Early American Historiograpy," *William and Mary Quarterly*, 3d ser., 39 (1982): 334–56; and Shalhope, "Toward a Republican Synthesis: The Emergence of an Understanding of Republicanism in American Historiography," *William and Mary Quarterly*, 3d ser., 29 (1972): 49–80. For the term "notorious debate," see Lance Banning, "The Republican Interpretation: Retrospect and Prospect," in *The Republican Synthesis Revisited: Essays in Honor of George Athan Billias*, ed. Robert D. Brown, Milton M. Klein, and John B. Hench (Worcester, Mass.: American Antiquarian Society, 1992), 92.

44. See, e.g., Joyce Appleby, *Capitalism and a New Social Order: The Republican Vision of the 1790s* (New York: New York University Press, 1984); and John Patrick Diggins, *The Lost Soul of American Politics: Virtue, Self-Interest, and the Foundations of Liberalism* (New York: Basic Books, 1985). More recent works include Joshua Foa Dienstag, "Serving God and Mammon: The Lockean Sympathy in Early American Political Thought," *American Political Science Review* 90 (1996): 497–511; Dienstag, "Between History and Nature: Social Contract Theory in Locke and the Founders," *Journal of Politics* 58 (1996): 985–1009; and Steven M. Dworetz, *The Unvarnished Doctrine: Locke, Liberalism, and the American Revolution* (Durham, N.C.: Duke University Press, 1990).

45. See, e.g., Bernard Bailyn, *The Ideological Origins of the American Revolution* (Cambridge, Mass.: Harvard University Press, 1967); Gordon S. Wood, *The Creation of the American Republic, 1776–1787* (Chapel Hill: University of North Carolina Press, 1969), and J. G. A. Pocock, *The Machiavellian Moment: Florentine Political Thought and the Atlantic Republican Tradition* (Princeton: Princeton University Press, 1975).

46. For a brief overview, see Robert E. Shalhope, "In Search of the Elusive Republic," *Reviews in American History* 19 (1991): 468–73. For the changed views of some of the original interlocutors, see, e.g., Joyce Appleby, "Republicanism in Old and New Contexts," *William and Mary Quarterly*, 3d ser., 43 (1986): 20–34; Lance Banning, "Jeffersonian Ideology Revisited: Liberal and Classical Ideas in the New American Republic," *William and Mary Quarterly*,

3d ser., 43 (1986): 3–19; and Banning, *The Sacred Fire of Liberty: James Madison and the Founding of the Federal Republic* (Ithaca, N.Y.: Cornell University Press, 1995). Like Banning, I "accept the risk of getting tangled in the current terminological confusion" and agree with him that eighteenth-century Americans might best be thought of as "liberal republicans." And, like him, I avoid the terms "civic humanism" and "classical republicanism," indicating that what I call the "republican" discourse in America drew most heavily on the *neo*classical tradition of the British Interregnum and later opposition thinking, with its priority of public liberty and the public good over private rights. See Banning, *Sacred Fire of Liberty*, 428n3 and 215–9.

47. See, e.g., Jeffrey C. Isaac, "Republicanism vs. Liberalism? A Reconsideration," *History of Political Thought* 9 (1988): 349–77; James T. Kloppenberg, "The Virtues of Liberalism: Christianity, Republicanism, and Ethics in Early American Political Discourse," *Journal of American History* 74 (1987): 9–33; and John Zvesper, "The American Founders and Classical Political Thought," *History of Political Thought* 10 (1989): 701–18.

48. Michael Zuckert, *Natural Rights and the New Republicanism* (Princeton: Princeton University Press, 1994),165 and passim. See also Jerome Huyler, *Locke in America: The Moral Philosophy of the Founding Era* (Lawrence: University Press of Kansas, 1995), 210, 277, and passim; and James H. Read, *Power versus Liberty: Madison, Hamilton, Wilson, and Jefferson* (Charlottesville: University Press of Virginia, 2000), esp. 6, 178n9.

49. Huyler, *Locke in America*, 28; see also 149, 306, and Zuckert, *New Republicanism*, 312. For "theory/practice," see Zuckert, *New Republicanism*, 165; and Huyler, *Locke in America*, 149.

50. Zuckert, *New Republicanism*, 165, quoting from Jefferson, "Minutes of the Board of Visitors, University of Virginia, 1822–25," 4 March 1825. Similarly, see Huyler, *Locke in America*, 225, 226, quoting *Cato's Letters*, #62.

51. Michael Lienesch, *New Order of the Ages: Time, the Constitution, and the Making of Modern American Political Thought* (Princeton: Princeton University Press, 1988), 8. See also, e.g., Isaac Kramnick, *Republicanism and Bourgeois Radicalism: Political Ideology in Late Eighteenth-Century England and America* (Ithaca, N.Y.: Cornell University Press, 1990), 261.

52. Huyler, *Locke in America*, 22.

53. Robert W. T. Martin, "Context and Contradiction: Toward a Political Theory of Conceptual Change," *Political Research Quarterly* 50 (1997): 413–36, esp. 425.

54. I use the term "evolution" here, despite the possible connotations of scientific positivism and predictability, both to remove any suggestion that these conceptual changes have a necessary, teleological direction and to stress that these transformations are natural (that is, an expression of human nature) and often unintentional.

55. For example, Lance Banning reveals that Madison frequently responded to criticism by rethinking his sophisticated if imperfect amalgamation of what we now call "liberal" and "republican" themes (Banning, *Sacred Fire of Liberty*, 84, 213, 232, and passim). In rare instances—slavery is a good example—criticisms and contextual shifts will make a contradiction manifest, yet people will live with the contradiction *uneasily* (continuing the Madison example, see Drew R. McCoy, *The Last of the Fathers: James Madison and the Republican Legacy* [Cambridge: Cambridge University Press, 1989], 253–322).

56. Kramnick, *Republicanism and Bourgeois Radicalism*, 261.

57. These overlapping literatures are vast but, as should soon be apparent, I have drawn most heavily from Richard D. Brown, *Knowledge Is Power: The Diffusion of Information in Early American History* (New York: Oxford University Press, 1989); Brown, *The Strength of a People: The Idea of an Informed Citizenry in America, 1650–1870* (Chapel Hill: University of North Carolina Press, 1996); Brown, "Shifting Freedoms of the Press in the Eighteenth Century," in *A History of the Book in America*, vol. 1 of *The Colonial Book in the Atlantic World*, ed. Hugh Armory and David D. Hall (Cambridge: Cambridge University Press, 2000), 366–76; Michael Warner, *The Letters of the Republic: Publication and the Public Sphere in Eighteenth-Century America* (Cambridge, Mass.: Harvard University Press, 1990); Charles E. Clark, *The Public Prints: The Newspaper in Anglo-American Culture, 1665–1740* (New York: Oxford University Press, 1994); Clark, "Early American Journalism: News and Opinion in the Popular Press," in Armory and Hall, eds., *Colonial Book*, 347–66; and Hall, *Cultures of Print*.

58. See, e.g, Kramnick's interesting essay, "Children's Literature and Bourgeois Ideology," in Kramnick, *Republicanism and Bourgeois Radicalism*, 99–132.

NOTES TO CHAPTER 1

1. For much of this history I rely on Fredrick S. Siebert, *Freedom of the Press in England, 1476–1776* (Urbana: University of Illinois Press, 1952).

2. William M. Clyde, *The Struggle for the Freedom of the Press from Caxton to Cromwell* (Oxford: Oxford University Press, 1934), 9.

3. Wentworth, quoted in Siebert, *Freedom of the Press*, 101.

4. Christopher Hill, *Milton and the English Revolution* (London: Faber and Faber, 1977), 152.

5. David D. Hall, *Cultures of Print: Essays in the History of the Book* (Amherst: University of Massachusetts Press, 1996), 81.

6. Siebert, *Freedom of the Press*, 89, 98–100.

7. Siebert, *Freedom of the Press*, 166, 173.

8. Elizabeth Skerpan, *The Rhetoric of Politics in the English Revolution*,

1642–1660 (Columbia: University of Missouri Press, 1992), 9; see also Siebert, *Freedom of the Press*, 203n1.

9. For the general background to these debates, see Christopher Hill, *The World Turned Upside Down: Radical Ideas during the English Revolution* (Middlesex, UK: Penguin, 1972).

10. John Lilburne, *A Copie of a Letter to Mr. William Prinne, Esq.* (London: 1645), 6. See John Milton, *Areopagitica* (1644; repr., London: Noel Douglas, 1927), 23, 26, 29, 39; see also the finale of Milton's sonnet *On the Forcers of Conscience* (1647?): "New Presbyter is but old Priest writt large," in *The Complete Poetry of John Milton*, ed. John T. Shawcross (New York: Doubleday, 1971), 212. See also William Walwyn, *A Helpe to the right understanding of a Discourse concerning Independency* (London: 1645), 1; and John Goodwin, *A Fresh Discovery of the High-Presbyterian Spirit*, 1641, appended to Clyde, *The Struggle for the Freedom of the Press from Caxton to Cromwell*, 336.

11. Milton, *Areopagitica*, 26, 4. See also Walwyn, *A Helpe*, 7, and John Goodwin, *Theomachia* (London: Henry Overton, 1644), 37; and Goodwin, *A Fresh Discovery*, 332–3. Cf. also Roger Williams, *The Bloudy Tenent of Persecution, for cause of Conscience*, 1644; repr., vol. 3 of *Publications of the Narragansett Club*, 6 vols., ed. S. L. Caldwell (Providence: Providence Press, 1866–74), 80.

12. William Haller, *Liberty and Reformation in the Puritan Revolution* (New York: Columbia University Press, 1955), 147; Goodwin, *Theomachia*, 1, 6–7, 11, 12; and Goodwin, *Fresh Discovery*, 331. See also Henry Robinson, *Liberty of Conscience* (London: 1644), 42.

13. Levellers' Petition of March 1647 and Petition of 11 September 1648, in *Leveller Manifestoes of the Puritan Revolution*, ed. Don M. Wolfe (New York: Thomas Nelson and Sons, 1944), 139, 289.

14. See, e.g., Walwyn, *The Power of Love*, A8; or Lilburne, *Copie of a Letter*, 3, 6.

15. See, e.g., Robinson, *Liberty of Conscience*, 59, 56. A frequent reference was to 2 Corinthians 13:8: "for we can do nothing against the truth, but for the truth."

16. Caroline Robbins, *The Eighteenth-Century Commonwealthman* (Cambridge MA: Harvard University Press, 1959), 46.

17. Haller, *Liberty and Reformation*, 187. See also Haller, *Tracts on Liberty in the Puritan Revolution, 1638–1647*, 3 vols. (New York: Columbia University Press, 1934), 1:7.

18. Milton, *Areopagitica*, 35, 36; Walwyn, *The Compassionate Samaritane* (London: 1644), 60. See also Walwyn, *The Compassionate Samaritane*, 14, 61; Goodwin, *Theomachia*, 33, and *Fresh Discovery*, 333, 335.

19. Levellers' Petition of 18 January 1649, in Wolfe, *Manifestoes*, 328; see

also their Remonstrance of Many Thousand Citizens (1646) and their Petition of 11 September 1648, both in Wolfe, *Manifestoes*, 128, 289.

20. See Hobbes, *Leviathan*, ed. C. B. Macpherson (Middlesex: Penguin, 1968), 527, 550.

21. Walwyn, *Compassionate Samaritane*, 7; Lilburne, *A Copie of a Letter*, 5.

22. Edmund S. Morgan, *Inventing the People: The Rise of Popular Sovereignty in England and American* (New York: Norton, 1988), 70.

23. Walwyn, *A Helpe*, 7, 4 (italics in original), seven.

24. Levellers' *Agreement of the People*, in Wolfe, *Manifestoes*, 227; Roger Williams, *Bloody Tenent of Persecution yet more bloody*, 1645; repr., vol. 4 of *Publications of the Narragansett Club*, 6 vols., ed. S. L. Caldwell (Providence: Providence Press, 1866–74), 189, 198–9.

25. Leonard Levy, *Emergence of a Free Press* (New York: Oxford University Press, 1985), 103; see also 336.

26. Walwyn, *Compassionate Samaritane*, A4; see also Milton, *Areopagitica*, 26.

27. Lilburne, *A Copie of a Letter*, 2–3.

28. Lilburne, *A Copie of a Letter*, 2. The number of newspapers published peaked in 1645 at 722. Siebert, *Freedom of the Press*, 203n1.

29. Walwyn, *Compassionate Samaritane*, 78–9. See also A4, 5; Walwyn, *Power of Love*, 43; Milton, *Areopagitica*, 37; and Lilburne, *A Copie of a Letter*, 2.

30. Hill makes this claim regarding Milton's argument; see *Milton and the English Revolution*, 151.

31. Lilburne, *Englands Birth-Right Justified* (London: 1645), 11. See also Walwyn, *Compassionate Samaritane*, A4, 39–40.

32. See Milton, *Areopagitica*, 1, 40; and the Levellers' Petition of 11 September 1648, in Wolfe, *Manifestoes*, 289.

33. Petition of 18 January 1649, in Wolfe, *Manifestoes*, 328–9.

34. See, for example, the Levellers' *Englands New Chains Discovered, The Second Part of Englands New-Chaines Discovered*, and *Walwyns Just Defence Against The Aspertion Cast Upon Him*, all in *The Leveller Tracts, 1647–1653*, ed. William Haller and Godfrey Davies (New York: Columbia University Press, 1944), 162, 167, 184, 384.

35. Williams, *Bloudy Tenent*, 198; see also 78–9, 96, 147, 163, 171, 384–5; and Williams, *Bloody Tenent Yet More Bloody*, 91, 111.

36. Walwyn, *A Helpe*, 8.

37. Siebert, *Freedom of the Press*, 243.

38. Lois G. Schwoerer, "Liberty of the Press and Public Opinioin: 1660–1695," in *Liberty Secured?: Britain Before and After 1688*, ed. J. R. Jones (Stanford: Stanford University Press, 1992), 213. The Miltonian pamphlet was

Charles Blount, *A Just Vindication of Learning and the Liberty of the Press* (London, 1679).

39. See, for example, Sidney, *Discourses concerning Government* (1698; repr., London: Arno Press, 1979), 9, 409, 424, 427, 451, 453. For Locke, see, for example, *Two Treatises of Government*, ed. Peter Laslett (Cambridge: Cambridge University Press, 1988), 409; and *A Letter concerning Toleration*, ed. James Tully (Indianapolis: Hackett, 1983), 46; see also *A Second Letter Concerning Toleration* (1690), in *The Works of John Locke*, 4 vols. (London: Ward, Lock, 1888), 3:42.

40. H. R. Fox Bourne, *The Life of John Locke*, 2 vols. (New York: Harper and Brothers, 1876), 2:315; see Locke's memo, reprinted in Peter King, *The Life and Letters of John Locke, with Extracts from his Journals and Commonplace Books* (London: George Bell and Sons, 1884), 376, 384. Locke also played a quiet role in the end of licensing in Virginia. The Royal Instructions of 1698, "which Locke did so much to draft" (Laslett, ed., *Two Treatises*, 284n), silently dropped the conventional licensing passage that continued to appear in other colonies' Instructions. See Leonard Woods Labaree, *Royal Instructions to the British Colonial Governors*, 2 vols. (New York: D. Appleton-Century, 1935), 2:495–6; also, Laslett, "John Locke, the Great Recoinage, and the Origins of the Board of Trade: 1695–1698," *William and Mary Quarterly*, 3d ser., 14 (1957): 369–402, esp. 398–401. But also cf. "The Fundamental Constitutions of Carolina" (1669), excerpted in Fox Bourne, *Life of John Locke*, 242.

41. Laurence Hanson, *Government and the Press: 1695–1763* (Oxford: Oxford University Press, 1936), 94.

42. John Asgill, *An Essay for the Press* (London: A. Baldwin, 1712), 2. See also Daniel Defoe, *An Essay on the Regulation of the Press* (1704; repr., Oxford: Basil Blackwell, 1948), 4.

43. Defoe, *A Letter to a Member of Parliament Shewing the Necessity of Regulating the Press* (Oxford: George West and Henry Clements, 1699), 41–3, 52; see also [Anonymous], *ARGUMENTS Relating to a Restraint upon the PRESS, Fully and Fairly handled in a LETTER to a Bencher, FROM a Young Gentleman of the* TEMPLE (London: R. and J. Bonwicke, 1712), 22.

44. [Anon.], *ARGUMENTS*, 19, 18; Defoe, *A Letter to a Member*, 41, 49.

45. Defoe, *A Review of the Affairs of France* (London), 8 November, 1705.

46. [Anon.], *ARGUMENTS*, 27.

47. Defoe, *A Letter to a Member*, 34, 61; [Anon.], *ARGUMENTS*, 14–5.

48. Samuel Johnson, quoted in David L. Jacobson, ed., *The English Libertarian Heritage* (Indianapolis: Bobbs-Merrill, 1965), liv.

49. See, for example, Tindal, *Four Discourses on the Following Subjects: viz . . . IV. Of the Liberty of the Press* (London: 1709) [a reprint of his *Letter to a Member of Parliament* (London: J. Darby, 1698)], 309.

50. Tindal, *Reasons against Restraining the Press* (London: 1704), 7; see also Tindal, *Four Discourses*, 294, 295.

51. Tindal, *Four Discourses*, 296, 294. See also Tindal, *Reasons*, 7, 4.

52. Tindal, *Four Discourses*, 323, 321.

53. Tindal, *Reasons*, 10; see also Tindal, *Four Discourses*, 324.

54. Tindal, *Reasons*, 13.

55. Tindal, *Reasons*, 9–10.

56. See Siebert, *Freedom of the Press*, 315–9, 321.

57. John Trenchard and Thomas Gordon, *Cato's Letters*, 4 vols. (London: Wilkins, Woodward, Walthoe, and Peele, 1724), 2:54–5 (#60), 74 (#62), 128 (#66).

58. Anthony Collins, *A Discourse of Free-Thinking* (London: 1713), 101 and passim.

59. I employ the terms *open* and *free* to distinguish these doctrines in anticipation of the colonists' frequent use of these terms. See this volume, chapters 2 and 3.

60. See, for example, Trenchard and Gordon, *Considerations offered upon the Approaching Peace* (London: J. Roberts, 1720), 6; or *Cato's Letters*, 1:99 (#15).

61. Trenchard and Gordon, *The Independent Whig* (London: J. Peele, 1721), 24 (#5), 75–6 (#11).

62. Trenchard and Gordon, *Cato's Letters*, 1:101 (#15), 1:261 (#32), 3:248 (#100).

63. Trenchard and Gordon, *Cato's Letters*, 3: 248 (#100); *Considerations*, 16.

64. Trenchard and Gordon, *Cato's Letters*, 1:259 (#32).

65. Trenchard and Gordon, *Cato's Letters*, 1: 99 (#15); 1:254 (#32); see also, 3:243 (#100).

66. Michael Zuckert, *Natural Rights and the New Republicanism* (Princeton: Princeton University Press, 1994), 165, 299; Jerome Huyler, *Locke in America: The Moral Philosophy of the Founding Era* (Lawrence: University Press of Kansas, 1995), 28, 224–5.

67. Trenchard and Gordon, *Cato's Letters*, 3: 326–31 (#115).

68. Trenchard and Gordon, *Cato's Letters*, 1: 268 (#33). But cf. Zuckert, *New Republicanism*, 311–2.

69. Trenchard and Gordon, *Cato's Letters*, 1:102 (#15); see also 3:243–4 (#100). In these *Letters*, freedom of speech and of the press are often referred to interchangeably.

70. Trenchard and Gordon, *Cato's Letters*, 3:242, 249 (#100).

71. Jacobson, ed., *The English Libertarian Heritage*, xli; Levy, *Emergence of a Free Press*, 118.

72. Trenchard and Gordon, *Cato's Letters*, 1:254–5 (#32); more generally, see 1:77–84 (#12).

73. Siebert, *Freedom of the Press*, 339.

74. Trenchard and Gordon, *Cato's Letters*, 1:252 (#32).

75. Trenchard and Gordon, *Cato's Letters*, 1:253–4 (#32); see also John Trenchard and Thomas Gordon, *The Character of an Independent Whig*, 4th ed. (London: J. Roberts, 1720), 19.

76. Trenchard and Gordon, *Cato's Letters*, 1:261 (#32); 3:244 (#100). See also 1:254 (#32); 3:248 (#100); 3:254 (#101). Cf. Levy's assertion (*Emergence*, 209) that "Junius Wilkes" was, in 1782, the "first to insist that the public's right to know outweighed the defamation of even a good official."

77. Trenchard and Gordon, *Cato's Letters*, 3:247 (#100).

78. Trenchard and Gordon, *Independent Whig*, 79 (#11); on ancient history, see, for examples, *Cato's Letters*, 1:97–105 (#15).

79. Trenchard and Gordon, *Cato's Letters*, 1:97 (#15).

NOTES TO CHAPTER 2

1. *Royal Instructions to British Colonial Governors, 1670–1776*, ed. Leonard Woods Labaree (New York: D. Appleton-Century, 1935), 2:495–6. See also Livingston Rowe Schuyler, *The Liberty of the Press in the American Colonies before the Revolutionary War* (New York: Thomas Whittaker, 1905), 34.

2. William Waller Hening, *The Statutes at Large Being a Collection of All the Laws of Virginia, 1619–1792*, 13 vols. (Richmond, Va: Samuel Pleasants, 1809–1823), 2:517; quoted on p. 2.

3. David D. Hall, *Cultures of Print: Essays in the History of the Book* (Amherst: University of Massachusetts Press, 1996), 99–100.

4. *Publick Occurrences* (Boston), 25 September 1690.

5. Clyde Augustus Duniway, *The Development of Freedom of the Press in Massachusetts* (New York: Longmans, Green, 1906), 33.

6. For more of the context surrounding Harris's venture, see Charles E. Clark, "Early American Journalism: News and Opinion in the Popular Press," in *The Colonial Book in the Atlantic World*, vol. 1 of *A History of the Book in America*, ed. Hugh Amory and David D. Hall (Cambridge: Cambridge University Press, 2000), 350–2; and Ian K. Steele, *The English Atlantic, 1675–1740: An Exploration of Communication and Community* (New York: Oxford University Press, 1986), 146–7.

7. Duniway, *Development*, 58.

8. Richard D. Brown, *Knowledge Is Power: The Diffusion of Information in Early America, 1700–1865* (New York: Oxford University Press, 1989), 16–41, esp. 36–41.

9. For example, a few unlicensed almanacs and pamphlets had been published; see Duniway, *Development*, 69n1.

10. Larry D. Eldridge, *A Distant Heritage: The Growth of Free Speech in Early America* (New York: New York University Press, 1994), 3.

11. Eldridge, *Distant Heritage*, 9. See also Brown, *Knowledge Is Power*, 16–41.

12. Extract from a letter from Conrade Adams to [Grove Hirst], 18 June 1713, Curwen Family Manuscript Collection, American Antiquarian Society, Box 2, Folder 1. More generally, see Norman L. Rosenberg, *Protecting the Best Men: An Interpretive History of the Law of Libel* (Chapel Hill: University of North Carolina Press, 1986), 25; and, most recently, Patricia U. Bonomi, *The Lord Cornbury Scandal: The Politics of Reputation in British America* (Chapel Hill: University of North Carolina Press, 1998).

13. Eldridge, *Distant Heritage*, 42.

14. See, e.g., Leonard Levy, *Emergence of a Free Press* (New York: Oxford University Press, 1985), xvi.

15. For example, when the jury acquitted William Bradford of seditious libel, largely on the basis of a technicality, the presiding judge punished the jury along with the (now formally acquitted) defendant; see James N. Green, "The Book Trade in the Middle Colonies, 1680–1720," in Amory and Hall, eds., *Colonial Book*, 211.

16. Eldridge, *Distant Heritage*, 65, 77, 79, 84, 137. For a similar assessment of the decreasingly draconian nature of penalties, see Rosenberg, *Protecting the Best Men*, 19, and Jane Kamensky, *Governing the Tongue: The Politics of Speech in Early New England* (New York: Oxford University Press, 1997), 181–9.

17. Isaiah Thomas, *The History of Printing in America*, 2d ed., 2 vols. (New York: Burt Franklin, 1874), 1:417, 423; Duniway, *Development*, 79.

18. Duniway, *Development*, 89, 89n1, 96; see also the *Boston News-Letter*, 3 April 1721, and the *Boston Gazette*, 6 April 1721.

19. *New-England Courant* (Boston), 11 June 1722.

20. Duniway, *Development*, 97–103, 163–6.

21. *New-England Courant*, 13 May 1723.

22. Jeffery A. Smith, *Printers and Press Freedom: The Ideology of Early American Journalism* (New York: Oxford University Press, 1988), mentions the role of juries rarely and only in passing; see, e.g., 87, 156. Levy, *Emergence*, notes that the jury's general verdict powers were "surprisingly accepted" by a court in 1692 and goes on to dismiss it as a fluctuating safeguard, ignoring its practical and theoretical significance; see 25, 128–9, 201.

23. On the Bradford case, see George Keith and Thomas Budd, *New-England's Spirit of Persecution Transmitted to Pennsylvania* (Philadelphia: William Bradford, 1693); Thomas, *History*, 1:211–23; and, more broadly, Green, "Book Trade in the Middle Colonies," 199–223, esp. 211. On the Maule case, see Theo. Philanthes [Thomas Maule], *New-England Persecutors Mauld with their Own Weapons* (New York, 1697); Duniway, *Development*, 70–3; and M. Halsey Thomas, ed., *The Diary of Samuel Sewall*, 2 vols. (New York: Farrar, Straus, and Giroux, 1973), 1:342n.

24. Case of Francis Mackemie discussed in Stanley Nider Katz, ed., *A Brief Narrative of the Case and Tryal of John Peter Zenger* . . . , by James Alexander (Cambridge, Mass.: Harvard University Press, 1972), 13, 208n34.

25. Harold L. Nelson, "Seditious Libel in Colonial America," *American Journal of Legal History* 3 (1959): 165n24; Fredrick S. Siebert, *Freedom of the Press in England, 1476–1776* (Urbana: University of Illinois Press, 1952), 273–4. On the general magnification of colonial jury powers, see Shannon C. Stimson, *The American Revolution in the Law: Anglo-American Jurisprudence before John Marshall* (Princeton: Princeton University Press, 1990); for seventeenth-century changes, see Eldridge, *Distant Heritage*, 79–85.

26. Duniway, *Development*, 107–11 and 166–71.

27. Henry Care, *English Liberties*, 5th ed. (Boston: James Franklin for Buttolph, Eliot, and Henchman, 1721), 4, 203; see also *New-England Courant*, 30 July 1722.

28. Eldridge, *Distant Heritage*, 80.

29. *Independent Advertiser* (Boston), 10 April 1749; see also 5 February 1749.

30. See, e.g., Stimson, *American Revolution*, 48, 71, and passim.

31. Willi Paul Adams, *The First American Constitutions: Republican Ideology and the Making of the State Constitutions in the Revolutionary Era* (Chapel Hill: University of North Carolina, 1980), 160.

32. *New-England Courant*, 11, 18 September 1721. For Cato's earlier letter on press liberty (#15), see 9 July 1722; for similar statements by the "Hell-Fire Club," see, e.g., 20 November, 4 December 1721, and 22 January 1722. The 115-day average for news crossing the Atlantic to Boston is in Steele, *English Atlantic*, 159.

33. *Boston Gazette*, 19 January 1722.

34. Brown, *Knowledge Is Power*, 34, 32.

35. Charles E. Clark, *The Public Prints: The Newspaper in Anglo-American Culture, 1665–1740* (New York: Oxford University Press, 1994), 131.

36. Jürgen Habermas, *The Structural Transformation of the Public Sphere: An Inquiry into a Category of Bourgeois Society* [1962], trans. Thomas Burger with Frederick Lawrence (Cambridge, Mass.: MIT Press, 1989) 36, 85.

37. Hall, *Cultures of Print*, 154, notes that satire enhanced the distance between the learned and the rabble and points out that the *Courant* used "'insider' verse" (152); but given the use to which the *Courant*'s satire was put (e.g., frequently lampooning Harvard), I argue that the effect was a questioning of the learned/rabble distinction.

38. *New-England Courant*, 7 August 1721. See also Michael Warner, *Letters of the Republic: Publication and the Public Sphere in Eighteenth-Century America* (Cambridge, Mass.: Harvard University Press, 1990), 66–7; Clark, *Public Prints*, 130–1; and David S. Shields, *Civil Tongues and Polite Letters*

in British America (Chapel Hill: University of North Carolina Press, 1997), 266–74.

39. *New-England Courant*, 7 August 1721.

40. Anon., *A Letter from a Freeholder, to a Member of the Lower House of Assembly* (Annapolis: William Parks, 1727), 4, quoted in Warner, *Letters of the Republic*, 38.

41. Warner, *Letters of the Republic*, 38–43, esp. 39. Though Warner is correct in noting that this negation of the individual accords with republican discourse in requiring that one forgo "any private views or Ends (inconsistent with the common Good)" (38, quoting *Letter from a Freeholder*), he overstates the relationship between "negativity" and printedness. Mechanical duplication neither required nor was required by nonattributed writing; anonymous tracts could be published via scribal production, and, of course, much printed discourse bore the author's name.

42. Clark, *Public Prints*, 169–70; see also, 4, 79, 129–31, 250–6, and Brown, *Knowledge Is Power*, 38–41.

43. [Thomas Walter], *The Little-Compton Scourge; Or, The Anti-Courant* (Boston: J. Franklin, 1721).

44. *New-England Courant*, 20 November 1721.

45. Samuel Sewall, quoted in Brown, *Knowledge Is Power*, 30.

46. But cf. the *American Weekly Mercury* (Philadelphia), 6 November 1740.

47. John Trenchard and Thomas Gordon, *Cato's Letters*, 4 vols. (London: Wilkins, Woodward, Walthoe, and Peele, 1724), 1:295–302 (#37), and, e.g., *South-Carolina Gazette* (Charleston), 29 July 1748; see also Trenchard and Gordon, *Cato's Letters*, 1:200–7 (#26).

48. Clinton Rossiter, *Seedtime of the Republic* (New York: Harcourt, Brace, 1953), 141.

49. See, e.g., the *South Carolina Gazette*, 12 June 1736, 16 July 1748, or the *Boston Gazette*, 21 April 1755, 26 April 1756.

50. *Boston Evening Post*, 30 March 1741. See also, e.g., the *South Carolina Gazette*, 2 February 1734; *Boston Gazette*, 26 May 1755, 2 January 1758; and *Connecticut Gazette* (New London), 7 February 1756.

51. Cf., e.g., Jonathan Mayhew, "Objections Considered," in his *Seven Sermons* (Boston: Rogers and Fowle, 1749), 71–4, and Mayhew, *A Discourse Concerning Unlimited Submission and Non-Resistance to the Higher Powers* (Boston: Fowle and Gookin, 1750), 38–40. For free press notions on their own, see, e.g., Obadiah Honesty, *A Remonstrance of Obadiah Honesty* (Philadelphia: 1757), 4. For open press, see, e.g., *Pennsylvania Gazette* (Philadelphia), 30 March 1738, 4 May 1740.

52. *Pennsylvania Gazette*, 6 June 1738, 30 March 1738. See also, e.g., A Lover of Truth and Liberty [Elisha Williams], *The Essential Rights and Liber-*

ties of Protestants (Boston: Kneeland and Green, 1744), 65; *South Carolina Gazette*, 1 August 1748; *Boston Gazette*, 10 May 1756; and *Pennsylvania Gazette*, 26 January 1758.

53. *Pennsylvania Gazette*, 18 May 1738; Richard Saunders [Benjamin Franklin], *Poor Richard Improved: Being an Almanack for 1757* (Philadelphia: Franklin and Hall, 1756).

54. *Independent Advertiser*, reprinted in the *Boston Gazette*, 8 March 1756. See also the *Connecticut Gazette*, 7 February 1756.

55. Katz, *Brief Narrative*, 1. For a recent reassertion of Zenger's prominence, see William Lowell Putnam, *John Peter Zenger and the Fundamental Freedom* (Jefferson, N.C. : McFarland, 1997).

56. See, e.g., Katz, *Brief Narrative*, 30; Levy, *Emergence of a Free Press*, 130; and Levy, "Did the Zenger Case Really Matter? Freedom of the Press in Colonial New York," *William and Mary Quarterly*, 3d ser., 17 (1960): 35–50.

57. *Pennsylvania Gazette*, 18 May 1738.

58. *New-York Weekly Journal*, 17 December 1733; see also *New-York Gazette*, 28 October 1734.

59. Katz, *Brief Narrative*, 9.

60. Warner, *Letters of the Republic*, 53.

61. DeLancey set bail at an unprecedented, impossible £400, forcing Zenger's continued imprisonment. For much of this history, see Katz, *Brief Narrative*, 8–9, 17–23, 41–56, 101–5; and the *New-York Weekly Journal*, 18 August 1735.

62. *New-York Gazette*, 21 January 1734.

63. James DeLancey, *The Charge of the Honourable James DeLancey to the Grand Jury [15 October 1734]* (New York: William Bradford, 1734), 7; *New-York Gazette*, 4 February 1734.

64. *New-York Gazette*, 28 October, 21 January 1734.

65. James Delancey, *The Charge of the Honourable James DeLancey to the Grand Jury [15 January 1734]* (New York: William Bradford, 173[4]), 2. See also, e.g., *New-York Gazette*, 28 October 1734.

66. See, e.g., Thomas Hobbes, *Leviathan*, ed. C. B. Macpherson (Middlesex: Penguin, 1968), 365.

67. *New-York Gazette*, 28 October 1734; concerning "snake stones," see Anthony Duche, *Advertisement. We do hereby Certify* (Philadelphia, 1743).

68. DeLancey, *The Charge [15 January 1734]*, 2; *New-York Gazette*, 4 February 1734.

69. *New-York Gazette*, 4 February, 28 October 1734. Cf. *New-York Weekly Journal*, 14 January 1734; *New-York Gazette*, 14 October 1734.

70. See, e.g., *New-York Weekly Journal*, 18 February (#15), 25 February, 4 March (#32), 9 December 1734 (#100).

71. *New-York Weekly Journal*, 12, 19 November 1733.

72. *New-York Weekly Journal*, 18, 25 February, 4 March 1734.

73. *New-York Weekly Journal*, 18 February 1734.

74. *New-York Weekly Journal*, 11, 18 February, 4 March 1734.

75. Katz, *Brief Narrative*, 90, 91, 84, and passim.

76. Anglo-Americanus [Jonathon Blenman], "Remarks on Zenger's Trial," in Katz, *Brief Narrative*, 158 [originally published in the *Barbados Gazette*, 20 July 1737].

77. X [James Alexander], *Pennsylvania Gazette*, 1, 8 December 1737; see also 17, 24 November 1737.

78. *Pennsylvania Gazette*, 26 January 1758; Nelson, "Seditious Libel," 170–1. For a similar assessment, placing the significance of the Zenger case not in legal precedent but in reflecting a changed political culture, see Rosenberg, *Protecting the Best Men*, 36.

79. See, e.g., *New-York Weekly Journal*, 3 December 1733, 8 April 1734; *Independent Advertiser*, 6 February 1749; and *Pennsylvania Gazette*, 26 January 1758.

80. For seventeenth-century circumvention of maritime laws by juries, see Eldridge, *Distant Heritage*, 141; for the role of lenient juries in the crisis of the 1760s, see this volume, chapter 3.

81. Laurence Hanson, *Government and the Press* (Oxford: Oxford University Press, 1936), 20; Shannon C. Stimson, *The American Revolution in the Law*, 54.

82. Katz, *Brief Narrative*, 31.

83. *South-Carolina Gazette*, 30 March 1747; see also Jeffery A. Smith, "Impartiality and Revolutionary Ideology: Editorial Policies of the *South-Carolina Gazette*, 1732–1775," *Journal of Southern History* 49 (1983): 519–20.

84. Thomas, *History*, 1:333–4, 2:48, 253; see also Nelson, "Seditious Libel," 168–9.

85. Clark, *Public Prints*, 184.

86. Warner (*Letters of the Republic*, 49–58) sees the Zenger jury as evincing a new principle of public *supervision*; this characterization overstates the case, anticipating the later development of a norm of continual, active direction of government officials by the public. In the 1730s, the jury was more broadly seen as a rear-guard defense, a "bulwark" against sporadically threatened public liberty.

87. For more on this point, see Stephen Botein, "'Meer Mechanics' and an Open Press: The Business and Political Strategies of Colonial American Printers," *Perspectives in American History* 9 (1975): 127–225; and "Printers and the American Revolution," in *The Press and the American Revolution*, ed. Bernard Bailyn and John Hench (Worcester, Mass.: American Antiquarian Society, 1980), 11–57.

88. Lawrence W. Leder, *Liberty and Authority: Early American Political*

Ideology, 1689–1763 (Chicago: Quadrangle Books, 1968), 22; cf. *American Weekly Mercury*, 6 November 1740.

89. Botein, "'Meer Mechanics,'" 142–3, 166, 171; "Printers and the American Revolution," 20n27.

90. Franklin's own *Pennsylvania Gazette*, 10 June 1731; see also *South-Carolina Gazette*, 14 October 1732.

91. Botein, "Printers and the American Revolution," 20n27; c.f. Clark, *Public Prints*, 210.

92. *Pennsylvania Gazette*, 10 June 1731.

93. *Pennsylvania Gazette*, 8 May 1740. Concerning Franklin's judgment, see also Thomas, *History*, 1:237.

94. *Virginia Gazette*, 10 August 1739.

95. *Pennsylvania Gazette*, 24 July 1740.

96. *Boston Evening Post*, 30 March 1741.

97. This commonplace view suggests the (republican) priority of the public good over individual property rights, though colonists were clearly trying to protect *both* "the *Publick*" press and private property.

98. *Connecticut Gazette*, 7 February 1756; see also, e.g., *Independent Reflector* (New York), 30 August 1753, and *New-England Magazine* 1 (August 1758): 38–40.

99. "Philo-Reflector" [William Livingston and William Smith], Preface to *The Craftsmen: A Sermon from the Independent Whig* (New York: J. Parker, 1753), ii, xii.

100. *Independent Advertiser* (Boston), 9 January 1749. Dwight Teeter is right to caution that the phrase "the public's right to know" is "so laden with twentieth-century connotations that it is difficult to use" in this context; still, he overstates the case when he writes that the phrase "does not seem to have had currency in the eighteenth century"; see Teeter, "From Revisionism to Orthodoxy" (a review of Levy, *Emergence*), *Reviews in American History* 13 (1985): 524.

101. *New-York Mercury*, 27 January 1755.

102. Jonathan Mayhew, "Objections Considered," in *Seven Sermons* (Boston: Rogers and Fowle, 1749), 74, 73. For a discussion of Mayhew's debt to Milton, see George F. Sensabaugh, *Milton in Early America* (Princeton: Princeton University Press, 1964), 52–66.

103. Though New Light forces were periodically rankled when a press proved open to Old Light forces. For one such press, see Clark, *Public Prints*, 263–5, Thomas, *History*, 2:48, and the *Boston Evening Post*, 30 March 1741.

104. "A Lover of TRUTH & LIBERTY" [Elisha Williams], *The Essential Rights and Liberties of Protestants* (Boston: Kneeland and Green, 1744), 6–7.

105. *Independent Advertiser* (Boston), 20 February 1749, 1 August 1748; c.f. Trenchard and Gordon, *Cato's Letters*, 1:286–95 (#36).

106. Mary G. Dietz, "Patriotism," in *Political Innovation and Conceptual Change*, ed. Terence Ball, James Farr, and Russell L. Hanson (Cambridge: Cambridge University Press, 1989), 177–93, esp. 187.

107. *Independent Reflector* (New York), 30 August 1753. See also the *New-England Magazine* (Boston), August 1758, 38–40 (partial reprint). Whether Smith or Livingston is the author of this particular essay is in dispute, but since they wrote together and generally agreed with each other, I have grouped them here. See William Livingston et al., *The Independent Reflector*, ed. Milton M. Klein (Cambridge, Mass.: Harvard University Press, 1963), 446–9.

108. *Independent Reflector* (New York), 30 August 1753.

109. As Lance Banning shrewdly observes, eighteenth-century readers were sensitive to nuances we easily miss; Banning, *The Sacred Fire of Liberty: James Madison and the Founding of the Federal Republic* (Ithaca, N.Y.: Cornell University Press, 1995), 397.

110. Botein, "'Meer Mechanics,'" 150.

111. Hall, *Cultures of Print*, 157–62.

112. See, e.g., Richard L. Bushman, *From Puritan to Yankee* (Cambridge, Mass.: Harvard University Press, 1967), 220, 143, and passim. More broadly, see Edmund S. Morgan, *Inventing the People: The Rise of Popular Sovereignty in England and America* (New York: Norton, 1988), 288–306, esp. 295–300.

113. Clark, *Public Prints*, 259.

114. For a discussion of the ways in which literacy statistics tend to underestimate access to the world of print, see Hall, *Cultures of Print*, 36–78, esp. 53–4, 54n63, and also 84, 95, and 125.

115. *New-York Mercury* 27 January 1755; *Independent Advertiser*, 4 January 1748. Similarly, in 1751, Jonathan Edwards explained the phrase "begging the question" to his "illiterate" [i.e., not academically trained] readers (Hall, *Cultures of Print*, 151). For the earlier, elitist view of the newspaper audience, c.f. *American Weekly Mercury*, 6 November 1740.

116. Jeffery A. Smith, "Impartiality and Revolutionary Ideology," 526.

117. For a particularly dramatic example of this shift, see Nathaniel Eells, *The Wise Ruler a Loyal Subject* (New London: Timothy Green, 1748). See also Bushman, *From Puritan to Yankee*, 282.

118. Mary Patterson Clarke, *Parliamentary Privilege in the American Colonies* (New Haven: Yale University Press, 1943), 123; see also Nelson, "Seditious Libel," 165–6.

119. *New-England Courant*, 6 May 1723.

120. Trenchard and Gordon, *Cato's Letters*, 1:126 (#24); see also, 3:234 (#99) and *South-Carolina Gazette*, 20 March 1749. On the mid-seventeenth-century origins of this claim, see Morgan, *Inventing the People*, 64, 85.

121. Alan Tully, *Forming American Politics: Ideals, Interests, and Institutions in Colonial New York and Pennsylvania* (Baltimore: Johns Hopkins Uni-

versity Press, 1994), 118; Clarke, *Parliamentary Privilege*, 128. See also, e.g., Tully, *Forming American Politics*, 467n147; Clarke, *Parliamentary Privilege*, 131, 222, 244; Elnathan Whitman, *Character and Qualifications of a Good Ruler* (New London: Timothy Green, 1745), 21; and *Pennsylvania Archives*, 8th ser. (Harrisburg: 1874–1935), 6:4701, 4839–40.

122. *Pennsylvania Archives*, 6:4708, 4712; see also, *Pennsylvania Gazette*, 26 January 1758.

123. Jeffery A. Smith estimates that there were more than 20 such cases in eighteenth-century America, while Mary Patterson Clarke figures that "literally scores, probably hundreds" were charged with breach of privilege during the entire colonial period. See Smith, "A Reappraisal of Legislative Privilege and American Colonial Journalism," *Journalism Quarterly* 61 (1984): 98; and Clarke, *Parliamentary Privilege*, 117.

124. Clarke, *Parliamentary Privilege*, 120 and passim.

125. Tully, *Forming American Politics*, 114.

126. Tully, *Forming American Politics*, 114. For much of this history, see Clarke, *Parliamentary Privilege*, 220–2, 240–6; Tully, *Forming American Politics*, 106–22.

127. See, e.g., *Pennsylvania Journal*, 23 February, 30 March 1758. See also Obadiah Honesty [author unknown], *A Remonstrance of Obadiah Honesty* (Philadelphia: 1757); *A Fragment of the Chronicles of Nathan Ben Saddi* (Constantinople [Philadelphia]: 5707 [1759]); and *The American Magazine and Monthly Chronicle* (Philadelphia) 1 (1757–8): 184–5, 196, 199–200, 210–227, 308.

128. For various accounts this history, see Daniel Fowle, *A Total Eclipse of Liberty* (Boston: Daniel Fowle, 1755); Thomas, *History*, 1:129–34; Duniway, *Development*, 115–9; and Levy, *Emergence*, 34–5.

129. *Extract from the Journal of House of Representatives of Massachusetts Bay* (Boston: Z. Fowle and Tyler, 1756), 2, 4–5. Fowle received £31/7/0 in 1765 and another £20 in 1766; see Duniway, *Development*, 118–9.

130. See, e.g., Levy, *Emergence*, 34–5. Smith, *Printers and Press Freedom*, mentions it only in passing; see 8. See also Smith, "Reappraisal," 101. Duniway, *Development*, however, provides a full account; see 115–9, 171–3.

131. Fowle, *A Total Eclipse of Liberty*, 10.

132. Daniel Fowle, *An Appendix to the late Total Eclipse of Liberty* (Boston: Daniel Fowle, 1756), 5.

133. *The Third Petition of Daniel Fowle* (1766) is reprinted in Duniway, *Development*, 171–3.

NOTES TO CHAPTER 3

1. William Blackstone, *Commentaries on the Laws of England*, 4 vols. (Oxford: Clarendon Press, 1765–9), 4:151–2. For a more Zengerian, though far

less influential, American view of press liberty, see [William Bollan], *The Freedom of Speech and Writing upon Public Affairs, Considered, with an Historical View* (London: S. Baker, 1765).

2. Blackstone, *Commentaries*, 4:150.

3. *Boston Gazette*, 9 January 1769, quoting Blackstone, *Commentaries*, 3:379; see also 3:350.

4. Blackstone, *Commentaries*, 4:354; see also, 3:378.

5. E.g., *New-York Journal*, 15 March 1770.

6. James Alexander, *A Brief Narrative of the Case and Trial of John Peter Zenger, Printer of the New-York Weekly Journal, for a Libel* (New York: John Holt, 1770).

7. *Boston Evening-Post*, 20 August 1770.

8. *Boston Gazette*, 10 December 1770; see also *New-York Journal*, 15 March 1770.

9. *An Interesting Appendix to Sir William Blackstone's "Commentaries on the Laws of England"* (Philadelphia: Robert Bell, 1772) and *The Palladium of Conscience* (Philadelphia: Robert Bell, 1773), Dated Pamphlets Collection, American Antiquarian Society.

10. *Palladium*, 34. See also Jeremy Bentham, *Fragment on Government* (1776), chap. 4, sec. xxiv.

11. Levy reads this passage as leaving it uncertain whether Furneaux thought the overt-acts test should apply to political expression; see *Emergence of a Free Press* (New York: Oxford University Press, 1985), 165.

12. Fowle implicitly referred to Wilkes in his last petition to the legislature. See Clyde Augustus Duniway, *Development of Freedom of the Press in Massachusetts* (New York: Longmans, Green, 1906), 118–9; see also 172.

13. See *An Authentick Account of the Proceedings against John Wilkes, Esq.* (Philadelphia: John Dunlap, 1763), Dated Pamphlets Collection, American Antiquarian Society.

14. "Contempt" and "breach of legislative privilege" were terms used interchangeably in colonial America, especially insofar as the breach was an expression that reflected on the dignity of the legislature; see Mary Patterson Clarke, *Parliamentary Privilege in the American Colonies* (New Haven: Yale University Press, 1943), 206–7.

15. *Boston Gazette*, 7 March 1768.

16. *Boston Gazette*, 14 March 1768. See also Arthur M. Schlesinger, *Prelude to Independence: The Newspaper War on Britain, 1764–1776* (New York: Knopf, 1958), 96–7.

17. *Massachusetts Spy* (Boston), 14 November 1771.

18. Isaiah Thomas, *The History of Printing in America* [1810], 2d ed., 2 vols. (New York: Burt Franklin, 1874), 1:166.

19. *Boston Gazette*, 18 November 1771. See also Thomas, *History*, 1:167–8.

20. *Boston Gazette*, 24 February 1772; see also Thomas, *History*, 1:168, and Schlesinger, *Prelude*, 142.

21. *Pennsylvania Gazette* (Philadelphia), 20 October 1773.

22. Jeffery A. Smith, "Impartiality and Revolutionary Ideology: Editorial Policies of the *South-Carolina Gazette*, 1732–1775," *Journal of Southern History* 49 (1983): 525.

23. *New-York Gazette*, 7 May 1770.

24. *Pennsylvania Gazette*, 3 January 1771.

25. Bernard Bailyn, *Ideological Origins of the American Revolution* (Cambridge, Mass.: Harvard University Press, 1967), 95.

26. Schlesinger, *Prelude*, 66.

27. *Pennsylvania Journal* (Philadelphia), 31 October 1765.

28. *Pennsylvania Gazette*, 11 September 1766.

29. Leonard Levy, *Emergence of a Free Press*, 154. Levy quotes from an excerpt in Duniway, *Development*, 128 n1, and is thus presumably unaware of the whole essay and the context; he therefore mistakenly reads it as an attack not on the Stamp Act but on subsequent restraint.

30. Fredrick S. Siebert, *Freedom of the Press in England: 1476–1776* (Urbana: University of Illinois Press, 1952), 323–45.

31. Rind's *Virginia Gazette* (Williamsburg), 16 May 1766; cf. Schlesinger, *Prelude*, 79. For use of this "common dodge of Whig editors" (Schlesinger, *Prelude*, 137), cf., e.g., the *Massachusetts Spy*, 10 December 1770 and thereafter. For an early suggestion of influence, cf. the *American Weekly Mercury* (Philadelphia), 6 November 1740.

32. *Pennsylvania Chronicle* (Philadelphia), 16 March.

33. *Pennsylvania Chronicle*, 13 April 1767; cf. 20 April 1767.

34. Benjamin Franklin, "An Apology for Printers," *Pennsylvania Gazette*, 10 June 1731.

35. Purdie's *Virginia Gazette* (Williamsburg), 7 April 1769.

36. *Boston Chronicle*, 26 October, 2 November 1769, and thereafter.

37. Manuscript note to *Boston Evening-Post*, 30 October 1769, Harbottle Dorr Annotated Collection of Boston Newspapers, Massachusetts Historical Society, microfilm.

38. Schlesinger, *Prelude*, 104–8; *Boston Evening-Post*, 30 October 1769. See also Pauline Maier, *From Resistance to Revolution: Colonial Radicals and the Development of Opposition to Britain, 1765–1776* (New York: Knopf, 1972), 127.

39. *Boston Gazette*, 1 February 1768.

40. *Massachusetts Spy*, 10 December 1770.

41. Cf., for example, the more mainstream Whig view (which was less dismissive of open press theory than was Thomas) exemplified in the *South-Carolina Gazette* (Charleston), 14 December 1769.

42. Bailyn, *Ideological Origins*, 117–8.

43. Schlesinger, *Prelude*, 222; cf. 240.

44. [John Drinker], *Observations on the Late Popular Measures, Offered to the Serious Consideration of the Sober Inhabitants of Pennsylvania* (Philadelphia: 1774), 24; see also, *New-York Gazetteer*, 2 February, 14 July 1774.

45. *New-York Gazetteer*, 12 May 1774; cf. 2 December 1773; also, the *Boston Post-Boy Advertiser*, 12 December 1774, 6–20 February 1775, and the *Boston Weekly News-Letter*, 16 February 1775.

46. The *Gazetteer* had a well-known "violently partisan cast" and had been accused of failing to include Patriot contributions (Schlesinger, *Prelude*, 190; see also 226).

47. Rivington thus reminds us of the inexact and ever-changing relationship between word and concept; see Quentin Skinner, "Language and Political Change," in *Political Innovation and Conceptual Change*, ed. Terence Ball, James Farr, and Russell L. Hanson (Cambridge: Cambridge University Press, 1989), 7–8; James Farr, "Understanding Conceptual Change Politically," in *Political Innovation and Conceptual Change*, ed. Terence Ball, James Farr, and Russell L. Hanson (Cambridge: Cambridge University Press, 1989), 26–8; and Robert W. T. Martin, "Context and Contradiction: Toward a Political Theory of Conceptual Change," *Political Research Quarterly* 50 (1997): 420.

48. *New-York Gazetteer*, 16 February 1775.

49. *New-York Gazetteer*, 8 December 1774; see also 14 July, 29 December 1774, 5 January 1775.

50. *Journals of the Continental Congress, 1774–1789*, ed. Wrothington C. Ford et al. (Washington, D.C.: U.S. Government Printing Office, 1904–37), 1:108 (24 October 1774; repr., *Boston Gazette*, 14 November 1774).

51. *New-York Gazetteer*, 15 December 1774; cf. 2 December 1773; also, the *Boston Weekly News-Letter*, 14 January 1773.

52. *New-York Gazetteer*, 20 April 1775; cf. 2 September 1774; also, the *Norwich Packet* (Connecticut), 25 November–2 December 1773.

53. Purdie's *Virginia Gazette*, 3 February 1775.

54. *Maryland Gazette* (Baltimore), 21 October 1773. The use of the term "professed" by this anti-British writer may be a bold appropriation of a derogatory Tory term; see Phillip Davidson, *Propaganda and the American Revolution, 1763–1783* (Chapel Hill: University of North Carolina Press, 1941), 294.

55. *Pennsylvania Journal*, 17 August 1774.

56. Even at this late date, some Patriots tried to maintain features of the older, received theory of the free and open press. Significantly, these texts also demonstrate an awareness of the increasingly distinct free and open press logics; see, e.g., *Pennsylvania Packet* (Philadelphia), 28 November 1774.

57. *New-York Journal*, 5 January 1775; cf. Rind's *Virginia Gazette*, 18 Au-

gust 1774. For a Tory, open press response to Holt, see the *New-York Gazette and Weekly Mercury*, 9 January 1775.

58. See Timothy Green's exclamation that his *Connecticut Gazette* (New London) was "sacred to *LIBERTY*," 19 August 1774.

59. Schlesinger, *Prelude*, 189.

60. *South-Carolina Gazette*, 19 December 1774.

61. Schlesinger, *Prelude*, 240–1, 257–8. Hugh Gaine's now-docile *New-York Mercury* remained, though under the Patriots' watchful eyes. New Tory papers emerged and past printers returned, but these papers were "narrowly circumscribed," effectively limited to areas held by the British Army (Davidson, *Propaganda*, 312).

62. *Pennsylvania Evening Post* (Philadelphia), 16 November 1776.

63. For an extensive—but by no means exhaustive—catalogue of such laws, see Claude Halstead Van Tyne, *The Loyalists in the American Revolution* (New York: Macmillan, 1902), 327–41.

64. Philadelphia *Pennsylvania Packet*, 15 October 1776.

65. James Madison to William Bradford, [early March 1775], *Papers of James Madison,* ed. William T. Hutchinson et al., 17 vols. (Chicago: University of Chicago Press, 1962–), 1:141. Lance Banning aptly characterizes this desire as "youthful innocence and bluster" (Banning, *The Sacred Fire of Liberty: James Madison and the Founding of the Federal Republic* [Ithaca, N.Y.: Cornell University Press, 1995], 82). But cf. Alexander Hamilton's more temperate reaction to the second mob attack on Rivington's printing office: Hamilton—four years Madison's junior and an equally avid Patriot—"cannot help disapproving and condemning this step," though he is "fully sensible how dangerous and pernicious Rivington's press had been, and how detestable the character of the man is in every respect" [Hamilton to John Jay, 26 November 1775, *Papers of Alexander Hamilton*, 27 vols., ed. Harold C. Syrett and Jacob E. Cooke (New York: Columbia University Press, 161–87], 1:176–7).

66. *Pennsylvania Gazette*, 27 September 1775; see also *Pennsylvania Evening Post*, 16 November 1776.

67. Schlesinger, *Prelude*, 257–8.

68. Journals of the Continental Congress, 4 (1779):18–20, reprinted in *The New-England Chronicle, or the Essex Gazette* (Cambridge, Mass.), 8 January 1776.

69. *Philadelphia Committee of Inspection and Observation*, "In Committee chamber, May 16, 1776" [broadside] (Philadelphia: William and Thomas Bradford, 16 May 1776), Broadsides Collection, American Antiquarian Society, Worcester, Mass.

70. Thomas R. Meehan, "The Pennsylvania Supreme Court in the Law and Politics of the Commonwealth, 1776–1790" (Ph.D. diss., University of

Wisconsin, 1960), 139. "Misprision of treason" is "an offense or misdeamour akin to treason or felony, but involving a lesser degree of guilt, and not liable to the capital penalty" (*Oxford English Dictionary*).

71. Schlesinger, *Prelude*, 261, 267, 298.

72. *Pennsylvania Packet*, 18, 25 March 1776.

73. Robert Bell, "The Printer to the Public: On the Freedom of the Press," appendix to *A Dialogue between the Ghost of General Montgomery Just Arrived from the Elysian Fields; and an American Delegate, in a Wood near Philadelphia* ([Philadelphia]: Robert Bell, 1776), Dated Pamphlets Collection, American Antiquarian Society.

74. Robert Bell, "A Few More Words, on the Freedom of the Press," appendix to Josiah Tucker, *True Interest of Britain* (Philadelphia: Robert Bell, 1776), Dated Pamphlets Collection, American Antiquarian Society. See also, e.g., *Pennsylvania Evening Post*, 3 January 1778.

75. *Pennsylvania Packet*, 31 July 1779; *Pennsylvania Evening Post*, 2 August 1779. See also *Pennsylvania Packet*, 29 December 1778.

76. Davidson, *Propaganda*, 334.

77. William Goddard, *The Prowess of the Whig Club* (Baltimore: [Mary K. Goddard], 1777), 12. *The Prowess* contains appendices reprinting a number of relevant documents; see also *Maryland Journal*, 25 February 1777; and Ward L. Miner, *William Goddard: Newspaperman* (Durham, N.C.: Duke University Press, 1962), 150–62.

78. Bernard Schwartz, *The Bill of Rights: A Documentary History*, 2 vols. (New York: Chelsea House, 1971), 1:284.

79. John Holt to William Goddard, 26 February 1778, Book Trades Collection, Box 1, Folder 6, American Antiquarian Society.

80. Dwight L. Teeter, "Press Freedom and the Public Printing: Pennsylvania, 1775–83," *Journalism Quarterly* 45 (1968): 446; Teeter, "A Legacy of Expression: Philadelphia Newspapers and Congress during the War for Independence" (Ph.D. diss., University of Wisconsin, 1966), 221.

81. *Maryland Journal* (Baltimore), 14 July 1779 (supplement to the *Journal* of 13 July 1779).

82. *Maryland Journal*, 27 July, 3 August 1779. For more on the "Queries" incident, see Miner, *Goddard*, 168–73.

83. Candidus [Samuel Adams], *Philadelphia Evening Post*, 3 February 1776; see Schlesinger, *Prelude*, 261.

84. Schlesinger, *Prelude*, 298.

NOTES TO CHAPTER 4

1. Gordon S. Wood, *The Radicalism of the American Revolution* (New York: Knopf, 1992).

2. Pauline Maier, *From Resistance to Revolution: Colonial Radicals and the Development of American Opposition to Britain, 1765–1776* (New York: Knopf, 1972), esp. 3–26.

3. Edward Countryman, *The American Revolution* (New York: Hill and Wang, 1985), 144.

4. Wood, *Radicalism*, 248.

5. Wood, *Radicalism*, 59.

6. See Michael Warner, *The Letters of the Republic: Publication and the Public Sphere in Eighteenth-Century America* (Cambridge, Mass.: Harvard University Press, 1990), esp. 42, 72.

7. Edmund S. Morgan, *Inventing the People: The Rise of Popular Sovereignty in England and America* (New York: Norton, 1988), 288–306; for the earlier, traditional view, see 134, 295–6.

8. Richard D. Brown, *Knowledge Is Power: The Diffusion of Information in Early American History* (New York: Oxford University Press, 1989), 64.

9. Wood, *Radicalism*, 86. For an interesting example of the continuing political importance of a gentleman's "honor," see Joanne B. Freeman, "Dueling as Politics: Reinterpreting the Burr-Hamilton Duel," *William and Mary Quarterly*, 3d ser., 53 (1996): 289–318.

10. Novanglus [John Adams], quoted in Gordon S. Wood, *The Creation of the American Republic, 1776–1787* (Chapel Hill: University of North Carolina Press, 1969), 63.

11. Eleazor Oswald to George Washington, 28 October 1778, quoted in Dwight L. Teeter, "The Printer and the Chief Justice: Seditious Libel in 1782–83," *Journalism Quarterly* 45 (1968): 260.

12. Bernard Schwartz, *The Bill of Rights: A Documentary History*, 2 vols. (New York: Chelsea House, 1971), 1:235; see also North Carolina *Declaration of Rights* (1776), 1:287.

13. Schwartz, *Bill of Rights*, 1:324.

14. Schwartz, *Bill of Rights*, 1:273.

15. William Blackstone, *Commentaries on the Laws of England*, 4 vols. (Philadelphia: Robert Bell, 1771), 4:151–2 (emphasis in original); Leonard W. Levy, *Emergence of a Free Press* (New York: Oxford University Press, 1985), 12–3.

16. Wood, *Creation*, 10. For a similar view that further qualifies Blackstone's influence, see Norman L. Rosenberg, *Protecting the Best Men: An Interpretive History of the Law of Libel* (Chapel Hill: University of North Carolina Press, 1986), 53.

17. Jefferson to James Madison, 17 February 1826, *Writings of Thomas Jefferson*, ed. Andrew A. Lipscombe and Albert Ellery Bergh, 20 vols. (Washington, D.C.: Thomas Jefferson Memorial Association, 1905), 16:156; see also Jefferson to Horatio Spafford, 17 March 1814, *Writings*, 14:120. Lord Chief

Justice Mansfield, in the Dean of St. Asaph's case in Britain (1783), reaffirmed the traditional interpretation of the common law of seditious libel that refused to admit truth as a defense and restricted the jury to a special verdict on the fact of publication only. Mansfield's interpretation was thus even more restrictive than Blackstone's, which at least included broader jury powers.

18. *Papers of Thomas Jefferson*, ed. Julian P. Boyd, 26 vols. (Princeton: Princeton University Press, 1950–), 1:363 [third and final draft]; see also 1:344–5, 353 [first and second draft].

19. Schwartz, *Bill of Rights*, 1:342 (MA), 1:378 (NH). For more on these and the other state constitutions, see James R. Parramore, "State Constitutions and the Press: Historical Context and Resurgence of a Libertarian Tradition," *Journalism Quarterly* 69 (1992): 105–23, esp. 110–2.

20. Robert R. Palmer, *The Age of the Democratic Revolution: A Political History of Europe and America, 1760–1800*, 2 vols. (Princeton: Princeton University Press, 1959), 1:520.

21. Oscar Handlin and Mary Handlin, eds., *The Popular Sources of Political Authority: Documents on the Massachusetts Constitution of 1780* (Cambridge, Mass.: Harvard University Press, 1966), 641, 724, 728, 749–50, 771, 789, and esp. 762.

22. See, e.g., John Trenchard and Thomas Gordon, *Cato's Letters*, 4 vols. (London: Wilkins, Woodward, Walthoe, and Peele, 1724), 1:126 (#24); see also 3:234 (#99).

23. Wood, *Creation*, 163.

24. Novanglus [John Adams] quoted in Wood, *Creation*, 165.

25. *Massachusetts Centinel* (Boston), 28 May 1785.

26. *Freeman's Journal* (Philadelphia), 13 June 1781.

27. *Independent Chronicle* (Boston), 11 January 1787; see also *Massachusetts Centinel*, 28 May 1785.

28. Schwartz, *Bill of Rights*, 1:234; *Pennsylvania Packet*, 3 July 1779; Handlin and Handlin, *Popular Sources*, 443.

29. Jean-Jacques Rousseau, *On the Social Contract*, in *Basic Political Writings of Jean-Jacques Rousseau*, ed. Donald A. Cress (Indianapolis: Hackett, 1987), Book 3, 198.

30. John Adams, *Thoughts on Government* (1776), reprinted in *American Political Writing during the Founding Era, 1760–1805*, 2 vols., ed. Charles S. Hyneman and Donald S. Lutz (Indianapolis: Liberty Fund, 1983), 1:403.

31. Wood, *Creation*, 191; Willi Paul Adams, *The First American Constitutions: Republican Ideology and the Making of State Constitutions in the Revolutionary Era* (Chapel Hill: University of North Carolina, 1976), 246.

32. Schwartz, *Bill of Rights*, 1:266, 287, 343.

33. Wood, *Creation*, 368.

34. Schwartz, *Bill of Rights*, 1:266, 273.

35. *Freeman's Journal*, 25 April 1781; 13 June 1781. Cf. a "constitutional-ist" printer's (Eleazor Oswald's) view, *Independent Gazetteer* (Philadelphia), 13 April 1782.

36. *Pennsylvania Journal* (Philadelphia), 4 June 1777.

37. *Maryland Journal* (Baltimore), 22 June 1787; see also 23 February 1787.

38. For a rare reference to this debate, see Clyde Augustus Duniway's single-paragraph discussion in *The Development of Freedom of the Press in Massachusetts* (New York: Longmans, Green, 1906), 136–7. Relying on Duniway, Levy is similarly curt and ignores the debate over the tax's disproportionate effect on ordinary readers (Levy, *Emergence*, 214).

39. Isaiah Thomas, "To the Customers for Thomas's <u>Massachusetts Spy</u> . . ." [broadside, 3 April 1786] (Worcester, Mass.: I. Thomas, 1786), Broadsides Collection, American Antiquarian Society, Worcester, Mass.; *Independent Chronicle*, 22 September 1785.

40. Petition of John Mycall, Book Trades Collection, Box 1, Folder 7, American Antiquarian Society (photocopy of Senate File 718–5, Massachusetts State Archives); see also Petition of Several Printers, Book Trades Collection, Oversize Manuscript Box, American Antiquarian Society (photocopy of Senate File 718, Massachusetts State Archives).

41. *Massachusetts Centinel*, 28 May 1785; see also *Independent Chronicle*, 11 August 1785, and *Pennsylvania Gazette*, 18 May 1785.

42. *Massachusetts Centinel*, 28 July 1787, reprinting from the *Independent Gazetteer*, 14 July 1787; see also *Essex Journal* (Newburyport, Mass.), 20 December 1786.

43. Wood, *Creation*, 367.

44. For a general discussion of the case, see Dwight L. Teeter, "The Printer and the Chief Justice: Seditious Libel in 1782–3," *Journalism Quarterly* 45 (1968): 235–42, 260.

45. *Pennsylvania Gazette*, 8 January 1783; *Pennsylvania Packet*, 25 January 1783.

46. *Pennsylvania Gazette*, 8 January 1783.

47. *Freeman's Journal*, 15 January 1783.

48. *Pennsylvania Gazette*, 22 January 1783.

49. Warner, *Letters of the Republic*, 72. More broadly, see Jürgen Habermas, *The Structural Transformation of the Public Sphere: An Inquiry into a Category of Bourgeois Society*, trans. Thomas Burger with Frederick Lawrence (Cambridge, Mass.: MIT Press, 1989), esp. 43–50.

50. *Independent Chronicle*, 4 June 1778.

51. Handlin and Handlin, *Popular Sources*, 641, 724, 728, 749–50, 789, and esp. 762.

52. See, e.g., *Independent Gazetteer*, 13 April 1782 and 7 December 1782; *Massachusetts Centinel*, 19 January 1785; 27 July 1787.

53. *Boston Evening Post,* 8 December 1781; *Massachusetts Centinel,* 24 September 1785.

54. *Independent Gazetteer,* 9 November 1782.

55. *Independent Gazetteer,* 7 December 1782; 14 December 1782.

56. Thomas Jefferson to John Jay, 25 January 1786, *Papers of Thomas Jefferson,* 9:239; see also Jefferson to James Currie, 28 January 1786, 9:215; and for John Jay's concurring view, see Jay to Jefferson, 5 May 1786, 9:450.

57. Thomas Jefferson to Abigail Adams, 25 September 1785, *Papers of Thomas Jefferson,* 8:548.

58. John Gardiner, quoted in Maryann Yodelis Smith and Gerald J. Baldasty, "Criticism of Public Officials and Government in the New Nation," *Journal of Communication Inquiry* 4 (1979): 66.

59. John B. Hench, "The Newspaper in a Republic: Boston's Chronicle and Centinel, 1782–1800" (Ph.D. diss., Clark University, 1979), 11.

60. Instructions of the Inhabitants and Freemen of Albemarle County to Their Representatives in the General Assembly, *Papers of Thomas Jefferson,* 6:288; see also *Freeman's Journal,* 27 March 1782.

61. Brown, *Knowledge Is Power,* 32–5. By the eighteenth century, elites were relegated to advising common folks to exercise caution; see 77.

62. See, e.g., *Independent Chronicle,* 21 October 1790; and *Pennsylvania Packet,* 9 August 1783.

63. *Freeman's Journal,* 10 April 1782.

64. *Independent Gazetteer,* 13 April 1782.

65. *Independent Chronicle,* 11 January 1787.

66. *Massachusetts Centinel,* 15 June 1785.

67. *Independent Gazetteer,* 9 November 1782.

68. *Independent Chronicle,* 17 March 1785, reprinting from Price's *Observations on the Importance of the American Revolution* (1784).

69. John Jay to Thomas Jefferson, 5 May 1786, *Papers of Thomas Jefferson,* 9:450.

70. For a brief discussion of this historiography, see Michael Lienesch, "In Defence of the Antifederalists," *History of Political Thought* 4 (1983): 65–87, esp. 65–8, 74–5, 81–2; for more detail, see Saul Cornell, "The Changing Historical Fortunes of the Anti-Federalists," *Northwestern University Law Review* 84 (1989): 39–73. For Kenyon's argument, see Cecelia Kenyon, "Men of Little Faith: The Anti-federalists on the Nature of Representative Government," *William and Mary Quarterly,* 3d ser., 12 (1955): 3–43.

71. Herbert J. Storing, *What the Anti-Federalists Were For,* vol. 1 of *The Complete Anti-Federalist,* 7 vols., ed. Storing (Chicago: University of Chicago Press, 1981); Lienesch, "Defence"; Christopher M. Duncan, *The Anti-Federalists and Early American Political Thought* (DeKalb: Northern Illinois University Press, 1995).

72. Saul Cornell, *The Other Founders: Anti-Federalism and the Dissenting Tradition in America, 1788–1828* (Chapel Hill: University of North Carolina Press, 1999). See also Cornell, "Aristocracy Assailed: The Ideology of Backcountry Anti-Federalism," *Journal of American History* 76 (1990): 1148–72. Following Cornell, I use the term "Anti-Federalist" (and its cognates) rather than "Antifederalist" or "anti-Federalist" to indicate a diversity of views within the general concord of Anti-Federalism; see Cornell, "Aristocracy Assailed," 1148n1.

73. Cornell, *Other Founders*, 84, 99; see also 115, 10.

74. Levy, *Emergence*, 221–233, 266; Leonard W. Levy, ed., *Freedom of the Press from Zenger to Jefferson: Early American Libertarian Theories* (Durham, N.C.: Carolina Academic Press, 1996).

75. David M. Rabban, "The Ahistorical Historian: Leonard Levy on Freedom of Expression in Early American History," *Stanford Law Review* 37 (1985) 795–856, esp. 841–8. But cf. David A. Anderson, "The Origins of the Press Clause," *U.C.L.A. Law Review* 30 (1983): 455–541, esp. 466–86.

76. But cf. Michael Lienesch, "Thomas Jefferson and the American Democratic Experience: The Origins of the Partisan Press, Popular Political Parties, and Public Opinion," in *Jeffersonian Legacies*, ed. Peter S. Onuf (Charlottesville: University Press of Virginia, 1993), 316–39.

77. Storing, *Complete Anti-Federalist*, 4:215n3. Storing's presumptive reading apparently relies on a single ambiguous Anti-Federalist statement and James Wilson's Blackstonian interpretation presented in the Pennsylvania Ratifying Convention. See 4:206–7, 215n3.

78. Levy, *Emergence*, 266, 221.

79. Cornell, "Changing Historical Fortunes," 70; Cornell, "Aristocracy Assailed," 1166. See also Cornell, *Other Founders*, 33.

80. See especially Hamilton's *Federalist* 84 and James Wilson's influential Speech in the State House Yard, 6 October 1787, reprinted in Merrill Jensen, ed., *The Documentary History of the Ratification of the Constitution* (hereafter *DHRC*), 18 vols. (Madison: State Historical Society of Wisconsin, 1976–), 2:167–72.

81. See, e.g., *Friends of the Constitution: Writings of the "Other" Federalists, 1787–8*, ed. Colleen A. Sheehan and Gary L. McDowell (Indianapolis: Liberty Fund, 1998), 41, 144, 247, 273, 318.

82. See, e.g., "Cincinnatus" I, *New York Journal*, 1 November 1787.

83. Wood, *Creation*, 485. More broadly, see Cornell, "Aristocracy Assailed."

84. Michael Lienesch, *New Order of the Ages: Time, the Constitution, and the Making of Modern American Political Thought* (Princeton: Princeton University Press, 1988), 162.

85. Russell Hanson, *The Democratic Imagination in America: Conversations with Our Past* (Princeton: Princeton University Press, 1985), 69. See also

Garry Wills, *Explaining America: The Federalist* (Garden City, N.Y.: Double-day, 1981).

86. Sherman preferred indirect election wherein the lower house would be chosen by the (directly elected) state legislators. *The Records of the Federal Convention of 1787*, 3 vols., ed. Max Farrand (New Haven: Yale University Press, 1911), 1:48; Jefferson to Edward Carrington, 16 January 1787, *Papers*, 12:48.

87. Wood, *Creation*, 562. Banning concedes that "for some, perhaps for many Federalists this characterization is apt"; see Banning, *The Sacred Fire of Liberty: James Madison and the Founding of the Federal Republic* (Ithaca, N.Y.: Cornell University Press, 1995), 252.

88. Thomas Lloyd, ed., *Debates of the Convention, of the State of Pennsylvania, on the Constitution proposed for the Government of the United States* (Philadelphia: Lloyd, 1788), 56 (1 December 1787). Since Wilson was a frequent and insightful critic of Blackstone's views, his use of Blackstonian language regarding the press is significant.

89. Certainly many Anti-Federalists saw little substance in Wilson's democratic rhetoric; see, e.g., An Officer of the Late Continental Army, *Independent Gazetter*, 6 November 1787. For a more sympathetic account of Wilson's democratic views, see James H. Read, *Power versus Liberty: Madison, Hamilton, Wilson, and Jefferson* (Charlottesville: University Press of Virginia, 2000), 89–117, and, more broadly, Mark David Hall, *The Political and Legal Philosophy of James Wilson, 1742–1798* (Columbia: University of Missouri Press, 1997).

90. Morgan, *Inventing the People*, 277–83.

91. Banning, *Sacred Fire of Liberty*, 243; see also 181.

92. George Mason to John Lamb, 9 June 1788, reprinted in *DHRC*, 9:821.

93. Helen E. Veit et al., eds., *Creating the Bill of Rights: The Documentary Record from the First Federal Congress* (Baltimore: Johns Hopkins University Press, 1991), 150–3 (reprinting from the *Congressional Register* for 15 August 1789). For an earlier exchange over instructions, see *Maryland Journal* (Baltimore), 22 June, 13 July, 3 August 1787.

94. Cornell, "Aristocracy Assailed," 1153.

95. See, e.g., "Uncus," *Maryland Journal*, 9 November 1787; James Madison to Thomas Jefferson, 17 October 1788, *Papers of Thomas Jefferson*, 14:19; and *The Federalist* 84.

96. "America" [Noah Webster], *New York Daily Advertiser*, 31 December 1787; see also "J.B.F.," *Maryland Journal*, 23 February 1787.

97. *Independent Gazetteer*, 2 October 1788, reprinting from the *Virginia Independent Chronicle* (Richmond), 18 June 1788; see also, e.g., "The Federal Farmer," Letters VI and XVI, reprinted in *DHRC*, 17:270, 343–4.

98. Jefferson to Madison, 15 March 1789, *Papers of Thomas Jefferson*,

14:659; Veit et al., eds., *Creating the Bill of Rights*, 84 (reprinting from the *Congressional Record* for 8 June 1789). "This is the single matter on which Jefferson unquestionably exercised a quite specific influence on his friend" (Banning, *Sacred Fire of Liberty*, 493n95).

99. Address of the Minority of the Maryland Convention, *Maryland Gazette* (Annapolis), 1 May 1788.

100. "The Federal Farmer," Letter XVI, reprinted in *DHRC*, 17:343. For earlier examples of declarations "defining and ascertaining" rights, see *The Essex Result* (1980), reprinted in Handlin and Handlin, eds., *Popular Sources*, 324, 332; and *Independent Gazetteer*, 19 October 1782.

101. Madison to Thomas Jefferson, 17 October 1788, *Papers of Thomas Jefferson*, 14:20. See also Veit et al., eds., *Creating the Bill of Rights*, 82 (reprinting Madison from the *Congressional Record* for 8 June 1789); and [Madison], "Public Opinion," *National Gazette* (Philadelphia), 19 December 1791.

102. Cornell, *Other Founders*, 11, 103.

103. Anderson, "Origins," 485.

104. Anderson, "Origins," 499.

105. James Wilson in Lloyd, *Debates*, 56; also *DHRC* 9:1136, 16:202; and Alexander J. Dallas, *Reports of Cases Ruled and Adjudged in the Courts of Pennsylvania, before and since the Revolution* (Philadelphia: T. Bradford, 1790), 325.

106. Anderson, "Origins," 490n211; John Adams to Thomas Cushing, 7 March 1789, reprinted in [Frank W. Grinnell, ed.], "Hitherto Unpublished Correspondence between Chief Justice Cushing and John Adams in 1789," *Massachusetts Law Quarterly* 27 (1942): 16.

107. *Pennsylvania Gazette*, 14 November 1787.

108. *DHRC*, 13:xvii, 315–22; 14:169; 16:540–96.

109. Cornell, *Other Founders*, 122; see also 121; Rosenberg, *Protecting the Best Men*, 57; and Charles E. Clark, "Early American Journalism: News and Opinion in the Popular Press," in *The Colonial Book in the Atlantic World*, vol. 1 of *A History of the Book in America,* ed. Hugh Amory and David D. Hall (Cambridge: Cambridge University Press, 2000), 365.

110. *Virginia Gazette and Winchester Advertiser*, 7 March 1788; see also the oft-reprinted "Centinel" II [Samuel Bryan], *Freeman's Journal*, 24 October 1787.

111. Jefferson to James Madison, 28 August 1789, *Papers of Thomas Jefferson*, 15:367; Jefferson also excluded false facts "affecting the peace of the confederacy with foreign nations."

112. "Amendments Proposed by William Paca in the Maryland Convention," (Baltimore) *Maryland Journal*, 29 April 1788, reprinted in *DHRC* 17:240–1. With at least forty-six reprintings, this text is possibly the single most reprinted Anti-Federalist item; see Cornell, *Other Founders*, 309.

113. Undated letter to Isaiah Thomas for the *Worcester Magazine* [1786–8],

Isaiah Thomas Papers, Box 15, Folder 3, American Antiquarian Society (underlining in manuscript).

114. *Gazette of the State of Georgia* (Savannah), 6 December 1787. See also, e.g., *Independent Gazetteer*, 27 October 1787, and A Friend to Harmony, *Candid Considerations on Libels* (Boston: Freeman and Andrews, 1789), 3.

115. *Independent Gazetteer*, 2 October 1788, reprinting from the *Virginia Independent Chronicle* (Richmond), 18 June 1788; Mentor, *Virginia Gazette and Petersburg Intelligencer*, 3 April 1788. See also Richard Henry Lee to Edmund Pendleton, 26 May 1788, reprinted in *DHRC*, 9:879.

116. Jefferson to Edward Carrington, 16 January 1787, *Papers of Thomas Jefferson*, 12:48.

117. Cornell, "Aristocracy Assailed," 1163.

118. "Federal Farmer," *Additional Letters*, Letter XVI, reprinted in *DHRC*, 17:350; "Philadelphiensis," VI, *Freeman's Journal*, 26 December 1787, reprinted in *DHRC*, 15:106; "Centinel" XVII, *Independent Gazetteer*, 9 April 1788.

119. Cornell, *Other Founders*, 106.

120. *National Gazette*, 19 December 1791 (italics in original).

121. Handlin and Handlin, *Popular Sources*, 333.

122. *Independent Gazetteer*, 3 December 1787.

123. "Cæsar" II, *Daily Advertiser* (New York), 17 October 1787.

124. Jefferson to Madison, 31 July 1788, *Papers of Thomas Jefferson*, 13:442; see also Jefferson to Noah Webster, Jr., 4 December 1790, *Papers of Thomas Jefferson*, 18:132.

125. "Federal Farmer," *Additional Letters*, Letter XVI, reprinted in *DHRC*, 17:350.

126. *Independent Gazetteer*, 27 September 1788; A Friend to Harmony, *Candid Considerations*, 8, 9, 17; see also Thomas Jefferson to Edward Carrington, 16 January 1787, *Papers of Thomas Jefferson*, 11:49.

127. Cornell, *Other Founders*, 112.

128. Rosenberg, *Protecting the Best Men*, 63.

129. Levy, *Emergence*, 211n118; more broadly, see 210–1, and Dallas, *Reports*, 319–31; also, *Pennsylvania Gazette*, 30 July, 3 September 1788. This is one of the few occasions when a conflict between a free press and a fair trial was discerned; accordingly, this issue received scant attention during the eighteenth century.

130. Saul Cornell is right to note that "the response to the Oswald case casts doubt on Leonard W. Levy's claim that 'in the entire body of Anti-Federalist publications no one had come to grips with any real problems connected with freedom of the press'" (*Emergence*, 244), but Cornell's claim that the Oswald case of 1788 was a "landmark in the history of the law of libel" (128) is slightly exaggerated. As we have seen, the case was part of a larger evolution in Anti-Federalist thought regarding press liberty.

131. Dallas, *Reports*, 324, 5. See also *Federal Gazette* (Philadelphia), 12 February 1789; and *Gazette of the United States* (New York), 13 March 1790. For a slightly different reading of McKean's views and the case more generally, see Rosenberg, *Protecting the Best Men*, 62–4.

132. *Independent Gazetteer*, 4 December 1787; see also *Massachusetts Centinel*, 10 November 1787.

133. Wood, *Creation*, 491.

134. Wood, *Radicalism*, 256; see also Cornell, "Aristocracy Assailed," 1156–68; and Wood, "Interests and Disinterestedness in the Making of the Constitution," in *Beyond Confederation: Origins of the Constitution and American National Identity*, ed. Richard Beeman, Stephen Botein, and Edward C. Carter II (Chapel Hill: University of North Carolina Press, 1987), 69–109. For an early critique of disinterestedness that may well have influenced early American thinking, see John Trenchard and Thomas Gordon, *Cato's Letters*, 4 vols. (London: Wilkins, Woodward, Walthoe, and Peele, 1724), 2:50–6 (#40).

135. Wood, *Creation*, 492.

136. See, e.g., *Independent Chronicle*, 4 October 1787; Boston *Massachusetts Gazette*, 16 October 1787; and *Independent Gazetteer*, 2 November 1787.

137. "Philadelphiensis," *Independent Gazetteer*, 7 November 1787. For Federalists cleverly using this argument against elite Anti-Federalists, see "Brutus," *Virginia Journal and Alexandria Advertiser*, 22 November 1787, reprinted in *DHRC* 14:152; and "Valerius," *Virginia Independent Chronicle* (Richmond), 23 January 1788.

138. See, e.g., *New Haven Gazette*, 22 November 1787; and "The Landholder" VIII, *Connecticut Courant* (Hartford), 24 December 1787.

139. *Massachusetts Centinel*, 10 October 1787; for an editor defending a contributor as not "concerned" in any present or future administration, see *Massachusetts Gazette*, 16 October 1787.

140. For a telling exchange over the relative importance of an author's "reasonings," see *Independent Gazetteer*, 7 November, 4, 5 December 1787.

141. *New York Journal*, 1 January 1788.

142. *Gazette of the United States* (Philadelphia), 14 December 1791.

143. Joyce Appleby, *Capitalism and a New Social Order: The Republican Vision of the 1790s* (New York: New York University Press, 1984), 21. For significant efforts to appreciate this fluidity, see Michael Lienesch, *New Order*, and Michael Lienesch, "Thomas Jefferson and the American Democratic Experience." For recent efforts to instead isolate liberalism and republicanism via a theory/practice distinction, see Michael Zuckert, *Natural Rights and the New Republicanism* (Princeton: Princeton University Press, 1994), and Jerome Huyler, *Locke in America: The Moral Philosophy of the Founding Era* (Lawrence: University Press of Kansas, 1995).

144. *Pennsylvania Packet*, 26 July 1788.

145. "The State Soldier" III, *Virginia Independent Chronicle*, 12 March 1788.

146. For a similar interpretation, see Banning, *Sacred Fire of Liberty*; and James H. Read, "'Our Complicated System': James Madison on Power and Liberty," *Political Theory* 23 (1995): 452–75.

147. Madison to Jefferson, 17 October 1788, *Papers of Thomas Jefferson*, 14:19.

148. Veit et al., eds., *Creating the Bill of Rights*, 77, reprinting from the *Congressional Register* for 8 June 1789.

149. *Gazette of the United States* (New York), 22 August 1789; Veit et al., eds., *Creating the Bill of Rights*, 188, reprinting from the *Congressional Record* for 17 August 1789.

150. *Gazette of the United States*, 22 August 1789; Veit et al., eds., *Creating the Bill of Rights*, 85, reprinting from the *Congressional Record* for 8 June 1789; Madison to Jefferson, 17 October 1788, *Papers of Thomas Jefferson*, 14:19.

151. *Journal of the First Session of the Senate* (New York: Gales and Seaton, 1789), 72.

152. "Philadelphiensis," *Independent Gazetteer*, 7 November 1787.

NOTES TO CHAPTER 5

1. John R. Howe Jr., "Republican Thought and the Political Violence of the 1790s," *American Quarterly* 14(1967): 147–65, esp. 150. For a more recent account of the dire political crisis of the 1790s, see James Roger Sharp, *American Politics in the Early Republic: The New Nation in Crisis* (New Haven: Yale University Press, 1993).

2. For a sense of this genuine and deep-seated apprehension, see William Manning, *The Key of Libberty* [1798], ed. Samuel Eliot Morison, *William and Mary Quarterly*, 3d ser., 13 (1956): 202–54.

3. Saul Cornell, *The Other Founders: Anti-Federalism and the Dissenting Tradition in America, 1788–1828* (Chapel Hill: University of North Carolina Press, 1999), 230.

4. Gordon S. Wood, "The Democratization of Mind in the American Revolution," in *Leadership in the American Revolution* (Washington, D.C.: Library of Congress, 1974), 81. More recently, Saul Cornell has aptly labeled the Sedition Act controversy a "watershed" (*Other Founders*, 13; see also 230–1).

5. "Exchange papers" traditionally swapped as a courtesy between printers would remain free; indeed, the Post Office Act formalized this custom and ensured that it was pursued impartially. See Richard R. John, *Spreading the News: The American Postal System from Franklin to Morse* (Cambridge, Mass.: Harvard University Press, 1995), 31–42.

6. *National Gazette* (Philadelphia), 28 May, 7, 14 July 1792; see also Don-

ald H. Stewart, *The Opposition Press of the Federalist Period* (Albany: State University of New York Press, 1969), 460–3.

7. Even Benjamin Franklin Bache, printer of the (Philadelphia) *Aurora* and opponent of the newspaper tax, thought the charge itself "trifling" (John, *Spreading the News*, 36).

8. The free delivery of all newspapers, the other proposal in the post office debates, would also have put the rapidly multiplying country newspapers, especially those in the South, at a severe disadvantage (John, *Spreading the News*, 39–40).

9. For much of this history, see Alfred F. Young, *The Democratic-Republicans of New York: The Origins, 1763–1797* (Chapel Hill: University of North Carolina, 1967), 476–95.

10. *Argus* (New York), 15 March 1796. See also *Timepiece* (New York), 22 December 1797; and *Aurora* (Philadelphia), 8 May 1798.

11. *Argus*, 6 April 1796.

12. *Argus*, 15 March 1796.

13. Stanley Elkins and Eric McKitrick, *The Age of Federalism* (New York: Oxford University Press, 1993), 847n12.

14. Elkins and McKitrick, *Age of Federalism*, 456.

15. Unable to resist concluding with a gibe at Federalists, the Society noted its fear that "their characters will exclude most men of the your [aristocratical] opinion." See the *Newark Gazette*, 26 March 1794, quoted in Philip S. Foner, ed., *The Democratic-Republican Societies, 1790–1800: A Documentary Sourcebook of Constitutions, Declarations, Addresses, Resolutions, and Toasts* (Westport, Conn.: Greenwood Press, 1976), 142.

16. *Declaration of the Political Principles of the Patriotic Society of New-castle County, in the State of Delaware*, quoted in Foner, *Democratic-Republican Societies*, 320.

17. *Independent Chronicle* (Boston), 16 January 1794; *Newark Gazette*, 31 December 1794, quoted in Foner, *Democratic-Republican Societies*, 148.

18. *Farmers' Library* (Rutland, Vt.), 23 April 1794, quoted in Foner, *Democratic-Republican Societies*, 285; *Independent Chronicle*, 16 January 1794. See also William Finley, *A Review of the Revenue System Adopted by the First Congress under the Federal Constitution* (Philadelphia: T. Dobson, 1794), Dated Books Collection, American Antiquarian Society, 103.

19. *Newark Gazette*, 12 March 1794, quoted in Foner, *Democratic-Republican Societies*, 144.

20. *General Advertiser* (later the *Aurora*) (Philadelphia), 26 January 1795; *New York Journal*, 31 May 1794.

21. But cf. *General Advertiser*, 26 January 1795.

22. *Annals of Congress*, 3d Congress, 934–5.

23. For a discussion of these trials, see James Morton Smith, *Freedom's*

Fetters: The Alien and Sedition Laws and American Civil Liberties (Ithaca, N.Y.: Cornell University Press, 1956), 188–220.

24. Elkins and McKitrick, *Age of Federalism*, 590.

25. Elkins and McKitrick, *Age of Federalism*, 592.

26. Cornell, *Other Founders*, 237; see also 173.

27. Elkins and McKitrick, *Age of Federalism*, 703.

28. *Annals of Congress,* 5th Congress, 2098.

29. Smith, *Freedom's Fetters*, 186.

30. Lance Banning, *The Sacred Fire of Liberty: James Madison and the Founding of the Federal Republic* (Ithaca, N.Y.: Cornell University Press, 1995), 385.

31. Elkins and McKitrick, *Age of Federalism*, 704.

32. See Smith, *Freedom's Fetters*, 277–306.

33. Smith, *Freedom's Fetters*, 270–4.

34. Elkins and McKitrick, *Age of Federalism*, 713.

35. See, e.g., *Aurora*, 6 June, 13 July 1798; *Independent Chronicle,* 14 June, 5 July 1798.

36. See Smith, *Freedom's Fetters*, 421–3, and Normal L. Rosenberg, *Protecting the Best Men: An Interpretive History of the Law of Libel* (Chapel Hill: University of North Carolina Press, 1986), 89.

37. Francis Wharton, ed., *State Trials of the United States during the Administrations of Washington and Adams* (Philadelphia: Carey and Hart, 1849), 692.

38. See, e.g., *Annals of Congress,* 5th Congress, 2153.

39. *Aurora*, 11 February 1799; John Thomson, *An Enquiry Concerning the Liberty and Licentiousness of the Press, and the Uncontroulable Nature of the Human Mind* (New York: Johnson and Stryker, 1801), 20, 21.

40. Banning, *Sacred Fire of Liberty*, 394. See also Cornell, *Other Founders*, 240; Sharp, *American Politics in the Early Republic*, 184; and Lance Banning, *The Jeffersonian Persuasion: Evolution of a Party Ideology* (Ithaca, N.Y.: Cornell University Press, 1978). Walter Berns long ago preferred to read Republican states' rights concerns as a preemptory defense of slavery, but even Leonard Levy, who stresses heavily the states' rights arguments, considers this contextualization "exaggerated" (*Emergence of a Free Press* [New York: Oxford University Press, 1985], 306n90). In fact, in the immediate context of 1800, the Republicans' "rhetoric of protest and liberty" if anything "stimulated slave unrest" (Sharp, *American Politics in the Early Republic*, 242). See Walter Berns, *The First Amendment and the Future of American Democracy* (New York: Basic Books, 1976), 80–147. See also Berns, "Freedom of the Press and the Alien and Sedition Laws: A Reappraisal," in *1970: Supreme Court Review*, ed. Philip B. Kurland (Chicago: University of Chicago Press, 1970), 109–59.

41. Impartiality was also expected of postmasters: efforts prior to the Post

Office Act to have only *selected* newspapers carried in the mail brought forceful opposition; similarly, government censorship of the mail, common in England and elsewhere, was not tolerated in America; see John, *Spreading the News*, 33–4, 41–2.

42. For the illustrative example of one newspaper's varying attempts at impartiality, see *Independent Chronicle*, 9, 16 May 1799; 15 May 1800; and John B. Hench, "The Newspaper in a Republic: Boston's Centinel and Chronicle, 1784–1801" (Ph.D. diss., Clark University, 1979), 273, 168, and passim.

43. William Collier and Thomas Stockwell, "PRINTING-OFFICE, south *of the* MEETING-HOUSE . . ." [broadside] October 1800, Broadsides Collection, American Antiquarian Society, Worcester, Mass.

44. Charles Pierce, "PROPOSALS *FOR EDITING, PRINTING AND PUBLISHING* The Oracle of the Day . . ." [broadside] 4 August 1798, Broadsides Collection, American Antiquarian Society, Worcester, Mass.

45. Elkins and McKitrick, *Age of Federalism*, 848n13. See also Stewart, *Opposition Press*, 15–6, and, on the post office, John, *Spreading the News*, 51.

46. Elkins and McKitrick, *Age of Federalism*, 365.

47. Thomas Jefferson to David Humphreys, 23 August 1791, *Writings of Thomas Jefferson*, 10 vols., ed. Paul Leicester Ford (New York: Putnam, 1892–7), 5:372–3.

48. *General Advertiser* (later the *Aurora*), 1 October 1790; James Tagg, *Benjamin Franklin Bache and the Philadelphia "Aurora"* (Philadelphia: University of Pennsylvania Press, 1991), 160, 297.

49. Jeffery A. Smith, *Printers and Press Freedom: The Ideology of Early American Journalism* (New York: Oxford University Press, 1988), 38–9.

50. Stewart, *Opposition Press*, 29.

51. Hench, "Newspaper in a Republic," 168. See also *Annals of Congress*, 5th Congress, 2106; *General Remarks, on the Proceedings Lately Had in the Adjacent Country, Relative to Infidelity* (Newburgh, N.Y.: David Denniston, 1798), 36.

52. *Bee* (New London, Conn.), 14 November 1797; cf. 14 June 1797.

53. *Annals of Congress*, 5th Congress, 2106. See also Stewart, *Opposition Press*, 28–9.

54. For examples, see Stewart, *Opposition Press*, 29–30.

55. *Aurora*, 1 March 1797; *Porcupine's Gazette* (Philadelphia), 3 April 1797. See also Charles Pierce, "PROPOSALS *FOR EDITING.*"

56. [Joseph Dennie], *Prospectus of a New Weekly Paper* ([Philadelphia: Joseph Dennie and Asbury Dickins, 1800]), 1–2, Dated Pamphlets Collection, American Antiquarian Society.

57. See, e.g., *General Remarks*, 36.

58. Smith, *Freedom's Fetters*, 146.

59. Elkins and McKitrick, *Age of Federalism*, 28, 27.

60. *National Gazette*, 20 December 1792.

61. John Rutledge, Jr. to Alexander Hamilton, 10 January 1801, *Papers of Alexander Hamilton*, 27 vols., ed. Harold C. Syrett and Jacob E. Cooke (New York: Columbia University Press, 1961–87), 25:309; Zephaniah Swift Moore, *An Oration on the Anniversary of the Independence of the United States of America* [1802], reprinted in *American Political Writing during the Founding Era, 1760–1805*, 2 vols., ed. Charles S. Hyneman and Donald S. Lutz (Indianapolis: Liberty Press, 1983), 2:1215. For Hamilton's similar claim that Jefferson was "too much in earnest in his democracy," see Hamilton to James A. Bayard, 16 January 1801, *Papers of Alexander Hamilton*, 25:319.

62. For a similar distinction (rendered "vigilance vs. responsibility") used in interpreting the thought of Alexander Hamilton (and detailing his stress on "responsibility"), see Karl-Friedrich Walling, *Republican Empire: Alexander Hamilton on War and Free Government* (Lawrence: University Press of Kansas, 1999), esp. 9–11, 54–60, and passim.

63. Richard Buel, Jr., *Securing the Revolution: Ideology in American Politics, 1789–1815* (Ithaca, N.Y.: Cornell University Press, 1972), 258.

64. Thomson, *An Enquiry*, 49; Cooper in *State Trials*, 665; *Annals of Congress*, 3d Congress, 934. See also St. George Tucker, *Letter to a Member of Congress* ([1799]), 36,7; *Argus*, 6 April 1798; *Independent Chronicle*, 8 January 1798; and Madison's "Virginia Report," in *The Virginia Report of 1799–1800* (Richmond: J. W. Randolph, 1850), 166.

65. Hamilton to Josiah Ogden Hoffman, 6 November 1799, in *Papers of Alexander Hamilton*, 24:5–6; *Observations on the Alien and Sedition Laws* (Washington, Pa.: John Colerick, 1799), 42–3; *State Trials*, 663. See also *State Trials*, 670; and Alexander Addison, *Liberty of Speech and of the Press: A Charge to the Grand Juries* (Washington, Pa.: John Colerick, 1798), 23–4, Dated Pamphlets Collection, American Antiquarian Society.

66. Hamilton to Jonathan Dayton, [October–November 1799], quoted in Sharp, *American Politics in the Early Republic*, 216; Sharp argues that this view "represented the considered conclusions of the Hamiltonian wing of Federalism" (324n29).

67. Elkins and McKitrick, *Age of Federalism*, 703.

68. *Columbian Centinel*, 21 September 1791; "T.L." [Hamilton], *Gazette of the United States*, 25 July 1792; Nathanael Emmons, *A Discourse Delivered on the National Fast* [1799], reprinted in *American Political Writing*, ed. Hyneman and Lutz, 2:1027.

69. *Massachusetts Magazine* 3 (1791): 156; *Annals of Congress*, 5th Congress, 2961.

70. Smith, *Freedom's Fetters*, 352. Cf. Jefferson's indiscriminate use of "country," "government," "nation," and "people" in his diplomatic correspondence; see Michael Lienesch, "Thomas Jefferson and the American Demo-

cratic Experience: The Origins of the Partisan Press, Popular Political Parties, and Public Opinion," in *Jeffersonian Legacies*, ed. Peter Onuf (Charlottesville: University Press of Virginia, 1993), 330.

71. Sharp, *American Politics in the Early Republic*, 216.

72. See, e.g., Finley, *Review of the Revenue System*, 103–4; and Annals *of Congress*, 5th Congress, 2110, 3010. See also, William Finley, *History of the Insurrection in the Four Western Counties of Pennsylvania* (Philadelphia: Samuel Harrison Smith, 1796), Dated Books Collection, American Antiquarian Society, 48–50; and Stewart, *Opposition Press*, 437.

73. Forrest McDonald, *The Presidency of George Washington* (Lawrence: University Press of Kansas, 1974), 93–4.

74. Elkins and McKitrick, *Age of Federalism*, 752.

75. *Commercial Advertiser* (New York), 3 July 1798; *Gazette and General Advertiser* (New York), 13 November 1798. See also *State Trials*, 672; *Philadelphia Gazette*, 27 March 1800, quoted in Smith, *Freedom's Fetters*, 316.

76. Addison, *Liberty of Speech*, 6; *Annals of Congress*, 6th Congress, 87.

77. See, e.g., *National Gazette*, 3 May 1792.

78. *Independent Chronicle*, 18 April 1799. See also, e.g., Thomas Cushing to Jedediah Morse, 1 December 1798, Book Trades Collection, Box 1, Folder 10, American Antiquarian Society; *Timepiece*, 23 August 1798.

79. Elkins and McKitrick, *Age of Federalism*, 420.

80. For Hamilton, see Julius Goebel, Jr., ed., *The Law Practice of Alexander Hamilton: Documents and Commentary*, 5 vols. (New York: Columbia University Press, 1964), 1:809; and this volume, Conclusion. For others, see, e.g., *Annals of Congress*, 5th Congress, 2148, 2967–8; Addison, *Liberty of Speech*, 8, 14; and *State Trials*, 332, 669.

81. *Independent Chronicle*, 9 December 1793, 5 July 1798; *National Gazette* 3 May 1792.

82. See, e.g., *Independent Chronicle*, 9 May 1799; *Argus*, 15 March 1796; Thomson, *Enquiry*, 21.

83. *Argus*, 15 March 1796. See also *Virginia Report*, 220 and St. George Tucker, ed., *Blackstone's Commentaries: with Notes of Reference*, 5 vols. (Philadelphia: William Young Birch and Abraham Small, 1803), 2:Appendix G, 3–30.

84. *National Gazette*, 14 July 1792; *Virginia Report*, 227; *Annals of Congress*, 5th Congress, 2110; *State Trials*, 665; Tucker, *Letter*, 45. See also, e.g., *General Advertiser*, 25 July 1793; *Virginia Report*, 221; Thomas Cooper, *An Account of the Trial of Thomas Cooper* (Philadelphia: John Bioren, 1800), Dated Books Collection, American Antiquarian Society, 46.

85. *Virginia Report*, 225.

86. John Park, "Boston, January 23, 1804. Repertory.: To the Publick . . ." [broadside] ([Boston: John Park, 23 January 1804]), Broadsides Collection,

American Antiquarian Society, Worcester, Mass.; *Independent Chronicle*, 4 March 1799.

87. Tucker, *Letter*, 45. See also, e.g., Tucker, *Blackstone's Commentaries*, 2:Appendix G, 16; Thomas Cooper to William Duane, 25 March 1800, reprinted in *Aurora*, 27 March 1800, quoted in Smith, *Freedom's Fetters*, 316.

88. *Annals of Congress*, 5th Congress, 2960. See also Alexander Addison, *Analysis of the Report of the Committee of the Virginia Assembly* (Philadelphia: Zachariah Poulson, 1800), 40, 42, 50.

89. See, e.g., *Independent Chronicle*, 5 July 1798, 18 April 1799; *Aurora*, 20 August 1798, 7 November 1798, 4 February 1799; *Annals of Congress*, 5th Congress, 2105.

90. Hortenius [George Hay], *An Essay on the Liberty of the Press, Respectfully Inscribed* . . . (1799; rep., Richmond: Samuel Pleasants, Jr., 1803), 5; *Bee*, 3 January 1798. See also *Independent Chronicle*, 5 July 1798, 11, 18 April 1799; *Aurora* 1 January, 4 February 1799; Thomson, *Enquiry*, 23.

91. Thomson, *Enquiry*, 69.

92. Richard Buel, Jr., "Freedom of the Press in Revolutionary America: The Evolution of Libertarianism, 1760–1820," in *The Press and the American Revolution*, ed. Bernard Bailyn and John B. Hench (Worcester, Mass.: American Antiquarian Society, 1980), 90. Cf., e.g., *Columbian Centinel*, 8 August 1798.

93. *Annals of Congress*, 6th Congress, 87.

94. *Annals of Congress*, 6th Congress, 409.

95. Alexander Hamilton, "The Reynolds Pamphlet," in *Papers of Alexander Hamilton*, 21:242.

96. Hay, *Essay*, 28–9; *Annals of Congress*, 5th Congress, 2143; Thomson, *Enquiry*, 83; "Inaugural Address," 4 March 1801, *Writings of Thomas Jefferson*, 8:3.

97. *Independent Chronicle*, 18 February 1799. See also e.g., *Massachusetts Magazine* 3 (1791): 156; Addison, *Liberty of Speech*, 16; Virginiensis [Charles Lee], *Defence of the Alien and Sedition Laws* (Philadelphia: John Ward Fenno, 1798), 25; *State Trials*, 478.

98. Saul Cornell sees this claim as "new" in 1788 (Cornell, *Other Founders*, 130), but, as we have seen, the claim had antecedents at least as old as *Cato's Letters* (#32): Libels are "an evil arising out of a much greater good"; and, just as the Nile cannot be rid of its "monsters" yet remains a "general blessing," so with libels and the press (John Trenchard and Thomas Gordon, *Cato's Letters*, 4 vols. [London: Wilkins, Woodward, Walthoe, and Peele, 1724], 1:259). Similarly, and even earlier, see John Milton, *Areopagitica* (1644; repr., London: Noel Douglas, 1927), 37: We must not compel conformity with what we take to be truth because "it is not possible for man to sever the wheat from the tares."

99. Marcellus [pseud.], *Essays on the Liberty of the Press* (Richmond: S. Pleasants, 1804); see also *Columbian Centinel*, 8 August 1798.

100. *Independent Chronicle*, 15 April 1799; *Aurora*, 22 August 1798; Thomas Jefferson, "Kentucky Resolutions" [1798], in *Virginia Report*, 163; Madison, *Virginia Report*, 222. See also, e.g., *Aurora*, 1 August 1798; Hay, *Essay*, 26–7; *Independent Chronicle*, 22 April 1799; and Tucker, *Letter*, 34 (where Tucker insists no government that was properly mindful of the American Constitution would ever "think it necessary to remove a wort by the amputation of a limb"). See also Madison's famous assertion, in *Federalist 10*, that it would be "unwise" to cure the mischiefs of faction by destroying liberty.

101. *Bee*, 27 August 1800; Madison, *Virginia Report*, 222. See also, e.g., An Impartial Citizen [James Sullivan], *A Dissertation upon the Constitutional Freedom of the Press* (Boston: Joseph Nancrede, 1801), 35.

102. *Timepiece*, 23 August 1798.

103. Cornell, *Other Founders*, 110, 208; see also Cornell, "Aristocracy Assailed," 1152.

104. *State Trials*, 322; *Annals of Congress*, 5th Congress, 2146; Addison, *Liberty of Speech*, 14; *Annals of Congress*, 5th Congress, 2989.

105. Smith, *Freedom's Fetters*, 228. See also Tucker, *Letter to a Member*, 31.

106. *Independent Chronicle*, 4 March 1799, 21 January 1796; *Bee*, 14 November 1798; Tucker, *Blackstone's Commentaries*, 2:Appendix G, 24. See also, e.g., Albert Gallatin, *The Speech of Albert Gallatin . . . [3 January 1795]* (Philadelphia: William W. Woodward, 1795), 5–7, Dated Pamphlets Collection, American Antiquarian Society, Worcester, Mass., and *Virginia Report*, 219.

107. Hay, *Essay*, 15; Tucker, *Blackstone's Commentaries*, 2:Appendix G, 18; Independent Chronicle, 2 May 1799. See also Pennsylvania House of Representatives, *Report of a Committee: The Committee Appointed on that Part of the Governor's Address Which Relates to Libels*([Lancaster, Pa.]:W. Hamilton, [1806]), 12–4, Dated Pamphlets Collection, American Antiquarian Society.

108. Thomson, *Enquiry*, 79.

109. Gordon S. Wood, *The Radicalism of the American Revolution* (New York: Knopf, 1992), 363.

110. *Aurora*, 30 January 1799. See also, e.g., *Independent Chronicle*, 9 May 1799; *Annals of Congress*, 5th Congress, 2162.

111. *State Trials*, 695; *Annals of Congress*, 5th Congress, 2967; Thomson, *Enquiry*, 68; *Annals of Congress*, 5th Congress, 2969; *Bee*, 26 March 1800. See also Addison, *Liberty of Speech*, 23; *State Trials*, 693.

112. *Gazette of the United States*, 5 May 1796.

113. Elkins and McKitrick, *Age of Federalism*, 518, 727, 729 (quoting Theodore Sedgwick).

114. Park, *Repertory*; *Bee*, 14 June 1797, 27 December 1797.

115. *Annals of Congress*, 5th Congress, 2154.

116. Pennsylvania House, *Report*, 8; Park, *Repertory*; Hyneman and Lutz, eds., *American Political Writing*, 2:1126 (characterizing Sullivan's *Dissertation*);

"An Impartial Citizen" [James Sullivan], *A Dissertation upon the Freedom of the Press* (Boston: Joseph Nancrede, 1801), 35, Dated Pamphlets Collection, American Antiquarian Society, Worcester, Mass. See also Thomson, *Enquiry*, 39, and, for an early intimation of this claim, the widely reprinted "Centinel" I, *Independent Gazetteer*, 5 October 1787.

117. For the failure of British and French thought to draw these connections among popular sovereignty, press freedom, and public opinion until decades later, see J. A. W. Gunn, "Public Opinion," in Terence Ball, James Farr, and Russell L. Hanson, eds., *Political Innovation and Conceptual Change* (Cambridge: Cambridge University Press, 1989), 259.

118. Elkins and McKitrick, *Age of Federalism*, 741. See also Banning, *Sacred Fire of Liberty*, 394; and Levy, *Emergence*, 273. But cf. Sharp, *American Politics in the Early Republic*, 243–9.

NOTES TO THE CONCLUSION

1. *The Bee* (New London, Conn.), 26 March 1800.

2. Leonard W. Levy, *Emergence of a Free Press* (New York: Oxford University Press, 1985), 332, 328. More recently, Saul Cornell has described Wortman's *Treatise* as "the cornerstone of a new theory of freedom of the press"; see Saul Cornell, *Other Founders: Anti-Federalism and the Dissenting Tradition in America, 1788–1828* (Chapel Hill: University of North Carolina Press, 1999), 254.

3. Jeffery A. Smith, *Printers and Press Freedom: The Ideology of Early American Journalism* (New York: Oxford University Press, 1988), 85; David M. Rabban, "The Ahistorical Historian: Leonard Levy on Freedom of Expression in Early American History," *Stanford Law Review* 37 (1985): 853.

4. Walter Berns reads Wortman as simply another Republican defender of states' rights. As Levy correctly observes, Wortman was only permitting state sovereignty over private defamation suits; his defense of political press liberty was absolute. See Levy, *Emergence*, 331n63; and cf. Berns, "Freedom of the Press and the Alien and Sedition Laws: A Reappraisal," in *1970: Supreme Court Review*, ed. Philip B. Kurland (University of Chicago Press, 1970), 139.

5. Tunis Wortman, *A Treatise Concerning Political Enquiry and the Liberty of the Press* (New York: George Forman, 1800), 33, 46, 76, 170, 26, 132; see also 157, 253–5, 266. See also, e.g., *Independent Chronicle* (Boston), 4 March 1799, 21 January 1796; and St. George Tucker, ed., *Blackstone's Commentaries: with Notes of Reference*, 5 vols. (Philadelphia: William Young Birch and Abraham Small, 1803), 2:Appendix G, 24.

6. See, e.g., *Bee*, 27 December 1797; Pennsylvania House of Representatives, *Report of a Committee: The Committee Appointed on that Part of the*

Governor's Address Which Relates to Libels ([Lancaster, Pa.]:W. Hamilton, [1806]), 8, Dated Pamphlets Collection, American Antiquarian Society; John Park, Boston, January 23, 1804. Repertory. : To the Publick . . ." [broadside] ([Boston: John Park, 23 January 1804]), Broadsides Collection, American Antiquarian Society, Worcester, Mass.

7. Wortman, *Treatise*, 48, 49, 55. See also 60, 62, 63–4, 66, 68–9, 91, 98, 110–1.

8. Wortman, *Treatise*, 203. Cornell correctly notes (*Other Founders*, 262) that Wortman would still have allowed civil suits for private libel (see also, Norman L. Rosenberg, *Protecting the Best Men: An Interpretive History of the Law of Libel* (Chapel Hill: University of North Carolina Press, 1986), 92–4), but Cornell overstates the impact of this limitation on political press liberty. Like current First Amendment jurisprudence, Wortman's analysis placed a heavy emphasis on the public nature of even a political *candidate's* seemingly private "morals" and "integrity"; Wortman likewise cautioned strongly against any civil action that might "[paralyze] the Liberty of Investigation" (Wortman, *Treatise*, 202–3, 205). Furthermore, Cornell substantiates this concern by erroneously claiming that "it was a private libel suit, not a criminal prosecution, that silenced Anti-Federalist printer Eleazer Oswald in 1788" (262; for a similar claim regarding St. George Tucker, see 266). As Cornell himself states, it was a contempt citation (and not the civil private libel charge) that Judge McKean used to rebuke his old nemesis Oswald (129). To be sure, the mere existence of civil remedies for private libel of public figures presents a potential danger to political press liberty (as does a judge's power to issue citations for contempt of court, which was found unconstitutional when applied to public criticism of the bench; see *Bridges v. California*, 314 U.S. 252 [1941] and *Pennekamp v. Florida*, 328 U.S. 331 [1946]). Still, it is worth noting that Wortman's defense of criticism of public figures went almost as far as current free speech law; indeed, in defending even "intentional misrepresentation" (*Treatise*, 204), he went farther (cf. *New York Times Co. v. Sullivan*, 376 U.S. 255 [1964] and *Garrison v. Louisiana*, 379 U.S. 64 [1964]).

9. Wortman, *Treatise*, 119, 120.

10. Wortman, *Treatise*, 122, 24.

11. Wortman, *Treatise*, 267; see also Pennsylvania House, *Report*, 8.

12. Wortman, *Treatise*, 266. For a very different account, one that reads Wortman as writing in "an anachronistic, nonparty context," see Rosenberg, *Protecting the Best Men*, 92.

13. The term is borrowed from David M. Rabban, "The First Amendment in Its Forgotten Years," *Yale Law Journal* 90 (1981): 514–95, and Rabban, *Free Speech in Its Forgotten Years, 1870–1920* (New York: Cambridge University Press, 1999).

14. Thomas Jefferson to Governor Thomas McKean, 19 February 1803, *Writings of Thomas Jefferson*, 10 vols., ed. Paul Leicester Ford (New York: Putnam, 1897), 8:218.

15. Jefferson goes on to say that the current "experiment" should be continued in which "improprieties" are left to "the censorship of Public Opinion"; see Second Inaugural, 5 March 1805, *Writings of Thomas Jefferson* (Ford ed.), 8:346. See also, Jefferson to Thomas Seymour, 11 February 1807, *Writings of Thomas Jefferson* (Ford ed.), 9:28–31; and Jefferson to Judge John Tyler, 28 June 1804, *Writings of Thomas Jefferson*, 20 vols., ed. Andrew Lipscomb and Albert Bergh (Washington, D.C.: Thomas Jefferson Memorial Association of the United States, 1904–5), 11:32–5. More broadly, see Leonard Levy, *Freedom of the Press from Zenger to Jefferson* (Durham, N.C.: Carolina Academic Press, 1996), 327–76; and, for an able defense of Jefferson, David N. Mayer, *The Constitutional Thought of Thomas Jefferson* (Charlottesville: University Press of Virginia, 1994), 175–84.

16. Julius Goebel, Jr., ed., *The Law Practice of Alexander Hamilton: Documents and Commentary*, 5 vols. (New York: Columbia University Press, 1964), 1:846n124. In light of the new law, the Court in 1805 awarded Croswell a new trial. This was a formality, as he had long before been freed and the prosecution declined to move for judgment on the original verdict.

17. Rosenberg, *Protecting the Best Men*, 114–5, and Levy, *Freedom of the Press*, 378.

18. Rabban, "First Amendment in Its Forgotten Years," 523–4 and passim.

19. Drew R. McCoy, *The Last of the Fathers: James Madison and the Republican Legacy* (Cambridge: Cambridge University Press, 1989), 12; see also 18.

20. Saul Cornell, *Other Founders*, 263–4. See also Levy, *Freedom of the Press from Zenger to Jefferson*, 318.

21. See, generally, Rosenberg, *Protecting the Best Men*, 130–78; Mark A. Graber, *Transforming Free Speech: The Ambiguous Legacy of Civil Libertarianism* (Berkeley: University of California Press, 1991), 17–49; and Rabban, *Free Speech in Its Forgotten Years*.

22. Wortman, *Treatise*, 266, 123.

23. Gordon Wood, *Radicalism of the American Revolution* (New York: Knopf, 1992), 296 (quoting Benjamin Latrobe to Philip Mazzei, 19 December 1806).

24. Wortman, *Treatise*, 103, 104, 144.

25. *Brandenburg v. Ohio*, 395 U.S. 449 (1969).

26. Douglas, con. op., *Brandenburg v. Ohio*, 395 U.S. 456 (1969).

27. *Independent Advertiser* (Boston), 9 January 1749; see this volume, p. 57.

28. Charles R. Lawrence III, "If He Hollers Let Him Go: Regulating Racist Speech on Campus," in *Words That Wound: Critical Race Theory, Assaultive Speech, and the First Amendment*, ed. Mari Matsuda et al. (Boulder, Colo.:

Westview Press, 1993), 80. See also Catharine A. MacKinnon, "Not a Moral Issue," *Yale Law and Policy Review* 2 (1984): 332, 340; and, more broadly, MacKinnon, *Only Words* (Cambridge, Mass.: Harvard University Press, 1993), and Mari J. Matsuda, "Public Response to Racist Speech: Considering the Victim's Story," *Michigan Law Review* 87 (1989): 2320–81.

29. The phrase is Quentin Skinner's; see Skinner, "Some Problems in the Analysis of Political Thought and Action," in Skinner, *Meaning and Context: Quentin Skinner and His Critics*, ed. James Tully (Princeton: Princeton University Press, 1988), 112.

30. MacKinnon, *Only Words*, 75–6, and "Not a Moral Issue," 336; and Lawrence, "If He Hollers," 77. Lawrence uses the now-common term "marketplace of ideas," which is frequently read back into eighteenth-century open press discourse. We have avoided the metaphor here, however, since it did not emerge until the more commercially minded nineteenth century.

31. Lawrence, "If He Hollers," 77, 77–9, 81, 83, 86; see also MacKinnon, "Not a Moral Issue," 336–7.

32. Lawrence, "If He Hollers," 83.

33. *New-York Journal*, 5 January 1775; see this volume, p. 86.

34. Most prominently, see James Fallows, *Breaking the News: How the Media Undermine American Democracy* (New York: Vintage, 1996).

35. *Independent Advertiser*, 4 January 1748; see this volume, chapter 2.

36. Much of this predicament was outlined with keen prescience by Jürgen Habermas in the early 1960s; see Habermas, *Structural Transformation of the Public Sphere: An Inquiry into a Category of Bourgeois Society*, trans. Thomas Burger with Frederick Lawrence (Cambridge, Mass.: MIT Press, 1989), esp. 159–75 [originally published in 1962]. More recently, see Habermas, *Between Facts and Norms: Contributions to a Discourse Theory of Law and Democracy*, trans. William Rehg (Cambridge, Mass.: MIT Press, 1996), esp. 373–9.

Bibliography

PRIMARY SOURCES

Manuscript Collections

Book Trades Collection. American Antiquarian Society, Worcester, Mass.

Curwen Family Manuscript Collection. American Antiquarian Society.

Dorr, Harbottle. The Harbottle Dorr Annotated Collection of Boston Newspapers. Massachusetts Historical Society, microfilm.

Thomas, Isaiah. Papers. American Antiquarian Society.

Newspapers and Periodicals (with Most Prominent Title and Publication Dates)

American Magazine and Monthly Chronicle (Boston), 1757–8.

American Weekly Mercury (Philadelphia), 1718–47.

Bee (New London, Conn.), 1797–1802.

Boston Chronicle, 1767–70.

Boston Evening Post, 1735–75.

Boston Gazette, 1719–98.

Boston News-Letter (later *Massachusetts Gazette and Boston Newsletter*), 1704–76.

Boston Weekly Post-Boy (later *Massachusetts Gazette and the Boston Post-Boy*), 1734–75.

Commercial Advertiser (New York), 1797–1831.

Connecticut Courant (Hartford), 1764–present.

Connecticut Gazette (continues *New London Gazette*), 1758–1844.

Constitutional Courant (Woodbridge, N.J.), 1765.

Daily Advertiser (New York), 1785–1836.

Essex Journal (Newburyport, Mass.), 1773–94.

Freeman's Journal (Philadelphia), 1781–92.

Gazette of the State of Georgia (Savannah), 1783–1802.

Gazette of the United States (New York, later Philadelphia), 1789–1847.

General Advertiser (later *Aurora*) (Philadelphia), 1790–1828.

Independent Advertiser (Boston), 1748–50.

Independent Chronicle (Boston), 1776–1831.

Independent Gazetteer (Philadelphia), 1782–96.

Independent Reflector (New York), 1752–3.

Maryland Journal and Baltimore Advertiser, 1773–99.

Maryland Gazette (Annapolis), 1745–1810.

Massachusetts (later *Columbian*) *Centinel* (Boston), 1784–1840.

Massachusetts Magazine (Boston), 1789–96.

Massachusetts Spy (Boston, later Worcester), 1770–1800.

National Gazette (Philadelphia), 1791–3.

New-England Chronicle, or the Essex Gazette (Salem, later Cambridge, Mass.), 1768–76.

New England Courant (Boston), 1721–7.

New England Magazine (Boston), 1758–9.

New Haven Gazette, 1782–6.

New York Gazette, 1725–44.

New-York Gazetteer, 1773–7.

New York Mercury, 1752–83.

New York Journal (later *The Argus*), 1766–1810.

New York Weekly Journal, 1733–51.

Norwich Packet (Connecticut), 1773–1804.

Pennsylvania Chronicle (Philadelphia), 1767–73.

Pennsylvania Evening-Post (Philadelphia), 1775–84.

Pennsylvania Gazette (Philadelphia), 1728–1821.

Pennsylvania Journal and Weekly Advertiser (Philadelphia), 1742–97.

Pennsylvania Packet (Philadelphia), 1771–1840.

Porcupine's Gazette (Philadelphia), 1797–1800.

Publick Occurences (Boston), 1690.

South Carolina Gazette (Charleston), 1732–73.

Timepiece (New York), 1797–8.

Virginia Gazette [Purdie and Dixon] (Williamsburg), 1736–80.

Virginia Gazette [Rind] (Williamsburg), 1766–76.

Virginia Gazette and Petersburg Intelligencer, 1786–1800.

Virginia Gazette and Winchester Advertiser, 1787–90.

Virginia Independent Chronicle (Richmond), 1780–95.

Books, Pamphlets, Broadsides, and Records

Adams, John. *Papers of John Adams.* 10 vols. Ed. Robert J. Taylor, Mary-Jo Kline, and Gregg L. Lint. Cambridge, Mass.: Harvard University Press, 1977–.

Addison, Alexander. *Analysis of the Report of the Committee of the Virginia Assembly.* Philadelphia: Zachariah Poulson, 1800.

———. *Liberty of Speech and of the Press: A Charge to the Grand Juries.* . . . Washington, Pa.: John Colerick, 1798.

Alexander, James. *A Brief Narrative of the Case and Trial of John Peter Zenger, Printer of the New-York Weekly Journal, for a Libel*. New York: John Holt, 1770.

Annals of the Congress of the United States, 1789–1824. 42 vols. Washington, D.C., 1834–56.

ARGUMENTS Relating to a Restraint upon the PRESS, Fully and Fairly handled in a LETTER to a Bencher, FROM a Young Gentleman of the TEMPLE. London: R. & J. Bonwicke, 1712.

Asgill, John. *An Essay for the Press*. London: A. Baldwin, 1712.

An Authentick Account of the Proceedings against John Wilkes, Esq. Philadelphia: John Dunlap, 1763.

Bell, Robert. "A Few More Words, on the Freedom of the Press." Appended to *True Interest of Britain*, by Josiah Tucker. Philadelphia: Robert Bell, 1776.

———. "The Printer to the Public: On the Freedom of the Press." Appended to *A Dialogue between the Ghost of General Montgomery just arrived from the Elysian Fields; and an American Delegate, in a Wood near Philadelphia*. [Philadelphia]: Robert Bell, 1776.

Blackstone, Sir William. *Commentaries on the Laws of England* 4 vols. Philadelphia: Robert Bell, 1771.

———. *Commentaries on the Laws of England* 4 vols. Oxford: Clarendon Press, 1764–9.

[Bollan, William]. *The Freedom of Speech and Writing upon Public Affairs, Considered, with an Historical View*. London: S. Baker, 1766.

Care, Henry. *English Liberties*, 5th ed. Boston: James Franklin for Buttolph, Eliot, and Henchman, 1721.

Collier, William, and Thomas Stockwell. "PRINTING-OFFICE, south *of the* MEETING-HOUSE . . ." [broadside]. Bennington, Vt." Collier and Stockwell, October 1800. Broadsides Collection, American Antiquarian Society, Worcester, Mass.

Collins, Anthony. *A Discourse of Free-Thinking*. London: 1713.

Continental Congress. *Journal of the Continental Congress, 1774–1789*. 34 vols. Ed. Worthington C. Ford et al. Washington, D.C., 1904–37.

Cooper, Thomas. *An Account of the Trial of Thomas Cooper. . . .* Philadelphia: John Bioren, 1800.

Dallas, Alexander J., ed. *Reports of Cases Ruled and Adjudged in the courts of Pennsylvania, before and since the Revolution*. Philadelphia: T. Bradford, 1790.

Defoe, Daniel. *An Essay on the Regulation of the Press*. 1704. Reprint, Oxford: Basil Blackwell, 1948.

———. *A Letter to a Member of Parliament Shewing the Necessity of Regulating the Press*. Oxford: George West and Henry Clements, 1699.

[Defoe, Daniel]. *A Vindication of the Press*. London: T. Warner, 1718.

DeLancey, James. *The Charge of the Honourable James DeLancey . . . to the . . . Grand Jury [15 January 1734]*. New York: William Bradford, 173[4].

————. *The Charge of the Honourable James DeLancey . . . to the . . . Grand Jury [15 October 1734]*. New York: William Bradford, 1734.

[Dennie, Joseph]. *Prospectus of a New Weekly Paper*. [Philadelphia: Joseph Dennie and Asbury Dickins, 1800].

[Drinker, John]. *Observations on the Late Popular Measures, Offered to the Serious Consideration of the Sober Inhabitants of Pennsylvania*. Philadelphia: 1774.

Duche, Anthony. *Advertisement. We do hereby Certify. . . .* Philadelphia: 1743.

Eells, Nathaniel. *The Wise Ruler a Loyal Subject*. New London: Timothy Green, 1748.

Extract from the Journal of House of Representatives of Massachusetts Bay. Boston: Z. Fowle and Tyler, 1756.

Finley, William. *History of the Insurrection in the Four Western Counties of Pennsylvania*. Philadelphia: Samuel Harrison Smith, 1796.

————. *A Review of the Revenue System Adopted by the First Congress under the Federal Constitution*. Philadelphia: T. Dobson, 1794.

Foner, Philip S., ed. *The Democratic-Republican Societies, 1790–1800: A Documentary Sourcebook of Constitutions, Declarations, Addresses, Resolutions, and Toasts*. Westport, Conn.: Greenwood Press, 1976.

Fowle, Daniel. *An Appendix to the late Total Eclipse of Liberty*. Boston: Daniel Fowle, 1756.

————. *A Total Eclipse of Liberty*. Boston: D. Fowle, 1755.

A Fragment of the Chronicles of Nathan Ben Saddi. Constantinople [Philadelphia]: 5707 [1759].

A Friend to Harmony. *Candid Considerations on Libels*. Boston: Freeman and Andrews, 1789.

Gallatin, Albert. *The Speech of Albert Gallatin . . . [3 January 1795]*. Philadelphia: William W. Woodward, 1795.

General Remarks, on the Proceedings Lately Had in the Adjacent Country, Relative to Infidelity. . . . Newburgh, N.Y.: David Denniston, 1798.

Goddard, William. *The Prowess of the Whig Club*. Baltimore: [Mary K. Goddard], 1777.

Goebel, Julius, Jr., ed. *The Law Practice of Alexander Hamilton: Documents and Commentary*. 5 vols. New York: Columbia University Press, 1964.

Goodwin, John. *Theomachia*. London: 1645.

————. *A Fresh Discovery of the High-Presbyterian Spirit*. 1641. Appended to William M. Clyde, *The Struggle for the Freedom of the Press From Caxton to Cromwell*. Oxford: Oxford University Press, 1934.

Grinnell, Frank W., ed. "Hitherto Unpublished Correspondence between Chief

Justice Cushing and John Adams in 1789." *Massachusetts Law Quarterly* 27 (1942): 12–6.

Haller, William. *Liberty and Reformation in the Puritan Revolution.* New York: Columbia University Press, 1955.

———, ed. *Tracts on Liberty in the Puritan Revolution, 1638–47.* New York: Columbia University Press, 1933.

Haller, William, and Godfrey Davies, eds. *The Levellers Tracts, 1647–53.* New York: Columbia University Press, 1944.

Hamilton, Alexander. *Papers of Alexander Hamilton.* 27 vols. Ed. Harold C. Syrett and Jacob E. Cooke. New York: Columbia University Press, 1961–87.

Handlin, Oscar, and Mary Handlin, eds. *The Popular Sources of Political Authority: Documents on the Massachusetts Constitution of 1780.* Cambridge, Mass.: Harvard University Press, 1966.

Hay, George. *An Essay on the Liberty of the Press. . . .* Philadelphia: Samuel Pleasants, 1799.

[Hayter, Thomas Bishop]. *An Essay on the Liberty of the Press. . . .* London: J. Raymond, [1755].

Hening, William Waller. *The Statutes at Large Being a Collection of All the Laws of Virginia, 1619–1792.* 13 vols. Richmond: Samuel Pleasants, 1809–1823.

Hobbes, Thomas. *Leviathan.* Ed. C. B. Macpherson. Middlesex, U.K.: Penguin, 1968.

Honesty, Obadiah [pseud.]. *A Remonstrance of Obadiah Honesty.* Philadelphia: 1757.

Hortenius [George Hay]. *An Essay on the Liberty of the Press, Respectfully Inscribed. . . .* 1799. Reprint, Richmond: Samuel Pleasants, Jr., 1803.

Hyneman, Charles S., and Donald S. Lutz, eds. *American Political Writing during the Founding Era, 1760–1805.* 2 vols. Indianapolis: Liberty Fund, 1983.

An Impartial Citizen [James Sullivan]. *A Dissertation upon the Constitutional Freedom of the Press. . . .* Boston: Joseph Nancrede, 1801.

An Interesting Appendix to Sir William Blackstone's "Commentaries on the Laws of England." Philadelphia: Robert Bell, 1772.

Jefferson, Thomas. *Papers of Thomas Jefferson.* 26 vols. Ed. Julian P. Boyd, Lyman H. Butterfield, Charles T. Cullen, and John Catanzariti. Princeton: Princeton University Press, 1950–.

———. *Writings of Thomas Jefferson.* 10 vols. Ed. Paul Leicester Ford. New York: Putnam, 1892–7.

———. *Writings of Thomas Jefferson.* 20 vols. Ed. Andrew A. Lipscombe and Albert Ellery Bergh. Washington, D.C.: Thomas Jefferson Memorial Association, 1905.

Jensen, Merrill, ed. *The Documentary History of the Ratification of the Constitution.* 18 vols. Madison: State Historical Society of Wisconsin, 1976–.

Keith, George, and Thomas Budd. *New-England's Spirit of Persecution Transmitted to Pennsylvania.* Philadelphia: William Bradford, 1693.

King, Peter. *The Life and Letters of John Locke, with Extracts from his Journals and Commonplace Books.* London: George Bell and Sons, 1884.

Labaree, Leonard Woods, ed. *Royal Instructions to the British Colonial Governors.* 2 vols. New York: D. Appleton-Century Co., 1935.

Lilburne, John. *A Copie of a Letter to Mr. William Prinne, Esq.* London: 1645.

———. *Englands Birth-Right Justified.* London: 1645.

Livingston, William, and William Smith. *The Independent Reflector.* Ed. Milton M. Klein. Cambridge, Mass.: Harvard University Press, 1963.

Lloyd, Thomas, ed. *Debates of the Convention, of the State of Pennsylvania, on the Constitution proposed for the government of the United States.* Philadelphia: Lloyd, 1788.

Locke, John. *A Letter Concerning Toleration.* Ed. James Tully. Indianapolis: Hackett, 1983.

———. *Two Treatises of Government.* Ed. Peter Laslett. Cambridge: Cambridge University Press, 1988.

A Lover of Truth and Liberty [Elisha Williams]. *The Essential Rights and Liberties of Protestants.* Boston: Kneeland and Green, 1744.

Madison, James. *Papers of James Madison.* 17 vols. Ed. William T. Hutchinson, William M.E. Rachal, and Robert Allan Rutland. Chicago: University of Chicago Press, 1962–91.

———. *The Virginia Report of 1799–1800.* 1800; repr., Richmond: J. W. Randolph, 1850.

Manning, William. *The Key of Libberty* [1798]. Ed. Samuel Eliot Morison. *William and Mary Quarterly*, 3d ser., 13 (1956): 202–54.

Marcellus [pseud.]. *Essays on the Liberty of the Press.* Richmond: S. Pleasants, 1804.

Mayhew, Jonathan. *A Discourse Concerning Unlimited Submission and Non-Resistance to the Higher Powers.* Boston: Fowle and Gookin, 1750.

———. *Seven Sermons.* Boston: Rogers and Fowle, 1749.

Milton, John. "On the Forcers of Conscience." In *The Complete Poetry of John Milton.* Ed. John T. Shawcross. New York: Doubleday, 1971.

———. *Areopagitica.* 1644; repr., London: N. Douglas, 1927.

Observations on the Alien and Sedition Laws. Washington, Pa.: John Colerick, 1799.

The Palladium of Conscience. Philadelphia: Robert Bell, 1773.

Park, John. "Boston, January 23, 1804. Repertory. : To the Publick . . ." [broadside]. [Boston: John Park, 23 January 1804]. Broadsides Collection, American Antiquarian Society, Worcester, Mass.

Pennsylvania Archives, 8th ser. Harrisburg: 1874–1935.

Pennsylvania House of Representatives. *Report of a Committee: The Commit-*

tee Appointed on that Part of the Governor's Address Which Relates to . . .
Libels. . . . [Lancaster, Pa.]: W. Hamilton, [1806].

Philadelphia Committee of Inspection and Observation. "In Committee chamber, May 16, 1776" [broadside]. Philadelphia: William and Thomas Bradford, 16 May 1776. Broadsides Collection, American Antiquarian Society, Worcester, Mass.

Philo-Reflector [William Livingston and William Smith]. Preface to *The Craftsmen: A Sermon from the Independent Whig.* New York: J. Parker, 1753.

Pierce, Charles. "PROPOSALS *FOR EDITING, PRINTING AND PUBLISHING* The Oracle of the Day . . ." [broadside]. Portsmouth, N.H.: C. Pierce, 4 August 1798. Broadsides Collection, American Antiquarian Society, Worcester, Mass.

Robinson, Henry. *Liberty of Conscience.* London: 1644.

Saunders, Richard [Benjamin Franklin]. *Poor Richard Improved: Being an Almanack for . . . 1757.* Philadelphia: Franklin and Hall, 1756.

Schwartz, Bernard, ed. *The Bill of Rights: A Documentary History.* 2 vols. New York: Chelsea House, 1971.

Sidney, Algernon. *Discourses Concerning Government.* 1698. Reprint, New York: Arno, 1979.

State Trials of the United States During the Administrations of Washington and Adams. Ed. Francis Wharton. Philadelphia: Carey and Hart, 1849.

Storing, Herbert J., ed. *The Complete Anti-Federalist.* 7 vols. Chicago: University of Chicago Press, 1981.

Thomas, Isaiah. *The History of Printing in America* [1810], 2d ed. 2 vols. New York: Burt Franklin, 1874.

———. "To the Customers for Thomas's Massachusetts Spy . . ." [broadside]. Worcester, Mass.: I. Thomas, 3 April 1786. Broadsides Collection, American Antiquarian Society, Worcester, Mass.

Thomson, John. *An Enquiry, Concerning the Liberty, and Licentiousness of the Press. . . .* New York: Johnson and Stryker, 1801.

Tindal, Matthew. *Four Discourses on the Following Subjects: viz . . . IV. Of the Liberty of the Press.* London: 1709.

———. *A Letter to a Member of Parliament. . . .* London: J. Darby, 1698.

———. *Reasons against Restraining the Press.* London: 1704.

Theo. Philanthes [Thomas Maule]. *New-England Persecutors Mauld with their Own Weapons.* New York: 1697.

Trenchard, John, and Thomas Gordon. *Cato's Letters: Or, Essays on Liberty, Civil and Religious.* 4 vols. London: Wilkins, Woodward, Walthoe, and Peele, 1724.

———. *The Character of an Independent Whig,* 4th ed. London: J. Roberts, 1720.

———. *Considerations offered upon the Approaching Peace.* London: J. Roberts, 1720.

Trenchard, John, and Thomas Gordon. *The Independent Whig.* London: J. Peele, 1721.

Tucker, St. George. *Blackstone's Commentaries: with Notes of Reference. . . ,* 5 vols. Philadelphia: William Young Birch and Abraham Small, 1803.

———. *Letter to a Member of Congress, respecting the Alien and Sedition Laws.* [Virginia?: 1799?].

Underhill, Edward Bean, ed. *Tracts on Liberty of Conscience and Persecution, 1614–1661.* London: Hanserd Knollys Society, 1846.

Veit, Helen E., Kenneth R. Bowling, and Charlene Bangs Bickford, eds. *Creating the Bill of Rights: The Documentary Record from the First Federal Congress.* Baltimore, Md.: Johns Hopkins University Press, 1991.

Virginiensis [Charles Lee]. *Defence of the Alien and Sedition Laws.* Philadelphia: John Ward Fenno, 1798.

[Walter, Thomas]. *The Little-Compton Scourge; Or, The Anti-Courant.* Boston: J. Franklin, 1721.

Walwyn, William. *The Compassionate Samaritane.* London: 1644.

———. *A Helpe to the right understanding of a Discourse concerning Independency.* London: 1645.

———. *The Power of Love.* London: 1644.

Whitman, Elnathan. *Character and Qualifications of a Good Ruler.* New London: Timothy Green, 1745.

Williams, Roger. *Bloody Tenent of Persecution yet more bloody.* 1645; repr., vol. 4 of *Publications of the Narragansett Club,* 6 vols., ed. S. L. Caldwell. Providence: Providence Press, 1866–74.

———. *The Bloudy Tenent of Persecution, for cause of Conscience.* 1644; repr., vol. 3 of *Publications of the Narragansett Club,* 6 vols., ed. S. L. Caldwell. Providence: Providence Press, 1866–74.

Wolfe, Don M., ed. *Leveller Manifestoes of the Puritan Revolution.* New York: Thomas Nelson and Sons, 1944.

Wortman, Tunis. *Treatise Concerning Political Enquiry, and the Liberty of the Press.* New York: G. Forman, 1800.

SECONDARY SOURCES

Adams, Willi Paul. *The First American Constitutions: Republican Ideology and the Making of the State Constitutions in the Revolutionary Era.* Chapel Hill: University of North Carolina Press, 1980.

Anderson, David A. "Levy v. Levy." *Michigan Law Review* 84 (1986): 777–86.

———. "The Origins of the Press Clause." *U.C.L.A. Law Review,* 30 (1983): 455–541.

Appleby, Joyce. *Capitalism and a New Social Order: The Republican Vision of the 1790s.* New York: New York University Press, 1984.

———. *Liberalism and Republicanism in the Historical Imagination*. Cambridge, Mass.: Harvard University Press, 1992.

Armory, Hugh, and David D. Hall, eds. *A History of the Book in America*, vol. 1, *The Colonial Book in the Atlantic World*. Cambridge: Cambridge University Press, 2000.

Bailyn, Bernard. *Ideological Origins of the American Revolution*. Cambridge, MA: Harvard University Press, 1967.

Baldasty, Gerald J. "Toward an Understanding of the First Amendment: Boston Newspapers, 1782–91." *Journalism History* 3 (1976): 25–30, 32.

Ball, Terence. "'A Republic—If You Can Keep It.'" In *Conceptual Change and the Constitution*, ed. Terence Ball and J. G. A. Pocock. Lawrence: University Press of Kansas, 1988.

———. *Transforming Political Discourse: Political Theory and Critical Conceptual History*. Oxford: Basil Blackwell, 1988.

Ball, Terence, and J. G. A. Pocock, eds. *Conceptual Change and the Constitution*. Lawrence: University Press of Kansas, 1988.

Ball, Terence, James Farr, and Russell L. Hanson, eds. *Political Innovation and Conceptual Change*. Cambridge: Cambridge University Press, 1989.

Banning, Lance. *The Jeffersonian Persuasion: Evolution of a Party Ideology*. Ithaca, N.Y.: Cornell University Press, 1978.

———. *The Sacred Fire of Liberty: James Madison and the Founding of the Federal Republic*. Ithaca, N.Y.: Cornell University Press, 1995.

Berns, Walter. *The First Amendment and the Future of American Democracy*. New York: Basic Books, 1976.

———. "Freedom of the Press and the Alien and Sedition Laws: A Reappraisal." In *1970: Supreme Court Review*, ed. Philip B. Kurland. Chicago: University of Chicago Press, 1970.

Blasi, Vincent. "The Checking Value in First Amendment Theory." *American Bar Foundation Research Journal* 2 (1977): 521–649.

Bonomi, Patricia U. *The Lord Cornbury Scandal: The Politics of Reputation in British America*. Chapel Hill: University of North Carolina Press, 1998.

Botein, Stephen. "'Meer Mechanics' and an Open Press: The Business and Political Strategies of Colonial American Printers." *Perspectives in American History* 9 (1975): 127–225.

———. "Printers and the American Revolution." In *The Press and the American Revolution*, ed. Bernard Bailyn and John B. Hench. Worcester, Mass.: American Antiquarian Society, 1980.

Bourne, H. R. Fox. *The Life of John Locke*. New York: Harper and Brothers, 1876.

Brandenburg v. Ohio, 395 U.S. 444 (1969).

Brown, Richard D. *Knowledge Is Power: The Diffusion of Information in Early American History*. New York: Oxford University Press, 1989.

Brown, Richard D. "Shifting Freedoms of the Press in the Eighteenth Century." In *A History of the Book in America*, vol. 1, *The Colonial Book in the Atlantic World*, ed. Hugh Armory and David D. Hall. Cambridge: Cambridge University Press, 2000.

Brown, Richard D. *The Strength of a People: The Idea of an Informed Citizenry in America, 1650–1870.* Chapel Hill: University of North Carolina Press, 1996.

Buel, Joy Day, and Richard Buel, Jr. *The Way of Duty: A Woman and Her Family in Revolutionary America.* New York: Norton, 1984.

Buel, Richard, Jr. "Freedom of the Press in Revolutionary America: The Evolution of Libertarianism, 1760–1820." In *The Press and the American Revolution*, ed. Bernard Bailyn and John B. Hench. Worcester, Mass.: American Antiquarian Society, 1980.

———. *Securing the Revolution: Ideology in American Politics, 1789–1815.* Ithaca, N.Y.: Cornell University Press, 1972.

Bushman, Richard L. *From Puritan to Yankee.* Cambridge, Mass.: Harvard University Press, 1967.

Chafee, Zechariah, Jr. *Free Speech in the United States.* Cambridge, Mass.: Harvard University Press, 1941.

———. "Free Speech in War Time." *Harvard Law Review* 32 (1919): 932–73.

Clark, Charles E. "Early American Journalism: News and Opinion in the Popular Press." In *A History of the Book in America*, vol. 1, *The Colonial Book in the Atlantic World*, ed. Hugh Armory and David D. Hall. Cambridge: Cambridge University Press, 2000.

———. *The Public Prints: The Newspaper in Anglo-American Culture, 1665–1740.* New York: Oxford University Press, 1994.

Clarke, Mary Patterson. *Parliamentary Privilege in the American Colonies.* New Haven: Yale University Press, 1943.

Clyde, William M. *The Struggle for the Freedom of the Press From Caxton to Cromwell.* Oxford: Oxford University Press, 1934.

Cornell, Saul. "Aristorcracy Assailed: The Ideology of Backcountry Anti-Federalism." *Journal of American History* 76 (1990): 1148–72.

———. *The Other Founders: Anti-Federalism and the Dissenting Tradition in America, 1788–1828.* Chapel Hill: University of North Carolina Press, 1999.

Corwin, Edward S. "Freedom of Speech and Press under the First Amendment: A Resume." *Yale Law Journal* 30 (1920): 48–55.

Countryman, Edward. *The American Revolution.* New York: Hill and Wang, 1985.

Davidson, Philip. *Propoganda and the American Revolution, 1763–1783.* Chapel Hill: University of North Carolina Press, 1941.

Dienstag, Joshua Foa. "Between History and Nature: Social Contract Theory in Locke and the Founders." *Journal of Politics* 58 (1996): 985–1009.

———. "Serving God and Mammon: The Lockean Sympathy in Early American Political Thought." *American Political Science Review* 90 (1996): 497–511.

Dietz, Mary G. "Patriotism." In *Political Innovation and Conceptual Change*, ed. Terence Ball, James Farr, and Russell L. Hanson. Cambridge: Cambridge University Press, 1989.

Duncan, Christopher M. *The Anti-Federalists and Early American Political Thought*. DeKalb: Northern Illinois University Press, 1995.

Duniway, Clyde Augustus. *The Development of Freedom of the Press in Massachusetts*. New York: Longmans, Green, 1906.

Eldridge, Larry D. *A Distant Heritage: The Growth of Free Speech in Early America*. New York: New York University Press, 1994.

Elkins, Stanley, and Eric McKitrick. *The Age of Federalism*. New York: Oxford University Press, 1993.

Farr, James. "Understanding Conceptual Change Politically." In *Political Innovation and Conceptual Change*, ed. Terence Ball, James Farr, and Russell L. Hanson. Cambridge: Cambridge University Press, 1989.

———. "Conceptual Change and Constitutional Innovation." In *Conceptual Change and the Constitution*, ed. Terence Ball and J. G. A. Pocock. Lawrence: University Press of Kansas, 1988.

Fiss, Owen M. *The Irony of Free Speech*. Cambridge, Mass.: Harvard University Press, 1996.

Formissano, Ronald P. "Deferential-Participant Politics: The Early Republic's Political Culture, 1789–1840." *American Political Science Review* 68 (1974): 473–87.

Foner, Philip S., ed. *The Democratic-Republican Societies, 1790–1800: A Documentary Sourcebook of Constitutions, Declarations, Addresses, Resolutions, and Toasts*. Westport, Conn.: Greenwood Press, 1976.

Freeman, Joanne B. "Dueling as Politics: Reinterpreting the Burr-Hamilton Duel." *William and Mary Quarterly*, 3d ser., 53 (1996): 289–318.

Green, James N. "The Book Trade in the Middle Colonies, 1680–1720." In *A History of the Book in America*, vol. 1, *The Colonial Book in the Atlantic World*, ed. Hugh Armory and David D. Hall. Cambridge: Cambridge University Press, 2000.

Habermas, Jürgen. *Between Facts and Norms: Contributions to a Discourse Theory of Law and Democracy*. Trans. William Rehg. Cambridge, Mass.: MIT Press, 1996.

———. *The Structural Transformation of the Public Sphere: An Inquiry into a Category of Bourgeois Society*, trans. Thomas Burger with Frederick Lawrence. Cambridge, Mass.: MIT Press, 1989.

Hall, David D. *Cultures of Print: Essays in the History of the Book*. Amherst: University of Massachusetts Press, 1996.

Hall, Mark David. *The Political and Legal Philosophy of James Wilson, 1742–1798*. Columbia: University of Missouri Press, 1997.

Hamburger, Philip. "The Development of the Law of Seditious Libel and Control of the Press." *Stanford Law Review* 37 (1985): 661–765.

Hamowy, Ronald. "Cato's Letters, John Locke, and the Republican Paradigm." *History of Political Thought* 11 (1990): 273–94.

Hanson, Laurence. *Government and the Press: 1695–1763*. Oxford: Oxford University Press, 1936.

Hanson, Russell L. "'Commons' and 'Commonwealth' of the American Founding: Democratic Republicanism as the New American Hybrid." In *Conceptual Change and the Constitution*, ed. Terence Ball and J. G. A. Pocock. Lawrence: University Press of Kansas, 1988.

———. *The Democratic Imagination in America: Conversations with Our Past*. Princeton: Princeton University Press, 1985.

Hench, John B. "The Newspaper in a Republic: Boston's Chronicle and Centinel, 1782–1800." Ph.D. diss, Clark University, 1979.

Hill, Christopher. *Milton and the English Revolution*. London: Faber and Faber, 1977.

———. *The World Turned Upside Down: Radical Ideas During the English Revolution*. Middlesex, U.K.: Penguin, 1972.

Horowitz, Morton. *The Transformation of American Law*. Cambridge, Mass.: Harvard University Press, 1976.

Howe, John R., Jr. "Republican Thought and the Political Violence of the 1790s." *American Quarterly* 14 (1967): 147–65.

Huyler, Jerome. *Locke in America: The Moral Philosophy of the Founding Era*. Lawrence: University Press of Kansas, 1995.

Isaac, Jeffrey. "Republicanism vs. Liberalism? A Reconsideration," *History of Political Thought* 9 (1988): 349–77.

Jacobson, David L., ed. *The English Libertarian Heritage*. Indianapolis: Bobbs-Merrill, 1965.

John, Richard R. *Spreading the News: The American Postal System from Franklin to Morse*. Cambridge, Mass.: Harvard University Press, 1995.

Kamensky, Jane. *Governing the Tongue: The Politics of Speech in Early New England*. New York: Oxford University Press, 1997.

Katz, Stanley Nider, ed. *A Brief Narrative of the Case and Tryal of John Peter Zenger . . .* , by James Alexander. Cambridge, Mass.: Harvard University Press, 1972.

Kenyon, Cecelia. "Men of Little Faith: The Anti-federalists on the Nature of Representative Government." *William and Mary Quarterly* 12 (1955): 3–43.

Kloppenberg, James T. *The Virtues of Liberalism*. New York: Oxford University Press, 1998.

———. "The Virtues of Liberalism: Christianity, Republicanism, and Ethics in Early American Political Discourse," *Journal of American History* 74 (1987): 9–33.

Kramnick, Isaac. *Republicanism and Bourgeois Radicalism: Political Ideology in Late Eighteenth-Century England and America*. Ithaca, N.Y.: Cornell University Press, 1990.

Kruman, Marc W. *Between Authority and Liberty: State Constitution Making in Revolutionary America*. Chapel Hill: University of North Carolina Press, 1997.

Laslett, Peter. "John Locke, the Great Recoinage, and the Origins of the Board of Trade: 1695–1698." *William and Mary Quarterly*, 3d ser., 14 (1957): 369–402.

Leder, Lawrence H. *Liberty and Authority: Early American Political Ideology, 1689–1763*. Chicago: Quadrangle Books, 1968.

Levy, Leonard. "Did the Zenger Case Really Matter? Freedom of the Press in Colonial New York." *William and Mary Quarterly*, 3d ser., 17 (1960): 35–50.

———. *Emergence of a Free Press*. New York: Oxford University Press, 1985.

———. "Freedom of Speech in Seventeenth-Century Thought." *Antioch Review* 57 (1999): 165–77.

———. *Jefferson and Civil Liberties: The Darker Side*. Cambridge, Mass.: Harvard University Press, 1963.

———. *Legacy of Suppression: Freedom of Speech and Press in Early American History*. Cambridge, Mass.: Harvard University Press, 1960.

———. "The *Legacy* Reexamined." *Stanford Law Review* 37 (1985): 766–93.

———. "On the Origins of the Free Press Clause." *U.C.L.A. Law Review* 32 (1984): 177–218.

———. *Origins of the Bill of Rights*. New Haven: Yale University Press, 1999.

———, ed. *Freedom of the Press from Zenger to Jefferson: Early American Libertarian Theories*. Indianapolis: Bobbs-Merrill, 1966; repr., Durham, N.C.: Carolina Academic Press, 1996.

Lienesch, Michael. "In Defence of the Antifederalists." *History of Political Thought* 4 (1983): 65–87.

———. *New Order of the Ages: Time, the Constitution, and the Making of Modern American Political Thought*. Princeton: Princeton University Press, 1988.

———. "Thomas Jefferson and the American Democratic Experience: The Origins of the Partisan Press, Popular Political Parties, and Public Opinion." In *Jeffersonian Legacies*, ed. Peter S. Onuf. Charlottesville: University Press of Virginia, 1993.

Maier, Pauline. *From Resistance to Revolution: Colonial Radicals and the Development of Opposition to Britain, 1765–1776.* New York: Knopf, 1972.

Martin, Robert W. T. "Context and Contradiction: Toward a Political Theory of Conceptual Change," *Political Research Quarterly* 50 (1997): 413–36.

———. "From the 'Free and Open Press' to the 'Press of Freedom': Liberalism, Republicanism, and Early American Press Liberty." *History of Political Thought* 15 (1994): 505–34.

Mayer, David N. *The Constitutional Thought of Thomas Jefferson.* Charlottesville: University Press of Virginia, 1994.

Mayton, William T. "From a Legacy of Suppression to the 'Metaphor of the Fourth Estate.'" *Stanford Law Review*, 39 (1986–7): 139–60.

———. "Seditious Libel and the Lost Guarantee of a Freedom of Expression," *Columbia Law Review* 84 (1984): 91–142.

McCoy, Drew R. *The Last of the Fathers: James Madison and the Republican Legacy.* Cambridge: Cambridge University Press, 1989.

McDonald, Forrest. *The Presidency of George Washington.* Lawrence: University Press of Kansas, 1974.

Meehan, Thomas R. "The Pennsylvania Supreme Court in the Law and Politics of the Commonwealth, 1776–1790." Ph.D. diss. University of Wisconsin, 1960.

Miner, Ward L. *William Goddard: Newspaperman.* Durham, N.C.: Duke University Press, 1962.

Morgan, Edmund S. *Inventing the People: The Rise of Popular Sovereignty in England and America.* New York: Norton, 1988.

Murphy, Paul L., ed. *The Historical Background of the Bill of Rights*, vol. 1, *The Bill of Rights and American Legal History.* New York: Garland, 1990.

Nelson, Harold L. "Seditious Libel in Colonial America," *American Journal of Legal History* 3 (1959): 160–72.

Nerone, John. *Violence against the Press: Policing the Public Sphere in U.S. History.* New York: Oxford University Press, 1994.

Palmer, Robert R. *The Age of the Democratic Revolution: A Political History of Europe and America, 1760–1800.* 2 vols. Princeton: Princeton University Press, 1959.

Parramore, James R. "State Constitutions and the Press: Historical Context and Resurgence of a Libertarian Tradition." *Journalism Quarterly* 69 (1992): 105–23.

Pocock, J. G. A. *The Machiavellian Moment: Florentine Political Thought and the Atlantic Republican Tradition.* Princeton: Princeton University Press, 1975.

———. *Virtue, Commerce, and History: Essays on Political Thought and History, Chiefly in the Eighteenth Century.* Cambridge: Cambridge University Press, 1985.

Post, Robert C. *Constitutional Domains: Democracy, Community, Management.* Cambridge, Mass.: Harvard University Press, 1995.

Rabban, David M. "The Ahistorical Historian: Leonard Levy on Freedom of Expression in Early American History." *Stanford Law Review* 37 (1985): 795–856.

———. "The First Amendment in Its Forgotten Years." *Yale Law Journal* 90 (1981): 514–95.

———. *Free Speech in Its Forgotten Years, 1870–1920.* New York: Cambridge University Press, 1999.

Rahe, Paul A. *Republics Ancient and Modern: Classical Republicanism and the American Revolution.* Chapel Hill: University of North Carolina Press, 1992.

Read, James H. "'Our Complicated System': James Madison on Power and Liberty." *Political Theory* 23 (1995): 452–75.

———. *Power versus Liberty: Madison, Hamilton, Wilson, and Jefferson.* Charlottesville: University Press of Virginia, 2000.

Robbins, Caroline. *The Eighteenth-Century Commonwealthman: Studies in the Transmission, Development, and Circumstance of English Liberal Thought from the Restoration of Charles II until the War with the Thirteen Colonies.* Cambridge, Mass.: Harvard University Press, 1959.

Rodgers, Daniel T. "Republicanism: The Career of a Concept." *Journal of American History* 79 (1992): 11–38.

Rosenberg, Norman L. "Another World: Freedom of the Press in the Eighteenth Century." *Reviews in American History* 16 (1988): 554–59.

———. *Protecting the Best Men: An Interpretive History of the Law of Libel.* Chapel Hill: University of North Carolina Press, 1986.

Rossiter, Clinton. *Seedtime of the Republic.* New York: Harcourt, Brace, 1953.

Schlesinger, Arthur M. *Prelude to Independence: The Newspaper War on Britain, 1764–1776.* New York: Knopf, 1958.

Schuyler, Livingston Rowe. *The Liberty of the Press in the American Colonies before the Revolutionary War.* New York: Thomas Whittaker, 1905.

Sensabaugh, George F. *Milton in Early America.* Princeton: Princeton University Press, 1964.

Shields, David S. *Civil Tongues and Polite Letters in British America.* Chapel Hill: University of North Carolina Press, 1997.

Siebert, Fredrick Seaton. *Freedom of the Press in England: 1476–1776.* Urbana: University of Illinois Press, 1952.

Skinner, Quentin. *Meaning and Context: Quentin Skinner and His Critics,* ed. James Tully. Princeton: Princeton University Press, 1988.

Skerpan, Elizabeth. *The Rhetoric of Politics in the English Revolution, 1642–1660.* Columbia: University of Missouri Press, 1992.

Smith, James Morton. *Freedom's Fetters: The Alien and Sedition Laws and American Civil Liberties.* Ithaca, N.Y.: Cornell University Press, 1956.

Smith, Jeffery A. *Franklin and Bache: Envisioning the Enlightened Republic.* New York: Oxford University Press, 1990.

———. "Impartiality and Revolutionary Ideology: Editorial Policies of the *South-Carolina Gazette*, 1732–1775." *Journal of Southern History* 49 (1983): 511–26.

Smith, Jeffery A. *Printers and Press Freedom: The Ideology of Early American Journalism.* New York: Oxford University Press, 1988.

———. "A Reappraisal of Legislative Privilege and American Colonial Journalism." *Journalism Quarterly* 61 (1984): 97–103, 141.

———. *War and Press Freedom: The Problem of Prerogative Power.* New York: Oxford University Press, 1999.

Smith, Maryann Yodelis, and Gerald J. Baldasty. "Criticism of Public Officials and Government in the New Nation." *Journal of Communication Inquiry* 4 (1979): 53–74.

Steele, Ian K. *The English Atlantic, 1675–1740: An Exploration of Communication and Community.* New York: Oxford University Press, 1986.

Stewart, Donald H. *The Opposition Press of the Federalist Period.* Albany: State University of New York Press, 1969.

Stimson, Shannon C. *The American Revolution in the Law: Anglo-American Jurisprudence before John Marshall.* Princeton: Princeton University Press, 1990.

Storing, Herbert J., ed. *The Complete Anti-Federalists.* 7 vols. Chicago: University of Chicago Press, 1981.

Tagg, James. *Benjamin Franklin Bache and the Philadelphia "Aurora."* Philadelphia: University of Pennsylvania Press, 1991.

Tarlton, Charles D. "Historicity, Meaning, and Revisionism in the Study of Political Thought." *History and Theory* 12 (1973): 307–28.

Teeter, Dwight L. "From Revisionism to Orthodoxy," *Reviews in American History* 13 (1985): 518–25.

———. "A Legacy of Expression: Philadelphia Newspapers and Congress during the War for Independence, 1775–1783." Ph.D. diss. University of Wisconsin at Madison, 1966.

———. "Press Freedom and the Public Printing: Pennsylvania, 1775–83." *Journalism Quarterly* 45 (1968): 445–51.

———. "The Printer and the Chief Justice: Seditious Libel in 1782–3." *Journalism Quarterly* 45 (1968): 235–42, 260.

Tully, Alan. *Forming American Politics: Ideals, Interests, and Institutions in Colonial New York and Pennsylvania.* Baltimore: Johns Hopkins University Press, 1994.

Van Tyne, Claude Halstead. *The Loyalists in the American Revolution.* New York: Macmillan, 1902.

Walling, Karl-Friedrich. *Republican Empire: Alexander Hamilton on War and Free Government.* Lawrence: University Press of Kansas, 1999.

Warner, Michael. *The Letters of the Republic: Publication and the Public Sphere in Eighteenth-Century America.* Cambridge, Mass.: Harvard University Press, 1990.

Wood, Gordon. *Creation of the American Republic, 1776–1787.* Chapel Hill: University of North Carolina, 1969.

———. "The Democratization of Mind in the American Revolution." In *Leadership in the American Revolution.* Washington: Library of Congress, 1974.

———. "Interests and Disinterestedness in the Making of the Constitution." In *Beyond Confederation: Origins of the Constitution and American National Identity,* ed. Richard Beeman, Stephen Botein, and Edward C. Carter. Chapel Hill: University of North Carolina Press, 1987.

———. *Radicalism of the American Revolution.* New York: Knopf, 1992.

Young, Alfred F. *The Democratic-Republicans of New York: The Origins, 1763–1797.* Chapel Hill: University of North Carolina, 1967.

Zuckert, Michael. *Natural Rights and the New Republicanism.* Princeton: Princeton University Press, 1994.

Zvesper, John. "The American Founders and Classical Political Thought," *History of Political Thought* 10 (1989): 701–18.

Index

Adams, John, 98–99; on Massachusetts Constitution's press clause, 113; as "mock Monarch," 141

Adams, Samuel, 92; and *Independent Advertiser*, 57, 165; on jury power, 41; redefines sedition, 58

Addison, Alexander, 148

Addison, Joseph, 42

"Address to Quebec," 83–84

Alexander, James, 48–53

Alien Acts, 131–32, 149. *See also* Sedition Act

Allen, John, 132

ambivalent legacy of suppression and liberation, 9, 15

Anne, Queen (of England), 29

Anti-Courant, 44

Anti-Federalists: and advantage argument, 117–18; on Bill of Rights, 110, 112–13; on people's role, 111–12; and "press of sovereignty," 114–17; scholarship on, 109–10, 196n. 72

"Apology for Printers" (Franklin), 55–56

Appleby, Joyce, 11

Areopagitica (Milton), 20, 45, 57

Asgill, John, 26

Aurora, 136

Bache, Benjamin Franklin, 136, 203n. 7

"bad tendency" of words, 24; brings less punishment than formerly, 38; in Cato, 31; in Sedition Act theory, 133. *See also* "direct tendency" of libel

Bailey, Francis, 101

Bailyn, Bernard, 11, 75

Banning, Lance, 172n. 46, 174n. 55, 186n. 109, 191n. 65

Bartigas, Matthew, 114

Bayard, James, 140, 146

Bee, 136, 147

Bell, Robert, 70, 90

Berkeley, Sir William, 2, 36

Bernard, Francis, 72

Berns, Walter, 203n. 40, 210n. 4

Bill of Rights (English), 39

black-market printing, 17, 25

Blackstone, Sir William, 6, 68–71; rejected during confederation, 97, 105

Blake, George, 142

Bloudy Tenent of Persecution, for cause of Conscience (Williams), 24–25

"bodily correction," 37

Bolingbroke, Henry St. John, Viscount, 29, 46

Boston Evening Post, 45–46, 87

Boston News-Letter, 39

Botein, Stephen, 9

Bradford, Thomas, 77–78, 85

Bradford, William, 40, 48, 77–78, 85

Brown, Richard D., 37

Bryan, George, 103

Buel, Richard, 9, 145

Burgh, James, 98

"Camillus Junius," 127

campaign finance reform, 167–68

Care, Henry, 40, 45, 64

Carlisle Gazette, 117

Cato: influence in early America, 44–47, 49, 51; and legislative privilege, 61–62; as Lockean liberal, 31

Cato's Letters (Trenchard and Gordon), 27, 29–35, 51, 147, 155

censorship, during Revolutionary War, 88–89

"Centinel," 113, 116

Charles II (king of England), 26

Chase, Samuel, 151

Church, Benjamin, 99
"Citizen of Georgia," 115
Clinton, George, 74
Cobbett, William, 136, 148
"Coercive" Acts, 81
Coke, Sir Edward, 45, 50
Collins, Anthony, 30
Columbian Centinel, 136
Commentaries on the Laws of England (Blackstone), 68–71
Commercial Advertiser, 141
"Commoners' right": claiming, 22–23, 28; extending, 23–24
Compassionate Samaritane (Walwyn), 22–23
conceptual history, 13–14, 190n. 47; evolution, 15, 173n. 54
confidence. *See* vigilance, versus confidence, as public virtue
conscience, freedom of, 30. *See also* "necessity of conscience" argument
contempt (of a legislature). *See* legislative privilege, breach of
contempt of court, 73, 118, 211n. 8
Continental Congress, 90
contradictions, in conceptual history, 13–14
Cooley, Thomas, 161
Cooper, Thomas, 139, 143
Cornell, Saul, 109–10, 115, 117–18, 196n. 72, 208n. 98, 211n. 8
corporal punishment. *See* "bodily correction"
Cosby, William, 48–49
Critical Race Theory, 165–66
Croswell, Harry, 160, 212n. 16
Culpeper, Lord, 2, 36

Declaration of Rights of Virginia (Mason), 96, 99
Declaratory Act, 76
defamation, private, 97. *See also* public/private distinction
Defoe, Daniel, 26–27
Delancey, James, 48–52
Democratic Societies, 128–31
Democratic Society of the City of New York, 130
democratic theory, and freedom of expression, 2, 156–57

Democratic-Republican Societies. *See* Democratic Societies
Dennie, Joseph, 137, 160
Dietz, Mary, 186n. 106
Diggins, John Patrick, 11
"direct tendency" of libel, 27, 50, 148–50; Blackstone on, 69. *See also* "bad tendency" of words
Discourses Concerning Government (Sidney), 26, 45
Dorr, Harbottle, 80
Douglass, William, 39
Drayton, William Henry, 73
Duane, William, 132, 141
Duncan, Christopher, 109–10
Dunmore, Lord, 88

Eldridge, Larry D., 37–38
Elkins, Stanley, 138, 151
Emergence of a Free Press (Levy), 6
Emmons, Nathanael, 140
ends/means distinction, 12–13, 31, 163, 201n. 143
English Liberties, or the Freeborn Subject's Inheritance (Care), 40
Essex Result, 116
Exclusion Crisis, 26

fact, as distinct from opinion. *See* opinion, as distinct from fact
fair trial, versus free speech, 200n. 129
Farr, James, 190n. 47
"Federal Farmer," 116–117
federalism. *See* states' rights
Federalists: use advantage argument, 147; on Bill of Rights, 110, 112; dominate press, 114; on people's role, 111–12, 116–17, 139–41, 151
Fenno, John, 136, 151
First Amendment, Madison's early versions, 122
Fleeming, John, 79–81
Fleet, Thomas, 45–46, 56, 87
Fowle, Daniel, 63–65, 89
Francklin case (in England), 53
Franklin, Benjamin, 39, 46, 55–56; as Poor Richard, 46
Franklin, James, 39
free and open press discourse: in Cato, 34; appears in colonies, 41; coherence un-

dermined, 76–78; coherent in colonies, 45–47, 59–60; coherent for James Franklin, 43–44; shifts its center, 59; in Zenger case, 50–53
free and open press tradition: bifurcated, 81–87; explained, 3–4, 170n. 9
Freedom of Information Act, 164
"Freeholder," 43
free press doctrine, in Buel, 9; in Cato, 32–34; explained, 3–4, 10, 170n. 9, 178n. 59; and legislative privilege, 62–65; becomes "press of freedom," 87–89; becomes "press of sovereignty," 98–103
free speech: for Members of Parliament, 17, 22–24; synonymous with press liberty, 14. *See also* press liberty
Freneau, Philip, 136
"Friend to Harmony," 117
Furneaux, Philip, 70–71

Gaine, Hugh, 56
Gallatin, Albert, 143
Gazette of the United States, 136
general verdict, versus special verdict, 40–41, 53, 69
Gill, John, 80
Glorious Revolution of 1688, 27
Goddard, William, 91–2
Goodwin, John, 19
Goodwin, Thomas, 160
Gordon, Thomas, 51. *See also* Cato; *Cato's Letters* (Trenchard and Gordon)
Great Awakening, 55–59
Greenleaf, Joseph, 72
Greenleaf, Thomas, 118, 120
Grenville, George, 75
Grimké, Frederick, 161

Habermas, Jürgen, 181n. 36, 195n. 49, 213n. 36
Hall, David D., 181n. 37
Hamilton, Alexander: in Croswell case, 160; on falsehood's power, 146; on people's role, 138–42, 205n. 61; on "press of freedom," 191n. 65; on seditious libel law, 142, 160; on Rivington, 191n. 65
Hamilton, Andrew, 52–53
Hancock, John, 79–80
Harris, Benjamin, 37

"hate speech," 1, 165–66
Hawkins, Sergeant William, 45
Hay, George, 145
"Hell-Fire Club," 39–44
Helpe to the Right Understanding of a Discourse concerning Episcopacy (Walwyn), 21, 25
Henry VIII (king of England), 17
history of the book in America, 14
Hobbes, Thomas, 20
Holt, Charles, 136, 152
Holt, James, 56
Holt, John, 86, 166
Holt, John Hunter, 88
Hudson, Barzillai, 160
Hughes, John, 77
Humphreys, Whitehead, 91
Hutchinson, Anne, 37
Hutchinson, Thomas, 72

impartiality, 134–37, 204n. 41. *See also* open press doctrine
Independent Advertiser, 57, 165, 167
Independent Chronicle, 136, 142
Independent Gazetteer, 103, 107
Independent Reflector, 58–60
"information revolution," 167–68
instructions, to legislators, 100

Jay, John, 108
Jefferson, Thomas: and advantage argument, 117; on Bill of Rights, 112; on ends/means distinction, 12; on government/administration distinction, 206n. 70; on informing the people, 111, 115; on private defamation, 97, 104, 108, 114; on public good, 162; on state seditious libel prosecutions, 159–60
Jensen, Merrill, 6
"Junius Wilkes," 105
jury power: Blackstone on, 69; expanding in early seventeenth century, 40–41; historians on, 180n. 22; limited in England, 53; in Oswald case, 103; solidified in Zenger case, 53; sometimes limited in seventeenth century, 38; threaten by vice-admiralty courts, 75–76

Kenyon, Cecilia, 109
Keteltas, William, 127

Lawrence, Charles R., III, 165–66
Lee, Charles, 91
Legacy of Suppression (Levy), 5–6
legislative privilege, breach of, 39, 61–65, 71–74, 103, 127–28, 141, 187n. 123, 188n. 14
legislative tyranny, 98–100
legislature, popular, as people's defenders, 61
Leinesch, Michael, 109–10, 201n. 143
L'Estrange, Sir Roger, 25
Levellers, 18–25, 161; Petition of 18 January 1649, 20, 24–25
Levy, Leonard W., 5–10, 78, 96–97, 179n. 76, 189n. 29, 195n. 38; on extension of Parliamentary free speech, 22; ignores practice of freedom of expression, 38; minimizes Anti-Federalists, 109–10; on Wortman, 157, 210n. 4
libel: Blackstone defines, 69; Cato defines, 33; and "poison" metaphor, 27, 50, 106, 114
libel, seditious: defined, 5; common law understanding of, 48; in McDougall case, 73
liberal/republican debate, 8, 10–15, 65, 119–21, 161–62, 172n. 46, 174n. 55, 185n. 97
"libertarian" interpreters. *See* Rabban, David; Smith, Jeffery A.
liberty, individual versus public, 95, 165–168, 185n. 97
liberty versus licentiousness. *See* licentiousness
licensing, colonial, of the press, 37–40
licentiousness: liberty and, 49–50; inseparable from liberty, 117, 147, 208n. 98
Lienesch, Michael, 13
Lilburne, John, 18, 21–22
Livingston, William, 56, 58–60, 186n. 107
Locke, John, 11, 26, 45, 177n. 40
Long Parliament, 22
Loudon, Samuel, 89–90
Lyon, Matthew, 149

Machiavelli, Niccolò, in Cato, 33, 61
MacKinnon, Catharine, 165–66
Madison, James: advantages of press liberty, 2, 147–48; on Bill of Rights, 112; demonstrates modern democratic press

liberty, 160–61; *Federalist Ten*, 111, 119; on majority tyranny, 121–22; on people's role, 138–40, 143; and "press of freedom," 89; on public sphere uniting the country, 116; on Rivington, 89; subsequent punishment, 3
Magna Carta, 40, 45, 64
Mansfield, Lord Chief Justice, 193n. 17
"marketplace of ideas," 165–66, 213n. 30
Martin Marprelate tracts, 17
Maryland Declaration of Rights, 91
Maryland Gazette, 85
Maryland Journal, 91–92
Mason, George, 96
Massachusetts Constitution, 99
master-servant relationship, between people and rulers, 99–101, 105, 114–15, 142–44
Mather, Cotton, 39, 44
Mather, Increase, 39, 42, 44
Maule, Thomas, 40
Mayhew, Jonathan, 57
McDougall, Alexander, 73–74
McKean, Thomas, 102–3, 105, 116, 118, 121, 148, 159
McKitrick, Eric, 138, 151
Mein, John, 79–80
Mill, John Stuart, 165
Milton, John, 18, 45; *Areopagitica*, 20, 45, 57
monarchical theory, 36, 44
Moore, William, 63
Morgan, Edmund, 111
Morris, Lewis, 48

National Gazette, 127, 137, 143
"necessity of conscience" argument, 20
New-England Courant, 39–44
New-York Gazetteer, 82–84, 88
New York Times Co. v. Sullivan (1964), 6, 211n. 8
New-York Weekly Journal, 47–54
Nicholas, John, 146
non-attributed writing, 119
"Notorious Debate." *See* liberal-republican debate

objectivity, 166–67
On Liberty (Mill), 165
open press doctrine: advantage argument,

2, 106–8, 117–18, 146–48, 158; in Botein, 9; in Cato, 30–31, 34; and economic context, 55; explained, 3–4, 10, 170n. 9, 178n. 59; made subordinate, 80–81, 84–85; and printer's judgment, 55–57, 78–79, 83; refined after "press of freedom," 89–92; Tories stress, 82–84; used against colonial Whigs, 79–81. *See also* "overt acts" argument

opinion, as distinct from fact, 134, 150–54
Oswald, Eleazor, 102–3, 105, 107, 118, 121
Otis, Harrison, 148
"overt acts" argument, 24–25; in Furneaux, 70–71; in Republicans, 148–50; in Supreme Court cases, 164; in Wortman, 157–58

Paine, Thomas, threatens critic, 91
Park, John, 144, 152
Parker, James, 73
parliamentary privilege. *See* legislative privilege, breach of
Pennsylvania Constitution (1776), 100–101
Pennsylvania Constitution (1790), 113
Petrikin, William, 115
"Philadelphiensis," 116, 123
Pocock, J. G. A., 11
poison, libels as, 50, 106, 114, 118
Political Society of Mount Prospect (New Jersey), 129
popular sovereignty: Federalists on, 141; and press liberty, 57, 111–12, 148–50
Porcupine's Gazette, 136–37
pornography, 1, 165–66
Port Folio, 137
Post, Robert C., 2
Post Office Act, 127
Powell, Thomas, 73
power versus liberty: in Cato, 32; in colonies, 46–47
practical/rhetorical arguments, in 1640s, 18–19
press liberty: as modern concept, 150–54, 156–59; as natural right, 29–30, 157–58
"press of freedom," 87–90
"press of sovereignty," 100–105, 114–17, 129–31
Price, Richard, 108
Printing Act of 1662, 25–26; expires, 38

Printing Ordinance of 1643, 16–18
Printing Ordinance of 1647, 20
privatization of liberty, 120–21
privilege, legislative, breach of. *See* legislative privilege, breach of
Prynne, John, 19
public opinion, 150–54, 158–59
public sphere: in Anti-Federalist thought, 116; colonial, 42–44, 66–67; early American, 14; expanded by non-attributed writing, 119; expands in post-Revolutionary America, 102–5; expands in 1790s, 135–36; and Great Awakening, 59–60; and press liberty, 164, 168
public/private distinction: advanced, 142–44; develops, 94–95; employed, 114; established, 104–105
Purdie, Alexander, 78, 85
Puritan theology. *See* theology, Puritan

Quakers, 88

Rabban, David, 7–8, 10, 157, 221n. 13
religion, freedom of, 70; and press liberty, 14, 63
religious toleration, and press liberty, 14
republicanism, and press liberty, 60–61
Republicans, on people's role, 142–44, 151–52
reputation, importance of in early America, 38, 50
Revenue Act. *See* Sugar Act
Revolution of 1800, 154, 159
Revolutionary War, transformations occasioned by, 93–95
"right to know," the public's, 57, 164–65, 185n. 100
Rind, William, 78
Rivington, James, 82–84, 87–89, 91
Rossiter, Clinton, 45
Rousseau, Jean-Jacques, 99
Royalist writings, 23
Russell, Benjamin, 118
Rutledge, John, 138

scribal publication, 36
Sears, Isaac, 88, 91
secularism: in Cato's works, 29–30; in eighteenth century, 29; increases in early America, 45; in Tindal, 28

Sedition Act, 126, 131–34, 149. *See also* libel, seditious
Seven Years War (1756–63), 75
Sewall, Samuel, 37, 42
Shays's Rebellion, 102–3
Sherman, Roger, 111
Shute, Samuel, 38
Sidney, Algernon, 26, 45
Smith, James Morton, 1, 138
Smith, Jeffery A., 8–10, 157, 180n. 22
Smith, William (New York), 49
Smith, William (Pennsylvania), 62–63, 90
Smith, William, Jr., 56, 58, 186n. 107
South Sea Bubble, in Cato, 32
special verdict, versus general verdict. *See* general verdict, versus special verdict
Stamp Act (Massachusetts, 1785), 101–2
Stamp Act (1765), 75–77
Stamp taxes, under Queen Anne, 29
standing armies, threat of, 75–76
Star Chamber, 24, 50
states' rights, 134, 204n. 40, 210n. 4
Steele, Richard, 42
Storing, Herbert, 109
subsequent punishment (versus previous restraint), 3, 68–69
Sugar Act, 75
"supervision," norm of, 102

Tacitus, as source for Cato, 31, 51, 60
Tea Act, 81
Teeter, Dwight, 185n. 100
theology, Puritan, 37, 42, 44
Theomachia (Goodwin), 19
theory/practice distinction. *See* ends/means distinction
Thomas, Isaiah, 72, 80–81
Thompson, Charles, 103
Thomson, John, 139, 145–46, 150
Timothy, Peter, 53
Tindal, Matthew, 26–29, 155
Total Eclipse of Liberty (Fowle), 64
Towne, Benjamin, 91
Townshend Duties, 76, 81
Tracy, Uriah, 145
treason, redefined by Livingston and Smith, 58–59

Treatise Concerning Political Enquiry, and the Liberty of the Press (Wortman), 157–59, 161–62, 168
Trenchard, John, 75. *See also* Cato; *Cato's Letters* (Trenchard and Gordon)
truth, as no defense in libel case: Blackstone on, 69; in Zenger, 50, 52
truth, as valid defense in libel case, 70, 105; in Sedition Act cases, 151–52; in Zenger case, 52–54
"truth shall prevail" argument: in Cato, 30; explained, 19–20; reexamined, 106–8, 129, 145–46; in Tindal, 28
Tucker, St. George, 143–44, 161, 209n. 100
Tucker, Thomas Tudor, on Madison's original press clause, 122

verdicts, jury power over. *See* general verdict, versus special verdict
vice-admiralty courts, 75–76
vigilance, as part of republicanism, 61, 129
vigilance, versus confidence, as public virtue, 139–44, 148–50
Virginia Report (Madison), 143
Virginia Resolutions, 147

Walwyn, William, 20–25, 28, 70
Warner, Michael, 43, 182n. 41, 184n. 86
Warren, Joseph, 72
Washington, George: criticized as general, 91–92; on loyal opposition, 141; on public information, 142
Webster, Noah, 116, 141
Wentworth, Peter, 17
Whig Club of Baltimore, 91
Wilkes, John, 71, 73
Williams, Elisha, 57
Williams, Roger, 21, 24–25, 37, 70
Wilson, James, 111, 113
Wood, Gordon, 11, 162, 164; on Anti-Federalists' attack on republicanism, 119–21; on fact/opinion distinction, 150
Wortman, Tunis, 157–59, 161–62, 168, 210n. 4, 211n. 8

Zenger, John Peter, 8, 47–54, 68
Zuckert, Michael, 12–13, 163, 201n. 143

About the Author

Robert W. T. Martin, Visiting Assistant Professor of Government at Hamilton College, teaches political theory, specializing in American political thought and democratic theory. He has written on those topics, among others, for such journals as *History of Political Thought* and *Political Research Quarterly*.